RIDER HAGGARD AND THE LOST EMPIRE

RIDER HAGGARD
AND THE LOST EMPIRE

TOM POCOCK

WEIDENFELD AND NICOLSON
LONDON

Typeset by Create Publishing Services Ltd, Bath, Avon
Printed in Great Britain by The Bath Press Ltd, Bath, Avon

For Randal and Alison Casson

Contents

Illustrations

On trek in Africa (*Norfolk Record Office*)
At home in Norfolk (*Norfolk Record Office*)
Lily Jackson (*Courtesy of Commander Mark Cheyne*)
Louisa Haggard (*Courtesy of Commander Mark Cheyne*)
William Meybohm Rider Haggard (*Courtesy of Commander Mark Cheyne*)
Jock Haggard, the son (*Courtesy of Commander Mark Cheyne*)
Rudyard Kipling (*National Portrait Gallery*)
The Egyptian inspiration (*Sotheby's*)
She by Maurice Greiffenhagen (*Longman, Green and Co.*)
Haggard's election handbill (*Courtesy of Chris Coquet Esq.*)
On the campaign trail (*Courtesy of Commander Mark Cheyne*)
Rider Haggard with his daughter Dorothy (*Norfolk Record Office*)
Theodore Roosevelt (*Courtesy of Commander Mark Cheyne*)
Rider Haggard's farewell to Egypt (*Courtesy of Commander Mark Cheyne*)

The author and publishers wish to thank the above copyright holders for permission to reproduce the pictures.

Introduction

THOSE WHO MET Sir Rider Haggard could not forget him any more than his readers could forget their discovery of his books. The man and his works threw echoes from deep instincts and emotions, rousing, it seemed, inherited memories and buried longings; an achievement that sounds trite but was true. That this should be so was all the more strange because the man was a robust Norfolk squire with a passion for farming his land. His books were, for the most part, considered to be thrilling yarns and it was not until the coming of psychoanalysis that the roots of their excitement became apparent and, with it, the realisation that their author was innocently unaware of the depths he was dredging.

His name often came to be associated with anywhere, anything, or anyone that seemed bizarre, beautiful or exotic and, above all, mysterious. Perhaps a view of distant mountains in a curious light – the lumpy hills of equatorial Africa, the Drakensberg of the Transvaal, or the Theban Hills above the Valley of the Kings in Egypt would recall Rider Haggard with a wondering of what might lie beyond. Perhaps a silent traveller in the wilds, or a beautiful, enigmatic woman would momentarily suggest *Allan Quatermain* or *She*. Reports in newspapers could sometimes suggest parallels: a search for Montezuma's treasure in Mexico, such as Haggard himself planned; or Dr Alan Ereira's discovery of the lost but surviving civilisation of the Kogi in the mountains of Santa Marta in Colombia. Any exploration, whether of unmapped terrain, or of the unknown qualities of the human brain and spirit, could bring Rider Haggard to mind. He was, like his friend Rudyard Kipling, one of the most famous writers of his time but, as his grandson, Mark Cheyne, has said, 'He was so much more than a novelist'.

That remark prompted this book. A preliminary look at the man and his life shows that he had relatively little regard for most of his own novels, belittling himself as a humble story-teller. His stories made him rich but he saw himself as one who should have been a shaper of destinies:

a statesman, politician, soldier, or imperial proconsul. Had his early life been different, he might have achieved such recognition. As it was, he made his own way, waging a lone crusade in what he saw as the ultimate cause, like one of the heroes of his own invention.

Haggard the author only attracted the attention of biographers after his youngest daughter, Lilias, published a charming memoir of him, *The Cloak That I Left*, in 1951. This was followed in 1961 by Dr Morton Cohen's thoughtful biography in which the author, an American academic, showed that he understood the attitudes and aspirations of the English rural gentry and the London literary circles a century past. In 1978, he was followed by Peter Beresford Ellis with *H. Rider Haggard: A Voice from the Infinite* and, in 1981, by D.S. Higgins's *Rider Haggard: the Great Storyteller*, the latter speculating on the psychological origins of Haggard's fantasies. Dr Cohen also published a collection of Haggard's correspondence with Kipling in 1965 and, in 1980, D.S. Higgins edited a selection from what the title described as *The Private Diaries of Sir Henry Rider Haggard*; misleadingly so because they had been written with a view to possible publication. Several academic books, or chapters of them, were devoted to Haggard and celebrated authors wrote essays about him. An active Rider Haggard Appreciation Society flourishes to this day.

This book attempts to look at Rider Haggard from a different standpoint, his own. He liked to see himself as a crusader for reform: first in agriculture, then in urban society and finally in the British Empire itself.

In studying him, I am, above all, grateful to Commander and Mrs Mark Cheyne for showing me their family papers, talking to me at length about Sir Rider and making me welcome at their charming house in Norfolk. Colonel and Mrs Richard Allhusen were also generous in their hospitality at the Haggards' old home, Bradenham Hall. Other authorities on Haggard were prodigal with their knowledge and time, particularly Dr Morton Cohen, Mr Peter Beresford Ellis, Colonel Denys Whatmore, Mr Chris Coquet, Mr Roger Allen and Mr David Binns. Mr Ben Burgess described the Norfolk of his youth, when he remembered meeting Haggard riding his bicycle through country lanes. Mr John Grigg pointed out the Lloyd George connection. In time past, the late Dr Philip Gosse imparted the stimulating flavour of his father's literary set and I am grateful to my father, the late Guy Pocock, for introducing me to the excitements of Haggard's novels when I was a boy and to my mother for introducing me to her county, Norfolk.

Introduction

My gratitude is also due to Miss Jean Kennedy, the Archivist of the Norfolk Record Office, which cares for the bulk of Haggard's papers, for her help and that of her staff, and the Librarian of Norfolk County Library. Thanks are also due to the Chief Archivist of the Manuscript Division of the Library of Congress in Washington, D.C., for identifying the Haggard correspondence among President Theodore Roosevelt's papers and the staff of the British Library for making it available on microfilm. Mr Michael Bolt of the University of Reading Archives enabled me to see the records of Haggard's publisher, Longman. The Librarian and staff of the London Library were as helpful as one has come to expect. Mr David Butters of the Swaffham Museum provided some unpublished Haggardiana and I am also grateful to Savills, the estate agents, for allowing me to explore the site of Didlington Hall and Mr Malcolm Cracknell for showing me round. Dr Irving Finkel of the Western Asiatic Division of the British Museum and Mr H.V.F. Winstone, the biographer of Howard Carter, helped with accounts of the Amhersts' collection of Egyptian antiquities. Colonel Denys Whatmore kindly read and commented upon the typescript and my wife, Penny, compiled the index.

Finally, like so many, I am grateful to Sir Rider Haggard himself for setting an example by sending his imagination leaping into the dark.

Tom Pocock
Chelsea, 1993

CHAPTER ONE

'Voices of thy distant home'

THE SUMMER DAY was long at Wood Farm. Standing on some of the highest land in the eastern counties of England – if only at three hundred feet above sea level – the small, thatched farmhouse was lit by the morning sun, and by its setting, long after the valleys below had fallen into shadow. Sunlight illuminated a panorama of gentle chalk downs, billowing tops of oaks and elms, church towers and, occasionally, great ornamental trees around a country house.

> An English landscape – green and bright –
> All smiling in the evening light,
> All bathed in sweet repose;
> A scene of vale and field and hill,
> And water – on whose bosom still,
> The sun-ray mirrored glows...[1]

The author of those lines was what might have been expected: a demure Victorian lady. Ella Haggard was staying at Wood Farm in the June of 1856 for the birth of her baby because Bradenham Hall, where she lived, was still let as it sometimes was during the family's absence in London or abroad.

The child she bore would one day describe her as 'near the standard of perfect womanhood'. He would praise her 'gentle sweetness' as one of the 'most charming ... most brilliant', who 'sang sweetly and drew with skill'.[2] She also wrote poetry but, during that summer, it was not what might have been expected:

> Faint, sick at heart, they tread their desperate way.
> Must they despair? They sadly gaze around;
> Death's icy robe enshrouds th' insensate ground;
> In the soul-piercing blast, they feel his breath;
> Before – behind – above – no choice but Death!
> Behold, his bloodhounds swarm along the way;
> From rocks, from caves, they spring upon their prey...[3]

This, she wrote in *Myra, or the Rose of the East*, a narrative poem of love and death in the Afghan War of 1842, in which a British expeditionary force was massacred and their women and children killed or captured by the fierce hillmen. Ella Haggard had been brought up in India and was nostalgic for its heat, mystery and excitement, confident of the British right – indeed, duty – to rule. Just before her little book was published in Norwich a year later she was to read news of more massacres when the Sepoys mutinied at the Meerut cantonment and the Indian Mutiny had begun. So she hurriedly added an Introduction about

> the drama now enacting in our Eastern possessions – the catastrophe of which we cannot, as yet, foresee ... For these foul acts ... RETRIBU-TION must and will be exacted; but when this bloody delirium has subsided, when the strong arm of England has been put forth effec-tively to crush the vipers she has nourished in her bosom – let us hope that then brighter days may again dawn for India.[4]

As Ella Haggard sat in the sun outside Wood Farm, placid in her long, flared dress, her kindly, wide-set eyes and sweet smile gave no hint of anger and anguish. All remarked on her equanimity and gentle-ness. When friends wondered how she could control her temper and make any contribution to conversation in her noisy, largely masculine, household, she would say, 'My dear ... I whisper! When I whisper, they all stop talking, because they wonder what is the matter. Then I get my chance'.[5]

On 22 June 1856, her sixth son (and eighth child, one of whom had died at birth) was born. Soon afterwards mother and baby were able to return to Bradenham Hall, where the infant was christened with con-secrated water from a large bowl of blue and white Lowestoft china and given the names of Henry Rider. He was sickly with jaundice and his survival was not expected.

He survived, born of hardy stock. His father William, the third Haggard to be squire of Bradenham, was a strongly built, bearded man of forty-three, forceful and intelligent but opinionated and short-tempered. The Haggards could be traced back to a family of Hertfordshire worthies of the sixteenth century but liked to claim more dramatic forebears. Although never able to prove that they were of distinguished Danish descent, they had some reason to believe that a Sir Andrew Haggard, or Agard, who had come to England from Aagaard in Denmark, was an ancestor. He had belonged to the Gyldenstjerne family, whose arms bore a star, as did those of the nineteenth-century Haggards.

More immediate injections of exotic genes into the family had come when the first Haggard of Bradenham married Frances Amyand. 'Wild blood' was reputed to give the Amyands their charm, excitability, footloose, sometimes unstable, ways, and their dash. The William Haggard born of this marriage entered the Amyands' banking house in St Petersburg and there met and married an Elizabeth Meybohm, whose father was similarly engaged and was of German-Jewish descent. Their eldest son was now squire of Bradenham.

There was a touch of the exotic in his wife's family, too. Ella herself increasingly cherished her memories of India amongst the cool beauty of the Norfolk countryside. She enjoyed describing its excitement to her more timorous English friends, as when she wrote,

> To the newly arrived European, a palanquin journey is at once novel and exciting. The confused and unceasing chatter around him, the flaring torches and wild and fantastic gestures of the unclothed Hamals, or bearers, who might, in the uncertain light, be well mistaken for Imps of Darkness, produce an effect calculated strongly to impress the imagination.[6]

Her father, Bazett Doveton of the Bombay Civil Service, had also been Governor of St Helena in the South Atlantic, but, before his time, the family had lived in India. Somewhere in the shadows of the early nineteenth century, they heard, was what some saw as a skeleton in the family's cupboard and others saw as the thrilling legend of Torlassi and 'the Begum'. Indeed evidence was later to be found that Ella's maternal grandfather, a Colonel Bond, had married a bride of mixed blood named Eleanor, who later deserted him and was divorced. Her father had been identified only by the name Torlassi but her mother was said to have been an Indian girl of high caste. In tune with the Victorian tendency to glamorise such ancestry, she was given the highest caste and spoken of as 'the Begum'. The subject was usually avoided amongst the Doveton and Haggard families because, as one of Ella's daughters said of her mother, 'She naturally did not care to speak about her grandmother's unedifying past, or the taint of black blood she imported into the family, but she could not deny the facts'.[7]

Thus Ella Haggard reflected the Victorian memsahibs' fear and jealousy of the sometimes beautiful and intelligent Indian women, who caught their menfolk's eyes. Similarly, her family referred to her mother-in-law, Elizabeth Meybohm, as having been Russian rather than German-Jewish although Ella was careful to refer in *Myra* to 'Jews . . . of beauteous mien'.[8] It was not that her attitude was what would later be called racist but that she was confident of Anglo-Saxon superiority. Brought up on her grandparents' stories of the savagery of the French Revolution, her own generation was steeped in the knowledge of the enterprise and gallantry with which their countrymen had taken possession of a quarter of the world to protect and civilise it. There was little awareness of the factors that had made other nations and races what they seemed to be; to her, history was romantic.

This self-confidence was the dominant factor in the Haggard family's attitudes; as it was in most others in the middle and upper classes. Squire Haggard presided over a relatively modest estate of hundreds, rather than thousands, of acres of farmland and woods from his square, pedimented red-brick house designed with the architectural confidence of the late eighteenth century.

Standing in this soft, rich countryside, six miles to the east of the Norfolk market town of Swaffham, Bradenham Hall seemed to have grown out of its surroundings. In one of its fields, a moated copse marked the site of a forgotten castle of the early Middle Ages, while a track, sheltered by high hedges, was known as Smugglers' Lane since it was said to have been the route for running contraband from the coast to Cambridge. The square-topped tower of the late-thirteenth-century church of St Andrew rose above the trees on the gentle slope towards the river Wissey and it was there that William and Ella had stood beside the little grave of their stillborn child.

The most famous visitor to the house had been Lady Hamilton, when she and her daughter Horatia had stayed with the former owners, Lord Nelson's sister Susannah and her husband Thomas Bolton, at the end of 1811. There were still elderly villagers who remembered her and her ghost was said to haunt the house, but the most poignant reminder was the lavender growing in the walled kitchen garden. Here, one old man remembered that, when a page at the Hall, he had been ordered to spread the late Lord Nelson's uniform upon the sun-warmed lavender hedge for an airing.

This was where the Haggards' sons grew up. Now the sixth, known as Rider rather than Henry, became aware of his surroundings: the nurseries behind the dormer windows in the mansard roof of the second floor;

the library on the first floor, facing south over the cedar-shaded lawns; the formal dining-room to the left of the front door. Outside, the mown grass and the flower-beds gave way to the west to fifty-five acres of the magnificent trees of the Great Wood and to the east to the Long Plantation, running down the hill to the sinister yew trees of the Dark Wood and beyond to a copse, Myra's Grove, newly named in honour of his mother's verse. More distant still to the south, beyond the little river, the land rose again to the Grazing Grounds, some two hundred acres of parkland without a house to surround, planted with oaks so many centuries before that the bole of one tree measured fourteen feet in diameter. These woods and plantations marked the child's first horizons.

Like all small children, Rider first saw himself as the centre of all things but this changed to seeing his parents as the heart of a social and emotional solar system. Around them circled the children – another daughter and son were born in 1858 and 1860 respectively – and, in orbit beyond them, relations, friends, neighbours and servants. The latter were not always beneficent, particularly one nurserymaid who would frighten the small Rider into obedience with stories about an ugly doll with boot-button eyes and a threatening leer which was kept at the back of a deep toy cupboard. This, she would say, would become horribly alive if he misbehaved and the doll became known as 'She-Who-Must-Be-Obeyed'.

It was feudal order, which, to participants, seemed divinely ordained, for religion commanded that each must accept their allotted place. Over this, William Haggard presided, reading prayers before breakfast in the dining-room, where the family assembled and the servants trooped in, all to kneel on chairs facing the wall. In church, it was he who occupied the squire's pew and, when parishioners were late, would turn, extract his watch from his waistcoat pocket and hold it up to them in silent rebuke. He seemed to enjoy reading a bloodthirsty lesson from the Old Testament and if he stumbled over some Hebrew or Hittite name would loudly repeat the entire passage.

At meals, the squire could be alarmingly unpredictable; perhaps, displeased with the soup, sending the tureen back to the kitchen with instructions that the cook drink it all herself. A customary rebuke to a son was to point to the door and shout, 'Out of the house, sir!'[9] Finding himself worsted in argument, he would storm out of the dining-room, slamming the door behind him, then out of the house by the front door and, his progress marked by further slamming of doors, return by another and finally to his place at the head of the table, equanimity restored. It was the same even beyond the crested gates of the drive, when as he raced his pony-cart to the railway station his bellows of 'Hold the train!'[10] could be heard half a mile away; indeed, it was said that Haggard males could be heard in conversation in the next field. In the midst of this uproar, Ella Haggard seemed, as Rider was to put it, like 'an angel that had lost her way and found herself in pandemonium'.[11] Yet, despite the high temperamental voltage around her, she loved her husband, as did all those who could put his outbursts down to high spirits.

The Haggard boys amused themselves with rural pastimes, according to their ages: playing around pond and stream, climbing trees, bird-nesting, riding and shooting. Despite their imposing house, it was a farming community and the slaughter of animals for food or sport was routine. Deaths of neighbours were part of their lives, too, and Rider was once taken into a cottage to be shown an old villager tucked up in his coffin and on display in the parlour. Yet, at the time, he did not connect mortality with his family, or with himself.

Throughout childhood he had grown close to his eldest sister, Ella, who was not only named after their mother but took after her in fertility of imagination. Years later, he was to write to her, 'While we were young; when faith knew no fears for anything and Death had not knocked upon our doors; when you opened to my childish eyes that gate of ivory and pearl, which leads to the blessed kingdom of Romance ... '[12] It was therefore appropriate, and not unexpected, that the first such knock upon his own door should come on the occasion of her marriage in the summer of 1869, when she was aged twenty-three and her adoring brother just twelve.

The house was full of guests for her wedding to a clergyman, the Reverend Charles Green, and Rider had given up his bedroom and slept in a small, stuffy room on the first floor. This was known as the Sandwich Room because it was squeezed between the library and a principal bedroom with doors to both but without its own access to the landing. Once it had been a dressing-room but now it was an annexe to the library with bookshelves reaching to the ceiling. It was claustrophobic, particularly on a hot July night, when only the hoot of owls in the Long Plantation and the bark of a fox broke the stillness once the festivities had ended.

He lay in bed with moonlight streaming through the tall window.

Raising his hand, he saw that it looked cold, white and chill, as if it were already dead. 'Then it was that suddenly my young intelligence for the first time grasped the meaning of death. It came home to me that I, too, must die', he would later recall. 'It was an awful hour. I shivered, I prayed, I wept. I thought I saw Death waiting for me by the library door ... '[13] This dread never left him; nor did the seeking of an alternative possibility to the unthinkable obliteration of the human spirit. It became the quest of a lifetime.

Although Bradenham was the setting for the lives of the Haggards, it was sometimes let for the pheasant-shooting and then the family would stay in London, or travel on the Continent. Indeed, Rider's formal education began at London day schools, while they were lodging at 24 Leinster Square in Bayswater. He was not particularly spirited, nor good-looking, and was bullied; he had to change schools and his work suffered. So his father decided to send him away for concentrated tuition to an Oxfordshire clergyman, who took a few boys as lodgers.

After the hubbub of Bradenham, Garsington rectory was a peaceful sanctuary. An old house, built long and low of grey stone, it was shielded by a high, dark yew hedge; a tall elm stood on its lawn and its tranquillity was enhanced by the cooing of doves from a dovecote in the walled garden. The rector and his wife were kindly and there were other new friends: 'a little, fair-haired girl' with whom he would climb inside a hollow elm, where they 'taught each other the rudiments of flirtation'. There were walnut shells to be floated on a stream, taken from a tree on land owned by a friendly farmer, 'a fine, handsome man of about fifty, with grey hair and aristocratic features that came to him probably enough with his Norman blood and he always wore a beautiful smock-frock'; his name was William Quatermain.

Rider was content, yet melancholy. One memory that stayed with him was of a December afternoon with the church 'standing out against the angry red of the setting light. Dark misty clouds hang about it, the grass is pale and sodden and the moisture is shaken by a chill wind from the solemn yew and cypress trees. Beyond the lych-gate stands the clergyman in white and fluttering robes',[14] waiting for a funeral cortège. Twenty years on, he was to recall that afternoon and remembered his mood: 'How vividly one recalls the hopes and fears, the joys and sorrows, the doubts and the fervid piety of boyhood!'[15]

On his return to Bradenham, his future education was to be decided. All his elder brothers had been given education suitable to sons of the rural gentry. Four had gone to public schools: the two eldest, William and Bazett, to Winchester (they were now undergraduates at Oxford and Cambridge, respectively); Alfred was at Haileybury and Andrew at Westminster, while John, or Jack, was now a midshipman in the Royal Navy.

It was no secret that Rider was the least-favoured son. He was said to lack concentration and had shown little interest in reading anything beyond *Robinson Crusoe*. He was considered 'not very bright', even by his adored mother, and to have little intellectual curiosity. Once, when the family was on holiday in Germany and had been taken cruising on the Rhine, Rider was seen to have gone below only to be dragged on deck by his father shouting, 'I have paid five Thalers for you to improve your mind by absorbing the beauties of nature and absorb them you shall!' In the hearing of his brother Andrew, his father had told him that he was 'only fit to be a greengrocer'. Seeking comfort from the brother, all he received was, 'I say, old chap, when you become a greengrocer, I hope you'll let me have oranges cheap!'[16]

In early adolescence he lacked his parents' good looks. He was tall and thin, his eyes protuberant, his nose long and his mouth and chin weak. He spoke loudly but with a lisp and pronounced *th* as *t'* and *r* as *w*. He was shy and 'highly-strung' and what self-confidence he had acquired in the manly recreations of his boyhood seemed to have been crushed by his father's disapproval.

It therefore came as confirmation of Rider's worst apprehensions, and the ultimate humiliation, when he alone was deemed unworthy of what was considered a gentleman's education; he to whom the most damning insult were the words, 'You are not a gentleman!' Rider had a high opinion of his father's judgement: 'I never knew anyone who could form a more accurate judgement of a person of either sex after a few minutes of conversation, or even at sight',[17] he was to write. Yet he was to be accorded an education appropriate for the sons of tenant farmers and tradesmen and was sent to Ipswich Grammar School. He told himself that the reason for his father's decision was the expense of the school fees but this rang hollow when, four years later, his younger brother Arthur was sent to Shrewsbury and then to Cambridge University.

Although schooling at Ipswich meant that he was unlikely to go on to university and thence into one of the gentlemanly professions such as the law, the church, the Army or Navy, or diplomacy, there were to be compensations. The education was probably as good as in most public schools and Rider quickly excelled in English composition. It was also a rough school, where boys soon learned to stand up for themselves. Rider – nicknamed 'Nosy' – had to fight bullies with his fists and, although he did not always win, acquired a reputation for integrity. He also discovered that boys from the social strata regarded as inferior to his own could be just as pleasant, or unpleasant, as any others.

In the holidays, the family still sometimes travelled to the Continent and in the summer of 1872, led by their father (wearing a tall white hat stuffed with damp cloths and cabbage leaves against sunstroke), it was to Switzerland. There Rider's abiding memory was not of the scenery but of a pretty chambermaid, who took him to the ossuary of the village church and produced her father's skull, which 'she polished up affectionately with her apron'.[18]

They travelled via Paris, which was then beginning to recover from the siege by the Prussians and the revolt of the Communards of 1871. 'The Column Vendôme was lying shattered on the ground', recalled Rider, 'the public statues were splashed over with the lead of bullets and great burnt-out buildings stared at me emptily'. He was horrified and fascinated to be taken to a high, bullet-pitted wall by a young Frenchman who had watched mass executions of Communards there a few months before. 'He told me that the soldiers fired into the moving heap until at length it grew still',[19] he noted with relish for the shocking detail.

William Haggard now thought that, despite his modest schooling, the Army might be a possible career for Rider so, on his return to Ipswich, he took the entrance examination and failed the mathematics paper. Setbacks only increased his father's determination and he decided that his boy should aim higher and try for a career in the diplomatic service. So he was to leave school at once, although not yet eighteen, and go to London for concentrated tuition before taking the Foreign Office examination in about three years' time.

But Norfolk had another educational experience to offer Rider Haggard. Around Bradenham were much larger estates, each supporting the mansion of a land-owning family and amongst the grandest of these were the Cokes of Holkham, the Walpoles of Houghton, the Townshends of Raynham and the Fountaines of Narford. But the most exotic were the Amhersts of Didlington, one of the great estates of Norfolk, where ten thousand acres of farmland and fifteen hundred of parkland surrounded a mansion overlooking a vast lake scattered with islands. Originally built in the seventeenth century and augmented by successive generations, the house stood in one of the most remote stretches of Norfolk and was reached down narrow roads across a flat landscape crossed by lines of twisted Scotch firs. Like Bradenham, it was on the little river Wissey, only at Didlington it was wider and stocked with trout.

The estate was also stocked with people. Three hundred men laboured on its acres; eight grooms and ostlers worked in the stables; there were troops of foresters and gardeners and the greenhouses were tended by twelve plantsmen; indoors, the housekeepers presided over nine men-servants and 'many maids'. All of this was to provide for the comfort and welfare of Mr William Amherst, High Sheriff of Norfolk, aspiring politician and amateur antiquary. He himself devoted much of his own time and energies to his private museum, already said to be the most distinguished in private hands.

Visitors accustomed to the stuffed English birds and tribal weaponry from the frontiers of the British Empire displayed in their own libraries and gunrooms, never forgot their first visit to Didlington.

A seven miles' drive through sandy 'breeks', hedges of Scotch fir and interminable rabbit warrens, brings you somewhat abruptly to the verdant oasis of Didlington [wrote one]. A dignified major-domo, who has been in the family for three and fifty years, receives you in the square hall and conducts you to the library ... The very door seems to form part of the ponderous walnut-wood bookcases which run round the walls; as it closes behind you with a spring, you see Mr Amherst ... The Squire of Didlington is in excellent spirits ... Keys are fetched ... a narrow door is opened and you are utterly bewildered at the sight which meets your view.

In the finest Gobelins tapestry you see all the victories of Louis the Great; a diploma signed by Charles XII and an Andrea Ferrara blade lie side by side on the glass case which covers the mummy of a royal priestess, buried at Thebes in the days of Joseph the Israelite ... a deed signed by Queen Isabella (the widow of luckless Edward II) when interned at Castle Rising, hangs over a superb collection of Egyptian figures, scarabs and cartouches ...

Outside the long, lofty hall sit in solitary state a row of basalt figures, holding in their hands the symbolic key of the Nile. For thousands of years these cat-headed goddesses were worshipped by the Egyptians; they have survived dynasties and empires to look down complacently on the trees which the Prince of Wales and the Duke of Edinburgh planted when they visited Didlington ... [20]

Egyptian antiquities predominated and amongst the statuary, ceramics, jewellery and mummies – both of people and of cats, crocodiles, ibises, hawks and even the head of a sacred bull – from Sakkara, Tel-el-Amarna, Thebes and the Valleys of the Kings and Queens were little figures of servants in glazed pottery or painted wood to be incarnated in the tomb to attend master, or mistress, in the afterlife. The sweetly serene face painted on one such maidservant is said to have caught Rider's eye, suggesting an alternative She-Who-Must-Be-Obeyed to the horrid doll at the back of the toy cupboard. At an age when so much experience seems to have sexual connotations, this exotic house held a strong erotic charge and adolescent fantasies involving a beautiful hostess – rather than a bearded landowner – behind the locked doors of a private museum lingered in his memory.

Egyptology had another appeal: not only was it a favourite subject of his mother's but it seemed to offer its own bizarre antidote to his fear of death. At Didlington were papyrus manuscripts and hieroglyphic inscriptions that described the journey of the soul in *The Book of the Dead* and the monotheist theories of the pharaoh Akhenaten; indeed, the Egyptians' trinity of Osiris, Isis and their son Horus could present startling parallels with Christian belief. Perhaps the solution to one mystery lay in another? Were all religions linked by human need, or by metaphysical reality?

But now the time had come to leave Norfolk and, on reaching the age of eighteen, Rider left for tuition in London, lodging in the Westbourne Grove district of Notting Hill. He remembered that his tutor and his wife quarrelled continually over religious principles: 'She told him that he would go to hell; fate would have its consolations'. After a year in this company, his father decided that to achieve the necessary academic standards Rider would move to a crammer's called Scoones, which specialised in aspiring diplomats.

Finding that new lodgings, kept by a young widow, were 'not respectable', Rider moved to others in Davies Street near Berkeley Square in Mayfair, which was more suitable to a socially ambitious young man about town. But his daily walks to and from Scoones in Garrick Street off St Martin's Lane led him through the streets around Leicester Square, the vortex of fast living and prostitution in London. Moreover some of his fellow students were well-to-do young blades, who regarded the district as recreational. Not surprisingly, the country-bred youth would later only admit that his brothers had once thrown him into the Rhine to teach him to swim and 'after nearly drowning, I learned to swim and, in a sense, the same may be said of my London life'.[21]

He never enlarged further upon his introduction to this, except in one unexpected area. One of the more affluent young men at the crammer's named Norris, introduced Rider to one of the most popular pastimes of the upper classes in mid-Victorian London: spiritualism. Arising in reaction to Darwin's theory of evolution and the attendant materialism, it seemed to combine hopes of religious truths with scientific enquiry. Rider, who showed abiding curiosity in any mystery that might offer guidance to the terrible prospect that had first overwhelmed him that summer night in the Sandwich Room, and had become fascinated by the Ancient Egyptians' preoccupation with death and the afterlife, was a natural recruit. Norris introduced him to several of the London hostesses who held séances in their drawing-rooms. Notable among these was Lady Caithness, a vice-president of the recently founded British National Association of Spiritualists, and Lady Poulett, who held frequent séances at her house in Hanover Square, a few minutes' walk from Davies Street.

These ladies were flattered that the young man should take their activities so seriously and, because of his talk about Egyptian beliefs and perhaps because of his odd looks – notably the hooded eyes – felt that he himself might prove psychic. He was not, at that stage, quite so solemnly interested as they expected. The setting of a séance was strange, as was intended: the lights were lowered and the last gleam lingered in the diamond necklace worn by Lady Caithness. At first, Rider was sceptical and on the verge of giggles; on one occasion when roses, wet with dew, materialised in the darkness, he and a confederate picked the hardest buds and shied them at the medium, who declared that the spirits were angry.

Yet it could not all be laughed away. The wraiths of beautiful young women were conjured up and seemed to change shape before their eyes. Finally several of the students at the crammer's determined to impose their own conditions at one of these meetings. Invited to a séance by Norris's rich uncle at his house in St James's, they determined to lay hold upon the medium – a feeble little man – and not to let go throughout the proceedings. It was of no avail. As Rider later described it,

We sat in the darkened dining-room round the massive table, which presently began to skip like a lamb. Lights floated about the room and with them a file of *Morning Posts*, which normally reposed in a corner.

Cold little hands plucked at the studs in our shirts and the feather fans off the mantelpiece floated to and fro, performing their natural offices upon our heated brows.

Finally the young men – still holding the medium in his chair –

became aware that heavy articles were on the move and the light showed us we were not mistaken. There, in the centre of the dining-table, piled one upon the other ... were the two massive dining-room armchairs and, on top of these, reaching nearly to the ceiling, appeared Mr Norris's priceless china candelabra.

It was as disturbing as it was startling and Rider became convinced that it involved 'some existent but unknown force' but that, whatever it was, it was 'harmful and unwholesome'.[22] He swore to attend no more séances, although he would keep an open mind on psychic phenomena; it was a subject for brooding rather than rational thought.

His social outings sometimes took a lighter path and one led to a ball at Richmond, to which he had been invited by a friend. That night he fell in love. Across the ballroom he saw a girl with blue eyes and curling hair and he was, as he put it, 'instantly and overwhelmingly attracted'.[23] She was aged twenty-one – a couple of years older than himself – and her name was Lily Jackson, the daughter of a prosperous Yorkshire farmer, now living with her mother at Leamington in Warwickshire. They were introduced and talked, finding they had something in common because their brothers had been at school and university together.

When the ball ended, Rider, already lovesick, escorted her out of the house, down a carpeted path across the garden to a floral arch, beyond which her carriage waited. Lily did not give her exact address but Rider later discovered the name of the street where she was staying and enquiries at the neighbouring butcher's finally produced the number of the house. He made the most of the slight family connection, was received by the girl's mother and permitted to pay court to the daughter, for, even if neither handsome nor rich, the son of a Norfolk squire was a worthy suitor for her daughter.

Then, just as Rider might have thought that his courtship was set fair, his father – presumably aware that his son was studying more than foreign languages in London – suddenly flung a thunderbolt, like Jupiter from Olympus. Indeed, he flung two. The first was his decision that Rider should continue his study of French in France and he arranged for him to

13

stay with another tutor at Tours. He had been there only a few weeks when the second blow fell.

William Haggard had heard that a neighbouring Norfolk landowner, Sir Henry Bulwer of Heydon – the nephew of Lord Lytton (the novelist Edward Bulwer-Lytton) – had been appointed Lieutenant-Governor of Natal. At the time, Africa was seen as the continent of opportunity for not only was its vast southern territory in a state of political flux but it was only seven years since a pretty pebble picked up on the shore of the Orange River had turned out to be a diamond. Southern Africa was the next sphere of expansion for the British Empire, where fortunes could be sought and won by young men of spirit.

So he wrote to Sir Henry, asking if there might be a place on his staff for his nineteen-year-old son. Bulwer had never met Rider Haggard but knew the family and it could be assumed that, unless he had heard otherwise, any young man brought up by that particular squire would be suited to a task involving enterprise and physical effort. So Sir Henry agreed and asked that Rider call upon him in London, which he did, meeting a courteous man of early middle age, to whom he quickly accorded the highest compliment by considering him 'my beau-ideal of what an English gentleman should be'.[24] Rider was told that, while no specific appointment, nor any pay, could be offered, he could join Sir Henry's suite as an aide, with duties in organising the commissariat; he was to start work at once by ordering French wines for shipment to Government House in Natal.

There were farewells to be made. To Lily he promised to return and declared, or implied, that when he did so he would propose marriage. Whatever her response – and it seems to have been encouraging – he took with him the memory of 'the girl with golden hair and violets in her hand'.[25]

The farewell from his mother and sisters was by letter, accompanied by advice about punctuality and checking his superiors' instructions. His mother wrote for 'my darling boy, in his new career' a poem inscribed, 'On leaving home, July, 1875'. This ran to seven verses, including,

> And thus, my son, adown Life's vernal tide
> Light drifting, has thou reached her troublous sea
> Where never more thy bark may idly glide,
> But shape her course to gain the far to be!

'Voices of thy distant home'

Rise to thy destiny! Awake thy powers!
Mid throng of men enact the full man's part!
No more with mists of doubts dim golden hours,
But with strong Being fill thine eager heart!

Nineteen short summers o'er thy youthful head
have shone and ripened as they flitted by:
May their rich fruit o'er coming years be shed,
And make God's gift of life a treasury . . .

But a few days: and far across the flood,
To stranger lands with strangers wilt thou roam;
Yet shall not absence loose the bonds of blood,
Or still the voices of thy distant home . . . [26]

CHAPTER TWO

'The most strange and savage sights'

TABLE MOUNTAIN STOOD above the Cape of Good Hope like an altar to the treasures and mysteries of Africa. Between its magnificence and the lost empire of Ancient Egypt far to the north, spread a continent that was unknown: much of it still unexplored and little of it understood by those arriving from Europe.

Its coasts had, of course, long been familiar from the sea-route to India and the East; the north had belonged to the Ancient World; but south of the Sahara was the heart of what was being called the Dark Continent. Equatorial Africa seemed too dangerous for white men because of tropical disease, the climate and its fierce tribes. But only now in the middle years of the nineteenth century was the nature of this terrain becoming known: five thousand miles from north to south, and four thousand at its greatest width, narrowing below that latitude to about two thousand, then tapering towards the Cape.

During the past twenty years more of the deep interior had been discovered by explorers – most famously by those seeking the source of the Nile: Livingstone and Stanley, Burton and Speke – but much of it remained blank on the map and the territory of speculation, even the source of its greatest river not yet being confirmed. It was known that there were jungles and deserts, grasslands, swamps and mountain ranges and vast lakes. Partly from ill-recorded observation and partly as a means of ruling a line between the half-known and the unknown it was said that the way north was barred by the great range known as the Mountains of the Moon.

Only in the extreme south and south-east did land seem suitable for European settlement and this had been achieved first by the Dutch in the seventeenth century and then by the British. While the former did seem to have severed their European roots and become a white African tribe, the British instinct was to establish ordered colonies rather than grow crops and raise livestock as settlers. So the latter gradually displaced the former, the Boer farmers, who trekked north to find new land and independence. By 1875, there were four separate territories: Cape Colony and to the north-east, Natal, were British; the Orange Free State and the South African Republic, or Transvaal, to the north, Dutch; the latter doggedly independent and ready to fight the African tribes, or, if necessary, the British, to hold what they had taken.

In the Transvaal and northward again, it had seemed, the challenges of distance, climate and terrain, hostile natives and disease were too great to be of value to any other Europeans; until, that is, the discovery of diamonds and the first traces of gold. Even that did not suggest settlement, but expeditions to plunder. Yet the British were developing a long-term ambition. Clearly, it seemed, the rough Boer farmers could no more found a modern state than could the tribes with whom they fought for land in the far north and north-east of the European advance; yet they were also a threat to British trade. But under the firm but benevolent rule of the British the whole of Africa from the Cape to the Zambezi river could be bound together in a federation of colonies such as they had achieved in Canada with such success in 1867.

This was the state of African affairs in the southern hemisphere when Rider Haggard arrived there in 1875. He was, as he saw himself,

> a tall young fellow, quite six feet and slight; blue-eyed, brown-haired, fresh-complexioned and not at all bad-looking ... Mentally I was impressionable, quick to observe and learn whatever interested me and could already hold my own in conversation. I was also subject to fits of depression and liable to take views of things too serious and gloomy for my age.[1]

Others took a less flattering view for even his fond sister Ella had, on his departure from England, considered him conceited. One who met him soon after his arrival in South Africa thought him as 'a leggy-looking youth, who seems the picture of weakness and dullness'.[2] Certainly his position on Bulwer's staff did not contribute to self-confidence for he was a general factotum, assigned to duties that nobody else seemed to want. 'My position is not an easy one', he wrote to his father, 'I find myself responsible for everything and everyone comes and bothers me ... I make a good many blunders ... '

After a few days of entertaining by 'the Cape Town aristocracy' and some stimulating conversation with the Bishop – 'a thorough specimen of muscular Christianity'[3] – they sailed for Durban, where, at the end of

August, they were landed through the surf rolling in from the Indian Ocean. This was the largest town in Natal but not the seat of government, which was inland at Maritzburg, yet here the senior British officials awaited them. The most important and impressive of these was Theophilus Shepstone, the Secretary for Native Affairs. An old Africa hand, he had been born there, spoke several tribal languages and had been in British service as an interpreter and then a political agent for forty years. Now approaching sixty, he was a saturnine man, with a strong jaw and shrewd, dark eyes. A fascinating companion, and an enthusiastic and practical botanist – he was to set up botanical gardens in Natal and acclimatise English fruit trees in his own garden there – he could tell strange stories of remote places and wild peoples.

It was in the company of Shepstone that Bulwer and his staff left Durban for Maritzburg at the beginning of September. Haggard recalled covering 'the fifty-four miles over most tremendous hills in five and a half hours, going at full gallop all the way, in a four-horse wagonette'. He did not enjoy the journey although 'some of the scenery was very fine', because the dust was so thick that they could not even see the road beneath the wheels. When it cleared and Haggard had time to observe the country, he was at once bewitched by

> the great plains rising by steps to the Drakensberg Mountains, the sparkling torrential rivers, the sweeping thunderstorms, the grass-fires creeping over the veldt at night like snakes of living flame, the glorious aspect of the heavens, now of spotless blue, now charged with the splendid and many-coloured lights of sunset and now sparkling with a myriad stars; the wine-like taste of the air upon the plains, the beautiful flowers in the bush-clad kloofs, or on the black veldt in spring – all these things impressed me.

Those Dutch words *kloof* and *veldt* – for ravine and prairie – were reminders that the other European occupants of this enormous country were the Boers, whose own country lay to the north across the Vaal river.

As they approached Maritzburg, citizens rode out to greet them and, as Haggard wrote to his mother, 'we entered in grand style amidst loud hurrahs. We galloped up to Government House, where the regiment was drawn up on the lawn and, as soon as the carriage stopped, the band struck up "God save the Queen"'.[4] Sir Henry Bulwer was at once caught up in a round of official welcomes, receptions and meetings and Haggard was given to understand that he would not, as he had hoped, be the

Lieutenant-Governor's secretary because he was too young; instead, he would continue to be responsible for the housekeeping and catering.

Maritzburg was a frontier town, its wooden buildings standing in wide, dusty streets, but its gardens bright with sub-tropical flowers. There was constant awareness of dangers beyond the horizon, not from the Boers, but from the warlike African tribes, notably the Zulus. Shepstone had made many expeditions into Zululand and commanded the respect of Zulus themselves, who had accorded him the flattering nickname of 'Sompseu' – 'The Mighty Hunter'. His interpreter, named Fynney, told Haggard about the great war-dances and parades held by the Zulu kings that he had seen. What seized his imagination was Fynney's account of a 'witch-finding' ceremony when potential traitors were 'smelled out'. He had seen five thousand plumed warriors drawn up in a circle in the centre of which the witch doctors pranced. 'Everyone was livid with fear', he said, 'and with reason, for now and again one of these creatures would come crooning up to one of them and touch him, whereupon he was promptly put out of the world by a regiment of the king's guard'.[5] Fynney had vainly tried to intervene and narrowly escaped execution himself.

Haggard had already been introduced to the local sport of hunting buck with hounds, or shooting them from horseback, but the real excitement was to come when he accompanied Sir Henry on an expedition to the frontiers of Zululand. He was to see at first hand what happened when, as he put it, 'the strong aggressive hand of England has grasped some fresh portion of the Earth's surface, there is a spirit of justice in her heart and head which prompts the question ... as to how best and most fairly to deal by the natives of the newly-acquired land'.[6] Zululand was, of course, nominally an independent African kingdom but as the Zulus and the Boers had been fighting for the ownership of land, it began to seem that the British might intervene and, if necessary, take control themselves for, as they saw it, the safety and benefit of all.

The Zulu king, Cetewayo, the heir to the fearsome rulers Chaka and Dingaan, still ruled the warrior nation from his capital of Ulundi. There he trained his armies, the ruthlessly disciplined impis, to run vast distances across the grasslands to 'wash their spears' – the stabbing assegais – in the blood of their enemies. But some Zulus were already under British 'protection', amongst them a chief named Pagáté and it was his kraal that Bulwer and his staff were to visit eight months after their arrival in Natal.

19

Pagáté's kraal stood on 'a high promontory that juts out and divides two enormous valleys ... The view is superb; two thousand feet below lies the plain encircled by tremendous hills bush-clad to the very top, while at the bottom flashed a streak of silver, which is the river'. There the visitors were invited to watch a war-dance, which Haggard was to describe as 'one of the most strange and savage sights I ever saw'. As he watched and later wrote home,

> the warriors arrived in companies singing a sort of solemn chant. Each man was dressed in his fierce, fantastic war-dress. One half wore heron plumes, the rest long black plumes; each company had a leader and a separate pattern of shield ... Each company as it arrived caught up the solemn war-chant ... The dance then commenced ... Company after company charged past looking for all the world like great fierce birds swooping on their prey. Assegais extended and shields on high, they flitted backwards and forwards, accompanying every movement with a shrill hiss something like the noise which thousands of angry snakes would make, only shriller, a sound impossible to describe but not easy to forget ... Then forth leaped warrior after warrior: advanced, challenged, leapt five feet into the air, was down, was up, was between his own legs, was anywhere and everywhere ... It was a splendidly barbaric sight ... [7]

Haggard was excited and moved by the confidence and physical magnificence of the warriors and described in detail one who stopped before them:

> a finely-built warrior arrayed in the full panoply of savage war. With his right hand he grasped his spear and, on his left, hung his large, black, ox-hide shield lined on its inner side with spare assegais ... As he stood before us with lifted weapon and outstretched shield, his plume bending in the breeze and his savage aspect made more savage still by the graceful, statuesque pose, the dilated eye and warlike mould of set features, as he stood there, an emblem and a type of the times and the things which are passing away, his feet resting on ground which he held on sufferance, and his hands grasping weapons impotent as a child's against those of the white man – he who was the rightful lord of all – what reflections did he not induce, what a moral did he not touch![8]

Then fear rippled through the plumed ranks: the 'witch-finder' – the seeker of traitors – had appeared.

Suddenly there stood before us a creature, a woman – tiny, withered and bent nearly double by age, but in her activity passing comprehension. Clad in a strange jumble of snake skins, feathers, furs and bones; a forked wand in her out-stretched hand, she rushed to and fro ... [9]

Rider Haggard never forgot her; his own immediate reflection was how astonished his friends at home would be to see what he saw. The very thought that spears, shields and witchcraft could offer the slightest resistance to rifle-fire, Gatling guns, rocket batteries and artillery would be funny were it not so pathetic.

The finale of the dance was both stirring and, in the light of such musings, prophetic. The companies of warriors assembled in formation before their chief and his guests and

at a given signal each man began to tap his ox-hide shield softly with the handle of his spear, producing a sound somewhat like the murmur of the distant sea. By slow degrees it grew louder and louder, until at length it rolled and re-echoed from the hills like thunder and came to its conclusion with a quick, sharp rattle ... One more sonorous salute with voice and hand and then the warriors disappeared as they had come, dropping swiftly over the brow of the hill in companies. In a few moments no sign or vestige of dance or dancers remained.[10]

Haggard's first impressions of the Zulus were romantic and so they remained. He saw them as 'the Romans of Africa' and although he heard and recounted ghastly stories of massacre and atrocity, he maintained that Cetewayo's 'manners, as is common among Zulus of high rank, are those of a gentleman'.[11] These were people he could understand, once some of their bloody customs were set aside, and he set about learning the Zulu language, quickly picking up its rhythms and almost biblical style, reminiscent of his father's readings from the Old Testament.

Shepstone, who had been recalled to London early in 1876, returned with a knighthood. Not only had he bowed the knee to Queen Victoria, but had discussed in the quiet committee rooms of Whitehall the planning and building of her Empire. The Prime Minister, Benjamin Disraeli, was an expansionist – 'imperialist' was the favoured word – and had an able executive in Lord Carnarvon, the Colonial Secretary. It was their intention that the four principal states of South Africa – two British, two Dutch – should become a federation under the British Crown.

There was also 'The Native Question'. Once the Zulus had fallen into line, the others would follow. Four years before, Shepstone had assured the succession of Cetewayo; indeed, had himself set the crown on his head at the coronation when the new king had sworn fealty of a sort to Queen Victoria. It was high time this loyalty was called to account and the continual threat of the Zulu impis to both British and Dutch finally removed. First it was vital that the Transvaal, the Boers' South African Republic, be brought into the fold. So Carnarvon had sent two men he could trust, Sir Bartle Frere and Major-General Sir Garnet Wolseley, as Governors of the Cape Colony and Natal respectively. To execute his scheme he sent Shepstone back to Maritzburg with orders to lead an expedition into the Transvaal, ostensibly to enquire into the situation there: on the state of the Boer administration, the welfare of the newly arrived gold prospectors and the abiding threat of attack by African tribes, notably the Zulus. If the circumstances were favourable, he could annex the Transvaal to the British Empire.

Seen as a simple diplomatic mission, this exercise appeared routine. His staff would number ten and, because Pretoria, the capital of the Transvaal, was nearly four hundred miles from Maritzburg across an open plateau, they would have an escort of an officer and twenty-five troopers of the Natal Mounted Police in addition to their African grooms and servants. The youngest European in the mission was to be Rider Haggard, now aged twenty, because Shepstone liked him and because, on arrival in Pretoria, he would need his help in entertaining.

The cavalcade rode out of Maritzburg just before Christmas, 1876, expecting to be about a month on trek. Trailing their cloud of dust across the plains, the horsemen and their baggage wagons, escorted by the jingling troop of police in their dark blue uniforms, whitened cross-belts and sun-helmets topped with brass spikes, headed north-west. Each night they would halt, the servants would make camp and cook dinner and the Europeans, stimulated by drink and tobacco smoke, would talk.

Inevitably they discussed Boers and Zulus. There was grudging admiration for the rough Dutch settlers, always qualified by their inability to come to terms with the African 'Kaffirs' they were either fighting, enslaving or dominating. There was admiration, tinged with apprehension rather than fear, for the Zulus and forecasts that, if the Boers were left to rule the Transvaal, it would be swept clear of them by Cetewayo's impis. Then Shepstone would talk of the bloody Zulu history and his political secretary, Melmoth Osborn, would again tell his own story of the great battle of Tugela between rival Zulu armies.

After such talk, Haggard was particularly fascinated by the head servant, a tall, lean man of about sixty; a son of a former King of Swaziland. He had been a great warrior when young, fighting with a long battle-axe, and his stories of tribal warfare – translated by Fynney, the interpreter – were even more beguiling than Osborn's. His name was M'Hlopekazi, or Umslopogaas, and in Haggard's imagination he assumed Arthurian stature.

Before Christmas dinner, the members of the mission, wearing frock coats or frogged uniforms, posed for a group photograph outside their mess tent, while Haggard sat cross-legged at their feet in his Norfolk tweeds. On entering the Transvaal, their progress became more military, with guards mounted at night, but more fascinating because this was relatively unknown, or at least unpredictable, country. Haggard was bewitched by 'the plains, the mountains, and the vast, rolling high veldt of the Transvaal territory ... the fearful sweeping thunderstorms that overtook us, to be followed by nights of surpassing brilliancy which we watched from beside the fires of our camp'. Their progress attracted visitors

the Boers ... big, bearded men with all the old Dutch characteristics, who made a greater show of religion than they practised, especially where Kaffirs were concerned ... The Old Testament was the standard by which they ruled their conduct. They compared themselves to the Hebrews marching from their land of bondage in Egypt, while the Kaffirs in the parallel filled the places of the Canaanites and Jebusites and other tribes that were unfortunate enough to stand in their way.[12]

After thirty-five days, the column reached Pretoria to a mixed reception of suspicion and relief: the former because the British had always been treading on the Boers' heels and the latter because there was real fear of imminent Zulu invasion from which only the British – and particularly Shepstone – seemed to offer any hope of rescue. There was the knowledge that, however small a British presence, there was always, some way behind it, however distant, the power of the British Army and the Royal Navy. Such thoughts could then have been confirmed by what was known to Shepstone, but probably not to his companions, that a battalion of infantry had been moved into Natal in readiness to cross into the Transvaal when the need arose and behind them were more British soldiers in South Africa and ready to embark in England.

Once the customary receptions and dinners were over, Shepstone began talking to the Boer leaders. He suggested that as only the British could save them from the hostile tribes, they should put themselves under the protection of the British Crown which would respect their political institutions. This was surprisingly well received until word came from the north that the most threatening tribal chieftain, Secocoeni, a Basuto,* had agreed to make peace and to accept the sovereignty of the existing Transvaal administration. If this were true, there would be no excuse for the planned annexation.

So to discover the truth a small mission was to be sent north to visit Secocoeni; this was to consist of Melmoth Osborn, Major Marshall Clarke and two Boer commissioners with Rider Haggard as secretary. They set out in March, taking a track high across the mountains rather than by the valleys, where fever was a risk, to the Basuto kraal. The latter was more elaborate and sophisticated than those of the Zulus, with paved courtyards, the huts decorated with painted spiral patterns: 'after the old Greek fashion', thought Haggard. Although their handsome women wore only a leather girdle, they loved ornaments and their hair was 'elaborately arranged and powdered with some metal that caused it to glitter and gave it a blue tinge ... These Basutos gave me the idea that they were sprung from some race with considerable knowledge of civilisation and its arts' but had now 'relapsed into barbarism'.[13]

Here they were formally received by the chief at an *indaba* watched by ranks of silent warriors. This was the British Empire of the adolescent imagination: the few white men, surrounded by savages' spears in the hot sun, keeping calm and laying down the law. The twist to this particular scene was that one half of the white men trusted the other half as little as both trusted the blacks. At this *indaba*, it was discovered that reports of a Basuto settlement with the Boer republic were untrue and that the threat to the Transvaal remained. This would be all that Shepstone needed to activate plans for annexation and the British members of the party decided to return at once to Pretoria.

Now the atmosphere changed. First the two Boer commissioners themselves left without warning, taking the party's guides with them. Then there was difficulty in finding new guides, or indeed any tribesman willing to give advice on the best track to follow south. Finally two Basuto boys were produced as guides but, as the party set out, they became agitated and tried to persuade the Englishmen to delay their journey.

Night had fallen when they arrived at the fork where the track divided

* In fact, a Bapedi, related to the Basutos.

into the high route they had followed on the outward journey and the low route through the valleys. Osborn and Clarke were for taking the familiar track but Haggard suggested the lower from which the moonlit mountains could be admired. The others agreed and they descended into a strange landscape that Haggard described as 'sombre, weird, grand. Every valley became a mysterious deep and every hill and stone and tree shone with that cold, pale lustre that the moon alone can throw. Silence reigned, the silence of the dead'.[14] So it might have become for the travellers. After riding in silence for some time, one of the Englishmen lit his pipe and the tiny flicker of flame brought on distant shouting high on the dark mountainside, where the higher track ran, and they could hear the blowing of war horns. It was only later, after they had reached the Transvaal, that they discovered that Secocoeni had, in collusion with unnamed but suspected Boers, laid an ambush on the road they were expected to take with orders that they be killed. Their escape was due to Rider Haggard's whim but he would always have the feeling that such instinct was not always the product of chance.

Pretoria was safely reached and the news of the continuing threat given to Shepstone. There was now no need to delay the annexation of the Transvaal on the pretext that the Boer administration was inefficient, bankrupt and unable to defend its European population against tribal invasion. There remained the main Zulu threat, although there were to be those who doubted it was as real as the British maintained. In any case, Shepstone sent a message to Cetewayo warning him to keep his impis at home because the Transvaal was now to be under the protection of Queen Victoria and received the reply:

> I thank my father Sompseu for his message, I am glad that he has sent it because the Dutch have tired me out and I intended to fight them once and once only and drive them over the Vaal ... My impis gathered to fight the Dutch ... Now I will send them back to their homes.[15]

Knowing that Shepstone was about to proclaim the annexation, Haggard decided that that would be the time to return home, propose marriage to Lily Jackson and return with her to Africa in triumph to take up what he expected would be a career as a colonial administrator. When he was told that no leave was available even for 'urgent private affairs', he confided in Shepstone that he 'desired to bring a certain love affair to a head by a formal engagement'.[16] Sir Theophilus sympathised and agreed, telling

Haggard that, when he reached London, he was to give Lord Carnarvon a verbal account of events in Pretoria. So a passage to England was booked, baggage sent ahead to the coast and Haggard wrote to his father, announcing his intention of returning to Norfolk in the early summer. He could then look upon the coming days with the anticipation of a story-teller recording excitements to be relayed to a wondering audience at home.

On 12 April 1877, a crowd in mixed moods had gathered in the market square of Pretoria. Most were British gold-prospectors and drifters and they seemed happy; the rest were Boers, silent and surly. While Sir Theophilus Shepstone remained in what was about to become Government House, Melmoth Osborn read out the proclamation of the annexation but was so nervous that his voice wavered and his hands shook so much that Haggard, standing beside him, had to hold the document for him. This was followed, as a formality, by the reading of the former Boer President's protest against his deposition. Then Haggard, standing behind Osborn, was handed the papers for delivery to Government House, but, as he began to cross the square, his way was barred by a group of large, sullen Boers. Trying to pass between two of them, neither would move until Haggard trod on the foot of one and he stepped back.

A few days later a letter reached him from Norfolk. It was his father's reply and it was not the letter of delight and promised welcome that he expected. It was a harsh letter, telling him that on no account could he abandon his career in Africa and pointing out that he had been subsidised by his father and, even so, his bank account was overdrawn by £25 so that there was no question of his returning until he had established himself in a career with a salary. Shocked and angered, Haggard tore up the letter. He was so hurt that he could not bring himself to reply and tell his father that he would be returning on a personal mission to brief the Foreign Secretary on the annexation of the Transvaal. Instead, he can-celled his passage home and returned to his duties.

Three weeks later, the British firmly impressed their stamp upon their new acquisition when a battalion of the 13th Regiment, which had been waiting in Natal, marched into the capital behind the thump and blare of its brass band. The final touch came on 24 May when, to mark Queen Victoria's birthday, the British flag was formally hoisted in Pretoria. As the military band played the national anthem and guns fired a royal salute, Rider Haggard was accorded the honour of hoisting the flag up its staff. 'I am very proud', he wrote to his mother. 'Twenty years hence it will be a great thing to have hoisted the union jack over the Transvaal for the first time'. Then he added sadly, 'My absence, which I remember we set down as five years at the most, is likely to be a long one now, my dearest Mother. The break from all home and family ties and the sense of isolation are very painful, more painful than those who have never tried them know'.[17]

His frustration was slightly mollified by the offer of his first salaried appointment. Shepstone was trying to cobble together an effective administration before the Afrikaners overcame their relief at rescue from Zulu invasion to realise that the British had again usurped their conquest. Osborn was appointed Colonial Secretary for the Transvaal with Haggard as his English Clerk on an annual salary of £250 with the prospect of promotion to Clerk to the Executive Council. This would not only make him almost independent of his father but also a suitor with prospects in his long-distance courtship.

He wrote home excitedly,

> It is far better to take service here than in Natal. In five years Natal will be to this country what Ireland is to England. To begin with, the Transvaal is six times its size. If the Transvaal at all realises what is expected of it, it will before long, with its natural wealth and splendid climate, be one of the most splendid foreign possessions of the British Crown and if, as is probable, gold is discovered in large quantities it may take a sudden rush forward and then one will be borne up with it.[18]

One of the many inherited weaknesses in the administration was a ramshackle and corrupt legal system and a start on imposing a new order had to be made. A new High Court was set up under a judge of high repute, John Kotzé, who together with a Master and a Registrar would attempt to rebuild a judicial system. But almost at once the Registrar died and Haggard, aged only twenty-one and without any legal experience, but, being considered a young man of initiative, was chosen as his successor.

The new appointment was demanding for he was the principal aide to the High Court; indeed he was the youngest official of his rank in the whole of South Africa. He and Judge Kotzé toured the country by spring-wagon drawn by eight oxen, sleeping under the stars when the Court was not sitting in a town. The itinerant life suited them. Haggard was not only a good shot but himself cooked the birds and game his gun brought down and, while in the wilds, they made their own entertainment, reading Shakespeare's plays aloud, each taking different parts.

One embarrassment was that Haggard had become a freelance journalist, sending articles about Africa to the *Gentleman's Magazine* and *Macmillan's Magazine*. His account of the Zulu war dance was innocuous enough, but another showed his initial contempt for the Boers. 'The whole house was pervaded by a sickly smell, like that of a vault', he wrote of one Boer farmhouse, 'whilst the grime and filth of it baffle description'.[19] This was signed with his initials but he was identified when one offending article, translated into Dutch, was reprinted in Afrikaner newspapers. 'The Boers are furious', he wrote. 'There are two things they cannot bear – the truth and ridicule'.[20]

He did not let this trouble him unduly for he was constantly busy and on the move. Travel and the law offered diversion although not always of an agreeable kind. Once, while out shooting, his horse bolted and when he regained control realised that he was lost and it was almost dark; only by firing his last round of ammunition did he attract the attention of his distant servant. Much of the legal work concerned squabbles over land but he was involved in the trial of a minor Swazi chief for the murder of a European. The African was condemned to death and Haggard had to attend the execution. Later Judge Kotzé said that Haggard had felt faint at the scaffold and, as the sentence was carried out, turned away. But Rider himself, unable to resist a dramatic story, told a different version: that the executioner was so drunk that he himself had to supervise the hanging.

On their return to Pretoria from one tour, they found prospects of continued peace darkening. The Boers were increasingly restive under British rule and the African tribes had been fighting amongst themselves and raiding Boer settlements. Sir Bartle Frere, now High Commissioner for South Africa, took so serious a view of these developments that he sent a British officer and a civil servant on a mission to the Matabele; Haggard, who knew both, sought permission to accompany them but this was refused. Meanwhile more important missions led by Shepstone and a staff officer, Major Clarke, attempted to pacify the Zulus and the Basutos respectively. Then news arrived that the two men sent to the Matabele had been murdered.

Haggard wrote to his mother that he now expected 'one last struggle between the white and black races ... The Zulus are brave men ... they are panting for war'. So at the end of 1878, he enlisted as a cavalry volunteer and was soon expecting to have to fight both the potential enemies. In March of the following year he wrote home that 'the Zulu business hangs fire, but that cloud will surely burst ... Our most pressing danger now is the Boers'.[21]

But quite a different blow fell. A letter arrived from Lily Jackson, telling him that she had decided to marry another. After two and a half years of waiting and no prospect of Rider's early return, she had become engaged to a stockbroker, the sole trustee of her family's considerable fortune. The date of the wedding had been set and there was no time for Haggard to make contact in the hope of changing her mind. 'All was over', he wrote later. 'It was a crushing blow, so crushing that at the time I should not have been sorry if I could have departed from the world'.[22] The only consolation – and one that took time to take shape in his imagination – was that, as his mother's poetry had insisted, love was eternal.

He abandoned thoughts of home. As his salary had been increased to £400, he decided to set up house with another bachelor, Arthur Co-chrane, in a tin-roofed bungalow they named 'The Palatial', surrounding it with blue gum trees and flowering shrubs. Attractive as Pretoria had become, with English roses added to its sub-tropical gardens, it did not offer much dissipation in which a heartbroken bachelor could lose himself. But there was some and he seems to have found it. Perhaps he ended the chastity imposed by the love of Lily and may for a spell have taken a mistress, possibly African; whatever occurred, it inspired guilt.

Yet this in turn was overcome by the mounting crisis. The Boers threatened revolt within the Transvaal and the Zulus were massing on its borders. For Cetewayo, the expansionist British had now replaced the Boers as his enemy and he was said to be contemplating war. His impis were believed to number forty thousand and, although they possessed few firearms, they were superbly trained in tactics which had almost always proved invincible. The Zulu impis could trot across the grass-lands for hours without a halt, before forming their fearsome battle formation: a central mass of warriors forming the 'chest' to assault from the front and two long, sharp 'horns' of running warriors to outflank, envelop and crush the enemy against the 'chest'. The only tactics with which even the best European troops could withstand such attacks had been developed by the Boers: controlled rifle fire from a strong defensive position such as interlocked wagons and thorn scrub.

This confrontation was brought to a head when Sir Bartle Frere arrived in Natal and issued an ultimatum to Cetewayo. The High Commissioner was feeling confident as military reinforcements had now arrived from England, including not only infantry but artillery and a rocket battery. Indeed he was confident enough in December, 1878, to deliver an ultimatum to Cetewayo which he must have known would not be accepted but would then provide the pretext to invade Zululand. This was that Cetewayo disband his impis, rescind the requirement for every young Zulu to 'wash his spear' in enemy blood before becoming eligible for marriage, that he pay reparations to the British for damage in frontier raids, and receive a resident British commissioner in Zululand. To accept such terms would have meant surrender and the absorption of the country into the British Empire as a minor province. Haggard considered the ultimatum 'a mistake'; instead, it would have been better to remonstrate with the Zulus because 'neither Cetewayo nor his people wished to fight the English'.[23]

At the beginning of 1879, a British expeditionary force under the command of Major-General Lord Chelmsford was deployed on the border of Natal and Zululand. It consisted of nearly sixteen thousand men, including five seasoned battalions of regular infantry, locally raised regiments, African infantry and cavalry and mounted volunteers; yet Haggard himself was required to stay in Pretoria. Morale was high and, amongst the regulars at least, the expectation was that if action followed it would be almost a sporting event – big-game hunting with plumed warriors instead of lions – but, in case there was none, they had loaded cricket gear into the baggage wagons.

Haggard was fearful for them. Melmoth Osborn, who had made a study of Zulu warfare, had sent a warning against over-confidence to Lord Chelmsford, also advising on tactics to be employed, but he received no reply. Haggard's apprehension increased as he saw many friends, including three of Shepstone's six sons, join the expedition and he knew many of the officers in the regular formations. He had heard that Chelmsford planned to advance in three parallel columns across open, rolling country towards Cetewayo's capital, Ulundi, and he feared for them. Unless they were trained to fight from tight, static defences, they would be vulnerable to the trotting impis.

Cetewayo had been given thirty days to respond to Frere's ultimatum and, when no reply had been received by 11 January, the army stirred into movement and next morning, a Sunday, crossed into Zululand: the

British infantry in their white sun-helmets and belts, their red tunics and blue, red-striped trousers; the naval brigade in wide-brimmed straw hats; the volunteers in riding breeches, bandoliers and bush-hats; the field guns and limbers bouncing and rattling behind their jingling horse teams and straining oxen dragging the great, creaking baggage wagons. Lord Chelmsford, a dignified, bearded figure surrounded by smartly tailored staff officers on magnificent horses, led the central column. Another exciting, satisfactory little colonial war seemed about to begin; surely, by next Christmas, Zulu shields and assegais would adorn the walls of the halls and trophy rooms of English country houses?

Rider Haggard was not alone in his fear for them. A few days after the frontier was crossed, a woman he knew in Pretoria told him of a nightmare she had experienced the night before: she had seen the British soldiers camped on a great plain in Zululand; snow had begun to fall, then turned red, burying the soldiers and their camp before melting in torrents of blood. Haggard put this down to 'the excited and fearful feeling in the air which naturally affected all who had relatives or friends at the front'. Then, on the morning of 23 January, he strolled across his garden from the verandah of 'The Palatial' to greet the old Hottentot washerwoman who had arrived to collect their laundry. She was agitated and told him that 'terrible things had happened in Zululand; that the "*rooibatjes*" – that is, redcoats – lay upon the plain "like leaves under the trees in winter", killed by Cetewayo'.[24] Haggard asked when this had happened and where had she heard the story. She replied that it had been the day before but would not say how she knew. Chelmsford's force was more than two hundred miles distant and there could be no communication over that distance in that time; even so, Haggard was impressed by her manner and rode over to the government offices. There he related the story to Osborn, who became worried because he felt that the old woman might have heard of some disaster that had happened several days before. Next day an exhausted horseman galloped into Pretoria with news which confirmed that the washerwoman's story and the date she had given were true. The town was struck silent; shops closed and men with frightened faces gathered in little groups. Gradually details began to arrive. Chelmsford's column had, after leaving a company of infantry to guard the ford at Rorke's Drift, marched another nine miles before making camp beneath the high, sphinx-like crag of Isandhlwana, which commanded a tremendous view over a wide, open valley towards hills, eight miles distant, beyond which lay Cetewayo's capital, Ulundi.

On the morning of 22 January, Chelmsford, leaving the bulk of his force in camp, led a detached column across the plain in a search for the Zulu impis. While he was away, a British cavalry patrol, riding along the crest of a huge, bare bluff a few miles from the camp, looked down its far slope into a natural arena and there they saw, squatting on the grass, a vast Zulu army. The British officer fired his carbine into the mass, reined his horse around and galloped back to the camp, while behind him there rose a sound like the stirring of a hornets' nest.

As British bugles sounded, the camp convulsed with activity. Colonel Durnford, who had been left in command, was aware that he had a reputation for caution and determined to live it down. As he watched sixteen thousand feathered Zulus line the summit of the long ridge and stream down into the valley before the camp, he did not draw up his men into a tight perimeter behind a semi-circle of wagons beneath the cliff of Isandhlwana, but ordered them to advance and take up an open formation half a mile in front of the camp. Then he watched to see what British rifle volleys, artillery fire and rockets could do to massed savages armed only with shields and spears.

What happened next only became clear as the few survivors were found and interviewed. Many of Haggard's friends had not survived: the dead included one of Shepstone's sons; Osborn's son-in-law; many volunteer and regular officers including Colonel Durnford and Captains Melvill and Coghill, who died together in a desperate attempt to save their regimental colours. One survivor, a Captain Essex, told Haggard how the 'horns' of the great impi had swept behind the camp and the mountain and when they had met, cutting off retreat, the 'chest' had charged. The extended line of British and African infantry shot down hundreds of the attackers, then began to run short of ammunition. More was rushed forward from the camp in upturned sun helmets but when this ran out and reserve stocks were called for, it was found that the wooden boxes were screwed down, the screws had rusted and no screwdrivers could be found. Then the African infantry, naturally more fearful of the Zulus' reputation, broke and ran and the impis poured through the gap. Soon the British were fighting in groups, back to back, until overwhelmed.

Haggard particularly remembered the account of one British officer of the 24th Regiment, facing the Zulus as they swept into the camp. Bracing his back against a wagon wheel, the officer drew his sword.

> Then the Zulu came at him with his shield up, turning and springing from side to side as he advanced [recorded Haggard]. Presently he lowered his shield, exposing his head, and the white man, falling into the trap, aimed a fierce blow at it. As it fell, the shield was raised again and the sword sank deep into its edge, remaining fixed in the tough ox-hide. This was what the Zulu desired; with a twist of his strong arm, he wrenched the sword from his opponent's hand and in another instant the unfortunate officer was down with an assegai through his breast.[25]

When it was over and the Zulus had stripped and ritually disembowelled their dead enemies, it was found that only fifty of some sixteen hundred men had escaped. The news was past imagining in its horror, even for Haggard, leaving only pride in the hopeless heroism and in the triumph of the detached company which had defended the post at Rorke's Drift all night against four thousand Zulus and survived. Writing home about the disaster, Haggard added,

> You and my mother must not be alarmed, my dear father, when I tell you that I shall very likely go down to the border with a volunteer troop shortly. The emergency is too great and mounted men are too urgently needed to hang back now ... If I should, and if anything should happen to me, it must be and I am sure will be your consolation that it will be in doing my duty.[26]

Haggard was appointed adjutant of the Pretoria Horse but orders for Zululand were countermanded when the Boers, seeing the British otherwise occupied, threatened rebellion and massed a force of three thousand men near Pretoria. There, Haggard had his own adventure when confronted by hostile Boers in a remote farmhouse, he bluffed his way out by telling them that dynamite was stored under the floorboards and one lighted match would destroy them all. Mostly, the Pretoria Horse were awaiting attacks that never came.

Sir Bartle Frere, not Shepstone, was now handling the crisis in Natal and the Transvaal and doing so in the manner of the imperious proconsul he had been in India. As Haggard saw it, he did not understand the complications of there being two European peoples faced by a diversity of African tribes:

I do not believe that he ever grasped the problem in its entirety as ...
Shepstone did. He saw the Zulu war cloud looming ... and determined
to burst it even if it should rain blood. But he did not see that by this act
of his, which, after all, might perhaps have been postponed, he was
ensuring the rebellion of the Transvaal Dutch ... Yonder was a savage
people, who threatened the rights of the Crown and the safety of its
subjects. Let them be destroyed![27]

But as British reinforcements poured into South Africa to take revenge
for Isandhlwana, the Boers realised that this was not the opportunity they
had imagined and their armed men faded away to their distant home-
steads. The Pretoria Horse was stood down but Haggard did not resume
his career as a civil servant. The Transvaal had changed. Shepstone
seemed to have been chosen as the scapegoat for the disaster in Zululand
and was recalled to London. The old order was passing and the British
Government, shocked by the humiliating slaughter of its soldiers – and
spurred by the realisation that the South African territories were likely to
be far richer in minerals than had been expected – would be sending out
new and favoured administrators.

Moreover Haggard was increasingly restless. The loss of Lily had
numbed his more delicate sensibilities and he bitterly regretted not
having defied his father and returned home to claim her. Now he was
trying – without success – to forget her by indulging the wildness that
comes naturally to a young unattached man far from home. He enjoyed
sharing a house with Arthur Cochrane and the two of them decided to
join those who were making money out of Africa; in their case not from
diamonds, or gold, but from ostrich feathers to make plumes for fine
ladies in England. So at the end of May, 1879, Haggard wrote to
Melmoth Osborn, resigning from the secretariat of the High Court.

The two young men sold their house in Pretoria but did not have to
search for suitable land for their project as Osborn himself sold them on
credit an estate of three thousand acres he owned near Newcastle, two
hundred miles from Pretoria. There was a house called Hilldrop below
one of the flat-topped hills characteristic of the landscape, and near to a
stream. The two friends bought their first ostriches but Cochrane went
alone to start work on the farm because Rider Haggard had finally
decided to return to England on leave. He did so without consulting his
father, whom he knew would disapprove. Africa and the edge of war had
given him the confidence he needed.

CHAPTER THREE

'Fresh as a rose and as sound as a bell'

RIDER HAGGARD REACHED London in August, 1879. He had changed. At twenty-three, he was upstanding, strong, and bore himself with confidence, a moustache adding a touch of authority. Yet, even so, he could not face what he knew would be his father's wrath at abandoning a promising career in the colonial service for the risks of ostrich-farming, which he would surely see as 'trade' at its most contemptible.

There was embarrassment, too, because his brother Jack, now a naval officer serving in the South Atlantic, had asked him to bring a huge, live turtle home to provide soup for their father; but this had been lost, or stolen, at the London docks and that had to be explained. So, instead of heading straight for Bradenham, he travelled down to Plymouth, where his brother Andrew's regiment was stationed, to ask and receive his support.

Fascinated by Rider's account of rebellious Zulus and Boers and magnificent, wild country, the wide-eyed Andrew caught the excitement and agreed to give his backing. On the 11th he wrote to their father:

> Rider has been stopping with me two or three days ... I have talked over his plans with him and am of the opinion that his step has been a very wise one. As far as I can judge, his speculation is a thoroughly sound one and I fancy that when you have seen him and hear what he has to say, you will agree that he has done well and not thrown up the service from mere caprice. I do not think he will ever return to Pretoria in an official capacity and I think it will make his stay at home a much pleasanter one to him if he is not pressed to do so.

Andrew then spoiled his plea by adding, 'He would "*entre nous*", like me to join him in his enterprise. If I could get the cash together, about a thousand – I should not be at all averse to doing so'. So now two of William Haggard's sons would be giving up honourable professions for trade! Andrew compounded his mistake by writing a second letter to their father soon after Rider had left for Bradenham:

> I hope you will agree with me that he is not such a fool as we thought him. I think more highly of his investment the more I think of it! ... I am living now in a state of genteel poverty, devilishly genteel but deucedly poor; why should not I have a little enterprise? You talked about a year ago with me about putting my money into land in England – yielding what? Three or four per cent. Well, I do not see in the least why Rider's concern (if he sticks to ostriches) should not yield forty or fifty per cent ... I have often heard you say that one must either be a man or a mouse. I have been a mouse long enough to hate the mouse-trap.[1]

So Squire Haggard's temper was well primed by the time Rider arrived at Bradenham. But he found that, while Andrew could be ordered to put such ridiculous thoughts out of his head and concentrate on soldiering, the newly confident Rider could no longer be brow-beaten. So, much of his father's bluster was ostensibly concerned with the loss of the turtle and the carelessness or dishonesty of whoever was responsible. But this finally led to the point at issue, William Haggard proclaiming that ostrich-farming would only lead to Rider becoming 'a waif and a stray' and dismissing his first ventures into journalism as making him 'a miserable penny-a-liner'.[2] Rider himself had no wish to spend his leave quarrelling with his father, who had, in any case, refused to invest in the ostrich farm and had forbidden Andrew to do so.

So, to humour him, and to keep open the possibility of financial support, he agreed to write to Melmoth Osborn and ask what vacancies there might be in the administration should he decide to give up ostrich-farming. It would be two or three months before a reply could be expected so a peaceful summer had been assured.

Rider's sister Mary was at home and he confided in her his unfaded longing for the lost Lily Jackson, now settled with her rich husband. To alleviate this she invited a succession of her former school-friends to stay in the hope that one would catch her brother's eye. Two of them did. One was Agnes Barber, an intelligent, opinionated girl, who talked about books and journalism with enthusiasm and imagination. But she was too strong a character for comfort and, he noted at the time, 'She will never marry till she finds her master'. But she did encourage him to write another article about his experiences in the Transvaal for the

Gentleman's Magazine; it was rejected because, in August, the reinforced expeditionary force, commanded by Lieutenant-General Sir Garnet Wolseley, had destroyed the Zulu army at Ulundi and captured Cetewayo; the Zulu War was over and no longer topical.

Then Mary invited a less daunting Norfolk friend to stay at Bradenham for a week. This was Louisa Margitson, aged twenty and an orphan, the only surviving child of Major Margitson of Ditchingham House near the Suffolk border in the far east of the county. She was 'not very pretty ... but she was a perfect specimen of a young English girl; fresh as a rose and as sound as a bell'.[3] She had none of Agnes Barber's imagination but was warmly sympathetic and Rider immediately identified with her loneliness. Both of them were accustomed to squirearchical life, enjoying its mixture of outdoor activity and indoor comfort, and understood and respected its customs.

They were instantly attracted to each other: he to her admiring, trusting manner and the glowing health of the young body within its cocoon of rustling silk from neck to ankle; she to this tall, sunburned young man with thrilling stories to tell about his adventures. She was also an heiress to the substantial, if not grand, Ditchingham estate of several houses and with land enough to keep a squire's family in comfort. For his part, William Haggard thoroughly approved of his son's interest on both social and financial grounds. Within a week Rider had proposed marriage to Louisa and been accepted.

It was not an infatuation such as Lily had inspired but it seemed to complete the pattern of their lives. He wrote to his brother Will, now a young diplomat at the British Embassy in Teheran, '*Je vais me marier* – to such a brick of a girl ... I love her sincerely, as I think she does me ... I think we have as good a prospect of happiness as most people. She is good and sensible and true-hearted ... a woman who can be a man's friend as well as his lover'.[4]

There followed a visit to Ditchingham, where the estate was managed by Louisa's uncle by marriage and guardian, William Hartcup, and his initial reaction was as enthusiastic as Squire Haggard's. The estate which Louisa would inherit on her twenty-first birthday in the following year stood along the low escarpment above the river Waveney, on the far bank from the Suffolk market town of Bungay. It was lusher country than that around Bradenham with south-facing slopes that had once been Norman vineyards above the water-meadows where cattle grazed among the buttercups. Ditchingham House was another square, red-brick Georgian house of about the same size as Bradenham and, because of the yellow lichen covering its roof, known locally as Mustard Pot Hall.

All seemed satisfactory until William Hartcup changed his mind. Again it was Rider's apparently feckless abandonment of a promising legal career for the absurd speculation in ostrich-farming and his consequent lack of prospects. Probably he had joked about the letters he had been receiving from Arthur Cochrane, which were full of comic complaints about the ostriches' behaviour – kicking or sitting upon their African keepers, refusing to grow feathers and breaking their necks – and serious problems with the farm's finance. It was intolerable that this young fortune-hunter should drag the heiress of Ditchingham to Africa to exchange the solid security of her estate for an ostrich farm in wild country terrorised by Boers and Zulus. So his opposition became implacable.

The young couple were defiant. 'We are not children to be played with, as the Kaffirs say', wrote Rider to Louisa, refusing to wait until her coming-of-age in the following October; one reason being that Arthur Cochrane seemed in desperation and had to be helped with the farm. As Rider wrote to Louisa, 'Two things are very clear. 1. That I do not see my way clear to stopping in England until next October. 2. That I will not leave England without you. So the sooner your Uncle makes up his mind to treat the matter on that basis the more comfortably we shall get on together'.[5] So, seeing that the girl agreed with her fiancé, Hartcup invoked the law and made her a ward in Chancery.

At once they were entangled with the lawyers but there Haggard was on familiar ground and refused to be over-awed. When their case came to court in London, the judge was sympathetic to the young couple and when Hartcup's counsel said that Rider had proposed within a week of meeting Louisa, snorted, 'Have you never heard of love at first sight?'[6] The couple won their case, the judge allowing the marriage on condition that Hartcup together with Louisa's more sympathetic aunts were guardians. Even so, her uncle succeeded in delaying the marriage, trying, but failing, to persuade the rector of Ditchingham not to publish the banns because she was under age. Finally he had to acknowledge defeat, but not before amassing legal bills amounting to £3,000, which had to be paid from Louisa's inheritance.

The battle with William Hartcup, and now victory, had given their match an excitement it would otherwise have lacked. Suited as they were in many ways, it was not to be a marriage of soulmates, not one forged by passion. During one of their brief separations, Rider wrote to Louisa, 'I hope and believe the step we are taking is entirely for our happiness, we are neither of us perfect and we must always try and remember that and bear with each other, for quarrels mean the destruction of love'.[7] This probably did not strike Louisa as lacking any necessary passion for she was unsentimental herself. Yet she could hardly have guessed that he was still longing for the lost Lily, whom he had not seen for five years but whom he had invested with superhuman qualities of beauty and sexuality. In moments of depression and hopeless longing, he had taken refuge in mysticism, a vague *mélange* of Christianity, Egyptian beliefs and spiritualism. The essence of this was that marriage was 'until death us do part' but then, as love was eternal, he and Lily would be reunited, either in another spiritual dimension or by reincarnation. Meanwhile he was determined to make the best of what he expected to be a satisfactory marriage to a thoroughly suitable girl.

Finally, on 11 August 1880, the couple were married in St Mary's Church at Ditchingham. It was a quiet wedding (without the attendance of the Hartcups), but they cut a dash afterwards by making the thirteen-mile journey to Norwich in an open carriage drawn by four grey horses with postilions; a final gesture of defiance planned by Louisa.

They travelled to the Lake District for their honeymoon, then to London to prepare for the voyage to South Africa. Haggard had had an encouraging reply from Melmoth Osborn, saying that he could probably be reinstated as Registrar of the High Court but that he would have to apply to Sir Garnet Wolseley, who was now Governor of the Transvaal. But on doing so at the beginning of the year he received a terse reply telling him that 'arrangements are in contemplation which prevent your reinstatement'.[8] So, initially at least, the couple would have to become ostrich-farmers.

There was a farewell visit to Bradenham, where William Haggard, delighted by his daughter-in-law, was at his most genial. The couple would take reminders of Norfolk to Africa with them: a middle-aged lady's maid, Lucy Gibbs, from Ditchingham and a young groom, Stephen Lanham, from Bradenham, who would be known, respectively, as 'Gibbs' and 'Stephen'. Lanham would maintain the light, folding carriage that had been especially built in Norwich, and care for the three dogs that would accompany them and, of course, the horses they would buy on arrival.

Finally there was Louisa's twenty-first birthday to celebrate in London and, consequently, much signing of legal documents connected with her inheritance. Gibbs and Stephen were sent ahead to the London docks with the luggage and the dogs. The ship was surprisingly small with only partitioned cabins leading off the saloon, the partitions open at the top so that every snore – and, in rough weather, every retch – could be heard. The first night on board was constantly disturbed by late-arriving passengers, bustle and chatter. The ship sailed before daybreak on 9 November and was off Dover at noon. Louisa, writing the first entry in the diary she planned to keep, noted 'Weather cold but fine and a little swell. Many people seedy, including Gibbs'.[9]

The ship stopped briefly at Dartmouth, where it rained, and Rider and 'Louie', as he now called her, could see each other in a less romantic light. 'Rider is in a great stew about himself, as feeling rather seedy', she wrote in her diary. 'He imagined he had caught the scarlet fever'. The ship called for a few hours at Madeira, where the passengers went ashore on arrival at one o'clock in the morning for nocturnal sightseeing and shopping before returning on board with wicker chairs, silver filigree-work and fruit. They sighted Tenerife on the horizon and then the long haul down the South Atlantic began with Louie confessing in her diary, 'Fight against it as I will, indolence overtakes me'.[10]

On Sunday, 12 December, they landed at Durban and the African adventure began. It took four days for their luggage to be landed and arrangements made with carriers to transport it in three wagons to the new railway line to Maritzburg. There they stayed with Sir Theophilus Shepstone, who had been retired from public service and now devoted himself to cultivating his sub-tropical garden. Other old friends had been overtaken by events: Sir Bartle Frere, the High Commissioner for South Africa, had been another scapegoat for the Zulu War and been dismissed and recalled to London for an enquiry; Melmoth Osborn had reluctantly accepted the appointment of Commissioner to Zululand and then left for England and retirement; even Judge Kotzé had been passed over and a more junior judge appointed Chief Justice. Without the support of such friends and mentors, Haggard's chances of returning to the ladder of official appointments were remote.

In view of the changed political climate in South Africa, Kotzé wrote to Haggard advising him to abandon all ideas of reinstatement. 'Why not read for the Bar?' he asked.

You have a *splendid* opening in the Cape Colony or at the Diamond Fields. You have a certain prospect of a judgeship and will, without much difficulty, get into the Cape Parliament. Mrs Haggard will be pleased with Grahamstown (which I would recommend in preference to Cape Town) and you will have a *fine* and *thoroughly independent* career before you ... Pretoria is no longer what it was ... Everybody at loggerheads with Government and his neighbours and the contractors in the meantime making fortunes.[11]

Haggard, however, was committed to the relief of Arthur Cochrane at the ostrich farm. The Shepstones insisted that the couple stay with them for Christmas and it was then that serious news arrived from the Transvaal. This was not unexpected. The destruction of Cetewayo's power by the British after the massacre at Isandhlwana had relieved the Boers of their fear of the Zulus and most of the British troops who had won the final victory had been sent home, leaving the way clear for a Boer rebellion. This had been aggravated in 1880, with Disraeli being succeeded as Prime Minister by Gladstone who, while in opposition, had favoured Boer independence in the Transvaal but, once in power, was having second thoughts.

Reports of tension, and even occasional violence, in Pretoria were reaching Maritzburg. On Sunday, 20 December, a column of the 94th Regiment, on their way to reinforce the small British garrison of Pretoria, was halted on the road by a strong force of armed Boers. The British, who had been marching at ease behind their band, eating peaches, were unprepared for trouble since their colonel had, when warned, said that if any hostile Boers appeared he would frighten them away with the big drum. A Boer horseman rode up to the colonel and told him that the South African Republic had been restored and that his further advance would be taken as an act of war. When his response was to order the regimental band to play *God Save the Queen*, the Boers, having taken cover behind rocks, opened fire. Eighty of the British, drawn up with their wagon-train on the road, were killed or died of their wounds. War had begun.

This presented the Haggards with a dilemma. Louie was now pregnant – although she never mentioned this in her diary – and the baby was due in the summer. The journey to their house, Hilldrop, was only a few miles from the Transvaal border and the journey would be difficult enough, even if raiding parties of Boers had not been reported inside Natal. But all their belongings had been sent ahead by wagon and they were committed to joining Arthur Cochrane. They decided to wait a few more days, or even weeks, while Haggard found some temporary work at the Government offices and Louie became his copying clerk.

Meanwhile all available British troops – only about one thousand – were concentrated at Newcastle, the nearest town to Hilldrop, under the command of Major-General Sir George Colley, who had succeeded Wolseley as Governor of Natal. On 10 January 1881, Sir George was to leave for Newcastle and, on the night before, he invited the Haggards to dine at Government House. With the general confidence of early success against the insurgents, it proved a jolly occasion, remembered particularly for the teasing of Colley's aide-de-camp, a Lieutenant Elwes, who, fresh out of Eton, had been responsible for writing the menu in French and had described mince pies as *'pâtés de mince'*. Also a Norfolkman, young Elwes touched thoughts of home when he told Haggard that only the other day he had seen his father talking to the barmaid in the buffet at King's Lynn railway station.

Four days later, the Haggard household set out themselves and almost at once suffered an accident. It had been raining and the roads were deeply rutted, causing the light 'spider' carriage – built with such care in Norwich – to lurch violently. Gibbs had been perched on the baggage holding their terrier Bob when, as Louie told her father-in-law in a letter, 'suddenly the carriage went into a hole, gave a lurch and nearly sent Bob flying. In her efforts to save him, out fell Gibbs right between the wheels'. Luckily the hole was filled with mud.

> Never shall I forget the splash she caused [Rider reported]. The spectacle of an elderly British lady's maid in that hole still clasping Bob to her bosom was almost weird. The hind wheels of the 'spider' went over her, grinding her deeper into the mire.
>
> 'Good God!' I said to Stephen, 'she is done for'.
>
> My further remarks were interrupted by a series of piercing yells.
>
> 'Lord bless you, sir', answered Stephen, 'if she can screech like that there ain't much the matter'.[12]

It took them eleven days to reach Hilldrop, camping or staying overnight in some small town. Rain had swamped or washed away the road, such as it was, and their way was sometimes barred by swollen torrents. Despite feeling 'seedy' from her pregnancy, Louie took the obstacles as they came, even picking up an occasional word of Afrikaans. 'About 5 o'clock came to an unexpected obstacle in the shape of a swollen *spruit*, which a man in charge of some wagons declared was too deep for us', she noted in her diary. 'However, we were not going to turn back over the fearful road we had come, so dashed bravely in and got through all right'.

They were met outside Newcastle by Arthur Cochrane – 'I am still feeling tired and seedy', noted Louie – and he accompanied them to Hilldrop, which they found 'in a fearful state of confusion' because they had not been expected so soon and so they returned to the town for the night. Arriving at the house next morning they 'got our room papered, cleaned and furnished, so were able to take up our abode'.[13]

Louie was enchanted by the house. It lay on a green apron of grass between two rocky knees of the flat-topped hill, overlooking a sweep of open country. Orange trees stood around it and the verandah of the stone-walled, thatched house was entwined with vines and moonflowers. Inside, a large drawing-room made them feel, once it was filled with their furniture from England, as much at home as they could ever feel in this vast and violent continent.

Even Gibbs began to feel settled until a tremendous thunderstorm burst over the house, reducing her to trembling terror. 'Don't be so foolish, Gibbs', snapped Louie. 'Look at me, I'm not frightened'.

'No, ma'am, I see you ain't', she replied, 'but I tell you straight *I* don't call it ladylike!'[14]

Haggard and Cochrane's work was outside the house with the farm and prospects there seemed better than expected, particularly since the arrival of mounted troops at Newcastle brought an urgent demand for hay. On the day of their arrival, General Colley had, in fact, ridden out of Newcastle with about a thousand men, heading for the Transvaal frontier, although no one expected that he would attempt to cross with so small a force. Later, when reinforcements arrived, he might try to force the pass through the Drakensberg Mountains known as 'the Nek' but now, defended by hundreds, or thousands, of Boer sharpshooters, it would clearly be folly.

On the third morning after their arrival, 28 January 1881, Louie was hanging pictures in the drawing-room when she heard the distant thump and roll of gunfire. That afternoon a messenger arrived from Newcastle with a note from the magistrate:

I am sorry to say the troops failed this morning in their attack on the 'Nek' and had to retire to their wagon laager after heavy loss ... I do not think Newcastle is in any danger. The signal for alarm in town is a bell; but should I think there is any occasion for it, I will send out a runner to warn you.[15]

He concluded by wishing he could have welcomed the Haggards more appropriately and assured Mrs Haggard that his wife would call on her as soon as possible.

Then more dreadful news arrived. Colley had ordered an assault on the pass by several hundred infantry; they had been shot down by two thousand Boers, sniping from the cover of rocks so presenting no targets for the supposedly irresistible British volleys of rifle fire. Seventy-seven British had been killed; amongst the seven dead officers was young Elwes, whose last recorded words, spoken to another young officer, were '*Floreat Etona*, we must be in the front rank'! But Haggard's friend Major Essex, who had escaped from Isandhlwana, survived again. It was difficult to believe that Dutch farmers could defeat the British Army and this view was widely attributed to their unsporting habit of shooting from cover rather than standing up in the open, like the British, and facing the enemy's fire like men. When the news reached London, *The Times* declared, 'The engagement was not a defeat. We simply failed to take the position'.[16]

> I do not think this place is in danger [Haggard wrote to his father], but still these are anxious times for us all ... We have got all our things up here safely and have made the place quite pretty but somehow one can take no pleasure in anything just now with blood being shed like water all round. Every time one sees a Kaffir runner coming to the house one feels anxious lest he should be the announcer of some fresh evil.[17]

At Hilldrop, the Haggards and Arthur Cochrane spent the next week papering the bedroom walls and cutting hay, listening for the distant rumble they did not now expect to be thunder. It came at mid-day on 8 February. The sound of the guns rolled and echoed round the hills less than a dozen miles away and, together with the crackle of rifle fire, swelled into continuous thundering. 'A most anxious time, I may say, an awful time', Haggard wrote to his mother. 'The air was alive with the roar of cannon and the crash of Gatlings'.[18] At dusk it slackened and ceased. Soon after, Haggard hailed a group of passing Africans, approaching from the hills, and asked for news. The British soldiers were surrounded, they said, 'their arms were tired'[19] and they would all be killed in the night.

It was cold, wet and windy and they waited with dread for the morning and the news they expected of another catastrophe, sleeping in their clothes, ready to ride to Newcastle, or, if the Boers were already there, down the long road to Maritzburg. General Colley, they would later hear, had advanced with five companies of the 60th Regiment, supported by artillery, and had suddenly been attacked and surrounded by mounted Boers. By nightfall he had lost about a hundred and fifty of his five hundred men killed and wounded and would have lost them all had the Boers attacked again that night, as the Africans had predicted. In these two defeats Colley had lost half of his thousand men and the survivors – again including Major Essex – were exhausted and demoralised.

So the triumphant Boers swept into Natal – five hundred of them occupying the farm next to Hilldrop – ready to ambush the British reinforcements marching up from Maritzburg. Haggard and Cochrane were torn between volunteering to fight as irregulars, or staying to defend the farm, which was now under immediate threat of attack. While they were talking of this in the garden, Louie came out of the house and told her husband, 'Don't consider me. Do what you think your duty. I'll take my chance'. He would have expected no less of her, despite her pregnancy, and always remembered her resolution as 'little less than heroic', adding, 'but of such stuff is she made'.[20]

She joined the men at rifle practice and at night they slept with revolvers under their pillows and rifles beside the beds. African look-outs were posted on the hill-top to warn of approaching Boers and six saddled horses were kept ready in the stables, day and night. A week later, the reinforcements had still not arrived; fifteen hundred Boers were said to be lying in ambush on the road they would have to take. There were even rumours that the attack was to be made on the Hilldrop estate and the Haggards and Cochrane were advised to leave at once for safety in Newcastle.

There, a friend put up a bed for Louie in her sitting-room and Rider slept on the floor. General Colley was back in the town, staying at an hotel while awaiting the reinforcements, which arrived three days later, unmolested. Sent from India, they presented a colourful, heartening sight, with the red coats and white sun-helmets of the English infantry, the kilts of the Gordon Highlanders – fresh from campaigning in Afghanistan – and the blue jackets and straw hats of sailors from the cruiser *Boadicea*, lying off Durban: about six hundred fighting men. Informed speculation suggested that, as the Boers were said to have mobilised seven thousand armed men, General Colley would be content to defend New-castle and Natal and make no move into the Transvaal until a further six thousand reinforcements arrived from England.

There was a sense of relief and the Hilldrop party returned to the farm, the men to continue haymaking and sowing vegetable seeds. Indeed the most alarming news was when Louie noted in her diary,

> This morning we discovered that someone had been stealing the feathers off two of the ostriches during the night and Mr Cochrane luckily discovered the offenders, who were taken into Newcastle to receive the just reward of their deeds, namely 20 lashes and two months hard labour.

That evening a mounted policeman galloped up to the house to warn that five hundred Boers were about to attack the farm. 'We did not believe it', noted Louie, determined not to be forced out of her house again, 'and, sure enough, no Boers made their appearance'.

Yet, two days later, on Sunday, 27 February, she recorded,

> Drove into church but found we were too late as service was at 10.15 instead of 11.30 as usual. Weather oppressively hot. In the afternoon, Rider thought he heard guns but we all said it was thunder. Presently he and Mr Cochrane rode into town and came back with the startling news that an engagement had taken place near the 'Nek', our loss was great and Sir G. Colley missing.
>
> We were all very anxious [she continued next day] for further particulars of the fight today so, as it was too wet for hay-making, Mr Cochrane went into Newcastle and brought back the following news. Sir George, having gone with 500 men to take possession of a hill commanding the 'Nek', was attacked by 7,000 Boers. Our men ... ran short of ammunition ... Sir George was shot through the head.[21]

The battlefield had been a dozen miles distant on Majuba Hill, rising to six thousand feet with the majesty of Gibraltar, with which it was often compared since it commanded the pass into the Transvaal. Perhaps General Colley believed that possession of the summit – and the panoramic view across Natal and to the Drakensberg peaks and the Transvaal beyond – would be accepted as the decisive, winning move. On that Saturday night, he had led some five hundred men up the steep southern slope of the mountain and, at dawn on Sunday, had seemed master of all he surveyed, including the Boer encampments below. Then those Boer riflemen – less than half the number of the British on the summit – swarmed up the gentler northern slope and opened fire.

Since Colley had decided his men were too exhausted by the climb to dig trenches and their uniforms were brightly coloured, they presented easy targets. Picked off in the open by riflemen, they retreated and the retreat became a rout as they ran and stumbled down the mountainside. The Boers shot them down 'like bucks',[22] as one told Haggard later, and amongst more than two hundred British killed and wounded, was General Colley himself.

'Poor Sir George Colley has paid dearly for his rashness', wrote Louie to her mother-in-law, 'but, humanly speaking, it was far better to die as he did, fighting bravely at the head of his men than to live with a lost reputation'. She and Rider mourned for Sir George, whom they remembered as a civilised soldier, much travelled, always with his water-colour sketchbook to hand; a linguist and former private secretary to the Viceroy of India; a cultivated gentleman, although, as Rider believed, 'He lacked patience. Or perhaps Destiny drove him on'. Now death had redeemed his folly but not that of those regular soldiers who had not been 'shot down like sheep', as Louie put it, and, although now safe in camp, were 'perfectly panic-stricken'.[23]

The final humiliation of the defeat on Majuba Hill shocked not only the British in Natal, but, as the news spread, the whole Empire. What made it all the more disastrous for the British was that the Government, not wanting a full-scale war in South Africa, had begun to make overtures to the Boer leadership before the battle and, early in March, the latter had announced an eight-day truce so that provisions could be sent to beleaguered townships. If a settlement were reached, inevitably it would be said to be the result of that one decisive battle. Not only had the British been defeated, they *felt* defeated. In the streets of Newcastle, Haggard recorded, 'I saw strong men weeping like children and heard English-born people crying aloud that they were "b—y Englishmen" no more. Soldiers were raging and cursing ... natives stood stupefied ... women wrung their hands'.[24]

At Hilldrop hay-making continued and the harvesting of ostrich feathers began, with Louie helping to wash, dry and dress them for packing; indeed the farm was flourishing. But the early optimism had been turned sour, not only by the succession of Boer victories. So many of their friends were lost: Shepstone, Osborn and Frere put aside as scapegoats and most of their army friends killed in action; of the thirteen who had sat down to dinner with General Colley in Maritzburg, only Rider, Louie and Lady Colley survived.

Neither peace nor war would satisfy them. Their own future prosperity was at risk, yet, in March, Louie wrote in her diary, 'There seems to be a real prospect of peace with the Boers much to our disgust'. Two days later, she heard from the magistrate in Newcastle that 'we are going to give back a great part of the Transvaal to the Boers and that there is to be two months cessation of hostilities and a commission formed to finally settle the terms of peace'.

By the end of the month, Sir Hercules Robinson, the President of the Royal Commission charged with the negotiations, arrived in Newcastle and, on the 29th, Louie noted that she had received a message asking 'if we should feel inclined to let Sir Hercules Robinson have this house to hold the conference in'.[25] They were offered a generous rent of £50 a week and agreed on condition that they could keep their own bedroom. The Commission used the house for about a month and Haggard was sharply aware that in his drawing-room they were discussing the surrender of the Transvaal, over which he himself had hoisted the British flag four years before.

At the beginning of May, he wrote to his mother,

> We are seriously debating clearing out of this part of the world. I am sorry to say that every day that has elapsed ... has only strengthened my conviction that henceforth we can look for no peace or security in South Africa ... I cannot tell you how sorry I shall be if we have to leave this place ... after two years' struggle we were just beginning to do well.[26]

In addition to the ostriches, they had assembled a steam-powered corn-mill, shipped from England, and had engaged an English engineer to run it. Hay, sold for the Army's horses at Newcastle, was profitable and a new venture, brick-making, a success. They had been joined by a young Englishman, George Blomefield, a ward of William Haggard's who had advised him to invest £1,000 in the farm and become a partner.

If a final omen were sought it was provided by Haggard's favourite horse, Moresco. He had owned the hunter since he first came to Hilldrop but, while he was away in England, the horse had been stolen. Cochrane had offered a reward for his recovery and learned that Moresco had been ridden twelve hundred miles to Cape Colony, but that his whereabouts were unknown. Six months later, he saw an emaciated horse in the pound at Newcastle: it was Moresco, who had found his way home, weak and covered with sores. When Haggard returned, the horse had recovered as much as he ever would and was kept as an honoured pensioner. But horse-sickness was rife in the district and one night they heard a thumping at the back door; Moresco, knowing that he was dying, had dragged himself over a four-foot wall to find his master. Nothing could be done for him and next morning the horse was dead.

Even if independence were granted to the Transvaal and the African tribes remained passive and the farm prospered, the standing of the British had suffered what seemed a mortal blow in Africa and Haggard could see only trouble ahead. He and Louie loved their pioneering life and, determined to continue it elsewhere. With a quarter of the land surface of the world within the British Empire to choose from, they selected Vancouver Island. Yet no sooner had they made this decision than Rider's brother Jack, who had just resigned from the Navy, came to stay at Hilldrop and, as Rider wrote to his father, 'His account of Vancouver Island is such as to make us abandon our idea of forming a company there, so I suppose we must stay on here and then come home'.[27]

They could not move until Louie's baby was born. On 23 May she mentioned her pregnancy in her diary for the first time: 'Baby was born at 1/4 to 6 a.m. Rider telegraphed home to announce the event'.[28] The child was delivered by an African woman, while Gibbs relapsed into hysterics. 'The child is a very perfect and fine boy', Haggard wrote to his father. 'He has dark blue eyes and is a fair child with a good forehead'.[29] On 11 June, Louie noted, 'Baby was christened Arthur John Rider ... Had a nice lunch afterwards and drank the youngster's health'.[30]

The father was more obviously delighted than the phlegmatic mother for Rider Haggard had a strong sense of dynasty and inheritance; now he had founded a new branch of his family and could ensure that his son would have all the advantages he himself had been denied. Yet, what, if anything, could they expect in Africa?

As he saw it, the British were the chosen rulers of these territories – including the Transvaal – for the benefit of all. The indigenous heirs were, of course, the African tribes and he recognised this fact. But, like all his contemporaries, he had been influenced by the evolutionary theories of Charles Darwin. The Africans were simply a few rungs down the evolutionary ladder from the Europeans – the Zulus only a very few rungs below – and they needed help in their ascent. 'In the case of the

Zulus', Haggard was to conclude, 'civilisation has one of its great opportunities, for certainly in them is a spirit which can be led on to higher things'.[31] The Zulu War, which he considered a tragic irrelevance, had only served to increase his admiration for them.

> By what exact right do we call people like the Zulus savage? [he asked]? Setting aside the habit of polygamy ... they have a social system not unlike our own. They have, or had, their king, their nobles and their commons. They have an ancient and elaborate law and a system of morality in some ways as high as our own and certainly more generally obeyed; they have their priests and their doctors; they are strictly upright and observe the rites of hospitality.
>
> Where they differ from us mainly is that they do not get drunk until the white man teaches them to do so, they wear less clothing, the climate being more genial, their towns at night are not disgraced by the sights that distinguish ours, they cherish and are never cruel to their children, although they may occasionally put a deformed infant or a twin out of the way, and when they go to war, which is often, they carry out the business with a terrible thoroughness ...
>
> Of course, there remain their witchcraft and the cruelties which result from their almost universal belief in the power and efficiency of magic ... Now let him who is highly cultured take up a stone to throw at the poor, untaught Zulu ... generally because he covets his land, his labour or whatever else may be his.[32]

The Boers were by now, he recognised, an African tribe themselves. There were some forty thousand of them in the Transvaal, outnumbering the British there by about ten to one and themselves outnumbered by the Africans by twenty-five to one. He admired their resolution, resilience and their cunning, while he deplored their exploitation of the Africans.

> The Boers are certainly a very peculiar people [he believed]. They are very religious but their religion takes its colour from the darkest portions of the Old Testament ... What they delight in are the stories of wholesale butchery by the Israelites of old; and in their own position they find a reproduction of that of the first settlers in the Holy Land. Like them, they think they are entrusted by the Almighty with the task of exterminating the heathen native tribes around them and are always ready with a scriptural precedent for slaughter and robbery ...
>
> Personally, Boers are fine men, but as a rule ugly. Their women-folk are good-looking in early life but get very stout ... He lives in a way

that would shock an English labourer at twenty-five shillings a week, although he is probably worth fifteen or twenty thousand pounds. His home is but too frequently squalid and filthy to an extraordinary degree. He himself has no education and does not care that his children should receive any. He lives by himself in the middle of a great plot of land, his nearest neighbour being perhaps ten or twelve miles away, caring but little for the news of the outside world and nothing for its opinions, doing very little work, but growing daily richer through the increase of his flocks and herds.[33]

So Haggard's sympathies were with the Zulus rather than the Boers. Once the Zulu males could be taught to work and exchange military training and warfare for work in the fields, instead of leaving that to their wives, they could not only become the Romans of Africa, but could attain British standards. For it was the British that he saw as most suited to rule and develop the primitive world to mutual benefit. Not every British male was suitable, of course, and there would be noble failures, too, like General Colley, but Britain was the nursery where rulers were bred.

The Englishman, and variations embodied in the Scot, the Welshman and the Anglo-Irishman, could be assessed according to patterns of behaviour. For Haggard, worth was not a reflection of social position at birth: the titled aristocrat *should* display chivalrous qualities but he was just as likely to be a wastrel, or a cad. The highest qualities were those of the gentleman – good manners, generosity and courage for a start: 'That unmistakable stamp of dignity and self-respect which, if it does not exclusively belong to, is still one of the distinguishing attributes of the English gentleman'.[34] Such qualities would be reflected down the social scale so that the British yeoman, or working man, was, like the Zulu, also on the ladder that could lead him, or his descendants, to ultimate gentlemanliness.

As Haggard saw it, the British had failed to do their duty in the Transvaal. Paradoxically, it had been Disraeli, the subtle Jewish Prime Minister, who had understood what was required of them and Gladstone, his Anglo-Scottish successor, who had not. When the Royal Commission left Hilldrop to continue negotiations in the Transvaal, it was known what the outcome would be. In anger and despair, Haggard wrote to Sir Bartle Frere:

The natives are the real heirs to the soil and surely should have some protection and consideration ... Leading all these hundreds of thousands of men and women to believe that they were safe for once and for ever the subjects of Her Majesty, safe from all violence, cruelty and oppression, we have handed them over without a word to the tender mercies of one, where natives are concerned, of the cruellest white races in the world.[35]

The signing of the Convention of Pretoria on 3 August 1881 came as no surprise for it only dressed the surrender in diplomatic language, granting the Transvaal 'complete self-government, subject to the suzerainty of Her Majesty'. The word 'suzerainty' saved face but meant little; after all, Queen Victoria had supposedly held it over the Zulus when Cetewayo was training his impis for war.

But already, on 1 August, Louie had written in her diary, 'Decided to leave here and return to England at once'. Immediately they began packing and arranging for the auction of their furniture. They would maintain a financial interest in the farm, which would now be run by George Blomefield as Arthur Cochrane, who had been suffering from chronic dysentery, would also be returning home. By the middle of the month their heavy baggage had been sent to Newcastle for carting 'down-country' and they broke off the final packing to celebrate their first wedding anniversary with 'a very jolly picnic'.

Africa required one last moment of attention when an African and his wives asked Rider for permission to settle on the farm as they had been attacked by Boers. This, he was convinced, was what happened once British control slackened. So, carrying out his own duty, he took down their statements and wrote letters reporting the incident. That was the end.

The auction was held at Hilldrop on 23 August and continued until dark, when the Haggards and Cochrane drove into Newcastle to stay for a couple of nights before leaving for the coast. Next day, while shopping, Louie noted, 'A hot dusty day, which made me look longingly towards the hill where Hilldrop stands but I had no time to waste in regrets'. A 'jolly dinner' was held for them at the Plough Hotel that night and, next morning, Louie wrote in her diary:

Felt rather seedy when I woke up at 5 a.m. this morning. The result, I suppose, of last night's orgie!! However up I got and managed to eat some breakfast, after which I felt better and we started about 6.30 on the first stage of our journey ... Baby seems to stand the travelling very well.[36]

The road to Maritzburg was even worse than it had been when they had covered it before. Now it was snowing and the passes through the hills were almost blocked. They had to dig their horses and carriage through several deep drifts and in one they saw a carter stranded with two wagons and thirty-one dead oxen, frozen to death the previous night. Early on the fifth day they reached Maritzburg only to find that their baggage, sent ahead, had not yet arrived, and that their terrier had died from poisoning. Thankfully, the journey on to Durban, where they would embark, could be continued by train.

On the dockside they bade farewell to the Shepstones – who gave them a basket of tropical fruit – and the invincible Major Essex. On 1 September 1881, the long voyage home began, calling at East London, Cape Town (where they landed for shopping), St Helena (where they inspected the town but did not have time to see Napoleon's house at Longwood), Ascension Island (where they were shown the turtle pens) and finally Madeira, where they disembarked for a holiday. They spent ten days ashore, travelling about the hilly island on sightseeing expeditions by palanquin, or sledge, before boarding another ship for London. Arriving on 15 October, they stayed briefly at the Union Hotel in Charles Street. Finally they travelled on to Norfolk and took up the seasonal life of Bradenham Hall.

It was a handsome little family that had returned home: Rider, a big confident man of twenty-five, with his smooth-faced young wife and their infant son, who was now known as 'Jock'. This time there were no recriminations from William Haggard because it was obvious that only the war, the humiliating peace and the certainty of future trouble had driven them from their African farm.

Africa was now behind them. 'There my son had been born', wrote Rider, 'there I had undergone many emotions of a kind that help make a man; there I had suffered the highest sort of shame, shame for my country; there, as I felt, one chapter of my eventful life had opened and closed ... '[37] As if to illustrate the total change of scene and prospect, Rider and Louie were plunged into the social life which absorbed their Norfolk contemporaries as totally as the affairs of the Transvaal had obsessed them. Rider had been out shooting almost every day, when friends at Heacham on the Wash coast of the county invited them to stay so they could attend the Prince of Wales's ball at Sandringham House. Louie was as thrilled as her husband had been when he first watched a Zulu war-dance. 'We arrived just too late to see the first quadrille', she noted in her diary. 'The princess looked lovely in pearl grey satin and was the prettiest women in the room with the exception of Lady Lonsdale, who is the finest woman I ever saw'.[38]

Rider Haggard's life was once more bounded by the oaks and elms of the Norfolk countryside, peopled by its familiar cast of characters: landowners and squires, parsons and doctors, farmers and millers, servants and labourers; yet, in his imagination, he was still beyond the Drakensberg at the courts of the savage gentlemen of Zululand.

CHAPTER FOUR

'A fine, weird imagination'

AMBITION, FUELLED BY frustration, was still the spur. Having overcome the educational disadvantages imposed by his father, Rider Haggard had twice achieved success – as a law officer and as a farmer – only to have it snatched away by circumstances beyond his control. His marriage was contented – Louie having proved herself a redoubtable companion in Africa – but the seductive memory of the lost Lily still glittered in his imagination. Even the birth of his son added edge to his frustration for he intended to become a man of achievement that his heir could admire and emulate.

One option was to live at Ditchingham House, his wife's inheritance, as a gentleman-farmer. But they were advised that the two hundred acres of the farm needed £2,000 spent on it and that, in any case, agriculture was suffering from a serious depression. So it was decided that both the house and the land there could continue to be let, the latter at a rental of £50 a year.

Rider was too active and ambitious to settle for life with the rural gentry. He wanted to carry on the work of his heroes, Shepstone and the other old Africa hands, which had been undone by lesser men for political and personal gain. He must play his part in maintaining the British Empire as the dominant civilising force in the world, powered by the energy and dedication of its sons.

> I was determined to make a success in the world in one way or another [he was to recall], and that of a sort which would cause my name to be remembered for long after I depart therefrom, and my difficulty was to discover in which way this could best be done.[1]

The one profession that might be open to him, despite his lack of educational qualifications, was the law, in which his time as Registrar of the High Court in the Transvaal had given him experience which Judge Kotzé had recommended as a career. Although he did not relish the prospect of a life spent in chambers and courtrooms, his father, who had himself been called to the Bar, was in favour; if Rider was successful, he could always apply for an appointment in the Empire. But, on making enquiries at Lincoln's Inn, he was told that none of his experience was considered a qualification and that, like any other aspiring lawyer, he must sit the entrance examination, which required a thorough knowledge of Latin. Even if he were successful, there would then follow a three-year course of study.

So, before Christmas, 1881, Haggard moved his wife and son to a furnished house in Norwood, a genteel suburb south of London, and began intensive tuition in Latin. But learning a dead language with a view to a life among the files and ledgers of a lawyer's chambers did not relieve his frustration or his energy. Considering himself an authority on South African affairs – one of the few in London – he wrote articles for *The South African* magazine and a succession of letters to *The Standard* and the *St James's Gazette* newspapers. When a letter he wrote to *The Times* was not published, he decided he must make his opinions known another way. With Cetewayo about to visit England prior to his possible reinstatement as monarch in Zululand, African issues would surely be talked about again. He decided to write a book.

First he bought the Government's recently published 'Blue Book' reports on South African affairs. Then, beginning with Cetewayo's imminent arrival, he wrote a vivid, often personal, account of the three-cornered struggle for power and land between the British, the Boers and the Zulus. He expressed his opinion that Cetewayo was a despot and that the British should annex and rule Zululand to allow its people to develop their potential in peace; similarly, the Boers were untrustworthy and brutal to the African natives so that the recent 'retrocession' of the Transvaal had been a tragedy. For the book's title, he chose *Cetewayo and his White Neighbours*.

Although it seemed topical, publishers maintained that it came too soon after the intense newspaper coverage of these events. Eventually a minor firm, Trübner, did show interest but, reluctant to take any risk, only offered to print an edition of seven hundred and fifty copies if the author would pay £50 towards the cost. He did and so, on 22 June 1882, the book was published.

It was not a commercial success for its potential readership was, as other publishers had feared, sated with commentaries on Africa; the British public was more stirred by the untimely death of Jumbo the circus elephant than by a catastrophe in the Transvaal. Yet it was reviewed respectfully in several journals, but the *Daily News*, spotting the author's principal prejudice, wrote tartly that he 'thinks we have not yet seen the end of the troubles in store for us, owing to our neglect to persevere in the work of exterminating the Boers'.[2] Such sarcasm was brushed aside by comments that mattered to him from his friends and former superiors. It was particularly gratifying to hear from Lord Carnarvon, who wrote congratulating him on having 'the courage to say what really did occur'.[3]

The book had given Haggard confidence in his ability to write more than magazine articles and he was further encouraged by his brother Andrew, who had spent off-duty hours writing a novel of contemporary social life, which he had read aloud to his family at Bradenham, soon after the return of Rider and Louie. Not to be outdone, Rider started to write one himself. If Andrew's example was one spur to write fiction, there was another. When Louie and he were attending a service in the parish church at Norwood, he noticed, near them in the pews, 'a singularly beautiful and pure-faced young lady'. He drew his wife's attention to 'the semi-divine creature'[4] and later remarked that, with such looks and bearing, she should be the heroine of a novel; indeed, he declared, he would make her the heroine of *his* novel. Then, perhaps to assure Louie that he was only showing a literary interest in the girl, he suggested that she try writing one, too.

Louie's novel came to a halt after a few hundred words but Rider's raced on for two thousand. His heroine he named Angela and, although he never saw her original again – and it is possible that using the unknown beauty in church so as not to arouse Louie's suspicions, he really had Lily in mind as his model – she inspired in him a furious energy as an outlet for his now unfocused drive. Louie was pregnant again and, before Christmas, they decided to move to her house at Ditchingham.

Rider's novel was, like Andrew's, to be set in contemporary society and, like most novelists, he drew on his own experience. But whereas his first book had presented the state of South Africa as seen through the eyes of an opinionated participant, the novel gave vent, probably unconsciously, to his own emotional history. Initially entitled *Angela*, after its heroine, the book was almost choked with three entwined plots. Set in the Norfolk countryside, its characters included a domineering father, who forbade his son to marry the girl of his choice and ordered his beautiful, but unloved, daughter Angela to spend a year apart from her lover when she wished to announce her engagement. Two other strong female characters complicated the plot: one who kept a collection of mummies in her private museum of Egyptology and another who dabbled in spiritualism. In the first draft, the hero was killed in an African war and Angela fell dead into an open grave; the lovers to be reunited in the hereafter.

Rider showed it to the publisher of his first book, Trübner, and they suggested he send it to the critic Cordy Jeaffreson, who not only wrote a letter of advice but invited Haggard to dinner to discuss his book over cigars. He insisted on a happy ending, adding that, if Haggard rewrote it,

> suppressing much, expanding much, making every chapter a picture by itself and polishing up every sentence so that each page bears a testimony to the power of its producer – the story will be the beginning of such a literary career as I conceive you to be desirous of running. Get the better of the common notion that novels must be dashed off – go to the Charles Dickens rooms at the S. Kensington Museum and observe the erasures, the insertions, the amendments of every paragraph of his writing.[5]

Then Rider showed it to his brother Andrew, who remarked, 'There is a little too much of your own personal experience in the book and, when you write another, I would, if I were you, draw a little more on your own imagination.'[6]

There was a third constructive critic, Agnes Barber, Louie's former school-friend, whom he had met at Bradenham just before he had become engaged. When Louie's first daughter was born on 6 January, and named Angela Agnes Rider, Agnes Barber arrived to keep Louie company and help with the baby. She stayed for six months and Rider and 'Aggie', as he called her, became close friends, she supplying the wit and imagination Louie lacked and offering such constructive criticism that Rider, when inviting it, described himself as a parched field longing for rain. Yet the idealised Lily still haunted him; she was living in style near Hyde Park in London with her husband and three small sons; their families were still in touch and that kept the wound open.

Haggard drove himself so hard on his novel and his law studies that it affected his eyesight; he began to fear he was going blind and was ordered to take a holiday by the sea. Yet, acting on the criticisms, his efforts proved worth while. Jeaffreson recommended it to the publishers Hurst and Blackett, as 'a thing of no ordinary power ... a tale of pathos, incident and *new ground*'.[7] They accepted it for publication; this time he was not asked for any financial contribution but was to be paid only £40 on the sale of four hundred copies and £30 on each hundred thereafter. The title *Angela* had been used before, so the novel was entitled *Dawn* when it was published in April, 1884.

On 25 March that year, a second daughter, Dorothy, had been born so that at the age of twenty-eight, Haggard had to support a family of five on the modest income from the Ditchingham estate. There was none other for, two years earlier, the partnership owning Hilldrop farm had been wound up. His first novel had brought mixed reviews but *The Times* had declared, '*Dawn* is a novel of merit far above the average. From the first page, the story arrests the mind and arouses expectation.'[8] That was encouragement enough and he decided to embark upon a second, drawing on his experiences in South Africa.

Again his own past was reflected. There were dominating squires and a beautiful, shining girl, whom the hero continues to love although both have married others. There is some dissipation such as he himself may have enjoyed in Pretoria, praise for the policies of his friends Shepstone and Osborn and a dramatic description of Isandhlwana. He called this book *The Witch's Head* and it came alive once the scene moved from Norfolk to Africa. To the public, it was thrilling to read a story about the sort of heroes and heroines to whom they were accustomed, in a setting for which so much dramatic news had prepared them. For those who knew the author it was embarrassingly clear that much was auto-biographical, from his pamphleteering approach to the political background to the acknowledgement that the hero had married his second choice.

This was moderately well received by the critics, who usually praised the African scenes, and one, his mastery of 'the art of truly patriotic and adventurous fiction'.[9] But commercially it was not a success. Indeed, his first and second novels had together earned him only £50, exactly the sum with which he had subsidised his first book. Again inspired by his brother Andrew, who had had an article about Egypt, where he was now serving, published by *Blackwood's Magazine*, he had written a short story – again dramatising his loss of Lily – and sent it to a magazine; it was returned. This realisation of failure coincided with the completion of his law studies when in January, 1885, he was called to the Bar.

It was time for a reassessment. He could not maintain his family at even a modest, middle-class standard of living by writing, or by the income from the Ditchingham estate, or even a combination of the two;

therefore he came to the conclusion, as he was to put it, that he would 'have to abandon the writing of fiction'.[10]

In the August of 1884, the Haggards had spent a few weeks by the sea, taking lodgings at Criccieth in North Wales. Haggard took a liking to their landlord's young nephew, David Lloyd George,* who was also studying law, and told him of his African adventures. Possibly the young Welshman talked of politics, for Haggard now speculated in a letter that he himself might stand for Parliament at the next general election. But that was no more than a possibility, therefore he would have to take the only practical course and become a lawyer. A distant connection by marriage, Henry Bargrave Deane, offered him a place in his chambers in London, so that was settled.

Once again Ditchingham House was let and the family moved to a small furnished house in West Kensington. This was 1 Fairholme Road, a four-storey, stucco'd, portico'd corner house – with just enough space for the family of five, two nursemaids from Norfolk, a grubby London cook and a French maid – in the genteel, unfashionable inner suburb near the new Gothic buildings of St Paul's School. Once settled in this tight maze of streets, so totally different from the great spaces he loved in Norfolk and Africa, Haggard began his daily journeys to practise in the Probate and Divorce Courts. The work struck him as unsavoury and demeaning but it did give him insights into the social attitudes and matrimonial problems of the time and was therefore material which might inspire plots for contemporary novels, should he ever return to authorship.

Yet he was already on the threshold of this. Even as he decided to forget his ambition to write, the talk of literary London was of the new novel for boys by Robert Louis Stevenson entitled *Treasure Island*. It was an immediate success and, after reading its reviews, Haggard was discussing it with one of his brothers on a train. As the brother praised the book, with the implication that that was the sort of novel he should be writing, Rider bridled, remarking that it was not as wonderful as was claimed. At this the brother bet him that he could not write anything to match it. Rider accepted the bet.

Amongst the few pieces of furniture brought to London from Norfolk

---

* 'The family took in lodgers at their new home, Morvin House, during the summer season, and one of them was Rider Haggard (from whom David Lloyd George may have received his first colourful impressions of South Africa).' – John Grigg, *The Young Lloyd George*, 1973. William George wrote in *My Brother and I* (1958), 'I remember how thrilled I was that the author of *King Solomon's Mines* was staying in the house with us,' and that he had 'made quite an impression on Dafydd and myself'.

was a pedestal desk, which was now set in the dining-room window. Each evening after he returned from his chambers in the Temple, Haggard sat writing there, letting his imagination loose. Again it galloped across the African plains but was not waylaid by memories of Maritzburg, Pretoria, or Hilldrop; instead it headed for the mountains, the jagged Drakensberg, perhaps, or the bluffs of Zululand, any of those great African ranges, which seemed both to warn and entice the traveller towards whatever lay beyond.

Other memories mixed the exotic with the cosily familiar. From his childhood visit to Garsington rectory he remembered the heavy gold ring worn by the rector and the story he had been told about it. It had come from a friend of the rector's who had been travelling in Peru, where he had happened upon the excavation of an Inca tomb. Within, they had opened a stone chamber, in which embalmed corpses were seated around a table and crumbled to dust as fresh air reached them. All that was left of the mummy at the head of the table was a golden ring from its finger – the ring now worn by the rector.

Another curious memory that bubbled to the surface was of visiting a cave in the Transvaal with Judge Kotzé and seeing there a formation of stalactites shaped like a cathedral pulpit. Also from Africa were the legends of strange tribes, whose ancestry linked them with past civilisations; and always rumours of gold, just over the horizon, there for the taking. A rich mulch of memories inspired the story now taking shape.

His characters sprang from memory and imagination, too. From Garsington, he took the farmer's name of Quatermain for the teller of his story *Allan Quatermain*, a character compounded of himself and, it was said, the explorer Frederick Selous, who had written of his African adventures. His own idealised Danish ancestry Haggard fashioned into another English gentleman of similar descent and enormous physical strength, Sir Henry Curtis. A third character he created from naval officers he had known through his brother Jack, the dapper and practical Captain Good.

This trio would head into unexplored Africa in search of legendary treasure. As he sat at his desk in the bay window each evening after his return from the Temple, the curtains drawn against the cold, gas-lit street, his imagination soared free across the great landscapes he conjured up. Unlike his earlier attempts at fiction, this was, like *Treasure Island*, for boys, so contemporary social realism could be forgotten. The story told of his heroes' quest for a missing explorer and how they found themselves in an unknown African country peopled by a tribe similar to the Zulus; how they became involved in a civil war of good against evil; and how they discovered an immense, hidden treasure. Of course, they only just escaped with their lives, leaving good triumphant and filling their pockets with jewels.

In six weeks it was finished and he had given it the title *King Solomon's Mines*. On a friend's advice he sent it to the poet W. E. Henley, who was connected with Cassell, the publisher of Stevenson's book, and he passed it for comment to the editor of *Harper's Magazine*, another poet and critic, Andrew Lang. He could not have picked a more stimulating critic and he soon decided that Lang, who modestly described himself as 'a hodman of letters', was '*par excellence* a *littérateur* of the highest sort, perhaps the most literary man in England or America' and 'the tenderest, the purest and the highest-minded of human creatures, one from whom true goodness and nobility of soul radiate in every common word or act, though often half-hidden in jest, the most perfect of gentlemen.'[11]

Lang had read the manuscript and written to Haggard, 'Seldom have I read a book with so much pleasure; I think it perfectly delightful. The question is, what is the best, whereby I mean the coiniest, way to publish it?'[12] This proved to be publication by Cassell, although Haggard had a narrow escape when he first agreed to the outright sale of the copyright, then acted on the whispered advice of a clerk in the publisher's office to change his mind and insist on royalties. Cassell knew that they would have a success on their hands, for the time was right. It was more than a boys' book, for much had recently been written about current affairs in Africa but little fiction had been set there and they believed that the public was tiring of novels about contemporary social life. There was topicality, too, because, just as Haggard was completing his book, the Berlin Conference on African Affairs had ended; convened by Bismarck, Chancellor of the new federal Germany, this had seemed to legitimise the division of Africa amongst the imperial powers of Europe in what came to be known as 'The Scramble for Africa'. So, on the eve of publication on 2 September 1885, they papered London with posters announcing: 'KING SOLOMON'S MINES – THE MOST AMAZING STORY EVER WRITTEN'.

The book seized the public imagination. It was not just the 'rattling good yarn' that was expected from a number of successful authors but was intensely visual. Until now Africa had seemed a distant, hot country of desert and jungle, but now Rider Haggard had brought the 'Dark

Continent' into vibrant colour. This was reflected in the reviews and Cassell sold 31,000 copies in the first year, a major sale by contemporary standards, more than a dozen editions being published in the United States.

To Haggard's delight, Robert Louis Stevenson wrote him a series of letters, but praise ('fine, weird imagination'; 'singularly fine') was mixed with sharp criticism: 'You should be more careful; you do quite well enough to take more trouble, and some parts of your book are infinitely beneath you', adding, 'excuse the tone of a damned schoolmaster.' But his third letter ended with the postscript, 'How about a deed of partnership?'[13] He could ask for no higher accolade.

Even before the novel was published he had started work on another, completing it in ten weeks, a month after *King Solomon's Mines* reached the bookshops. It was named *Allan Quatermain* after its hero, who was once more accompanied by the country gentleman of Danish descent, the unruffled naval officer and also by a magnificent African warrior, Umslopogaas, a character drawn directly from Shepstone's escort in the Transvaal. Again the explorers discover a lost people, but this time they are white and their adventures are more bizarre. Shaking himself free from the constraints of geography, history and anthropology, he sends his characters, led by Quatermain, into Africa, 'the land whereof none know the history, back to the savages, whom I love, although some of them are almost as merciless as Political Economy'.[14]

There, after a succession of testing ordeals, they discover the hidden civilisation of Zu-Vendis, chivalrous yet cruel in custom and ruled by two sisters. Civil war breaks out between good and evil factions and, after colossal carnage, good prevails and Sir Henry Curtis marries the righteous queen and elects to remain as guardian against the corrupt world outside.

Haggard dedicated the book to his son Jock

> in the hope that in days to come, he, and many other boys whom I shall never know, may in the acts and thoughts of Allan Quatermain and his companions, as herein recorded, find something to help him and them to reach to what, with Sir Henry Curtis, I hold to be the highest rank whereto we can attain – the state of dignity of English gentleman.

Yet there was a curiously gratuitous sadness about the book for, at the beginning, Quatermain's own son, Harry, a young doctor, dies of an infection, devastating his father: 'I have just buried my boy, my poor

handsome boy of whom I was so proud and my heart is broken ... The
great wheel of Fate rolls on like a Juggernaut and crushes us all in turn,
some soon, some late – it does not matter when, in the end it crushes us all
... Poor Harry, to go so soon!' It was almost as if the author were
imagining the death of his own son, such was the emotion with which he
described Quatermain's grief at his country house 'not five hundred yards
from the old church where Harry is asleep' – about the distance from
Ditchingham House to St Mary's – and his having to go to the wilds of
Africa, where he 'should be able to think of poor Harry lying in the
churchyard without feeling as though my heart would break in two'. The
death of Harry Quatermain was not vital to the plot, so the feelings which
Haggard described seemed oddly morbid.

The book ended with the death of Quatermain himself in Zu-Vendis,
after he had described how 'the dark draws nearer and the light departs.
And yet it seems to me that through the darkness I can already see the
shining welcome of many a long-lost face. Harry is there, and others; one,
above all, to my mind, the sweetest and most perfect woman that ever
gladdened this grey earth ... ' Then he speaks his final words to his
friends: 'I am going on a stranger journey than any we have taken
together ... I shall wait for you.'[15]

In writing this story, Haggard had, perhaps unconsciously, dredged to
the surface his deepest longing and dread: his longing for the imagined
perfection of the lost Lily and fear for his adored only son. Other worries
– particularly over money – faded with his rising success. He put his work
in the hands of an agent, A. P. Watt, who recommended that his books
could be serialised in magazines before publication and that he should
transfer from Cassell to Longman, which he did.

While these negotiations were in hand, he wrote another novel. Again
set in Africa, its time was the present and, instead of fantasy, it presented
dramatic realism. The characters were British and Boer settlers and
African natives. The villain was a Boer half-breed, as might have been
expected, but the original of his English heroine was less recognisable
since she was not an unattainable, golden-haired goddess, but an intelligent, independent-minded young woman, pale and dark-eyed. In
settings he remembered in Natal, the heroine, Jess, nobly refuses to
become her sister's rival for the love of a British officer, then, in a
melodrama of love and passion, kills the Boer villain before herself
expiring from exhaustion. The British officer marries the younger sister,
patiently awaiting his own death and the hereafter where 'Jess is waiting

to greet him at its gates'.[16] Only those who knew something of Haggard's own life would recognise the original Jess as the amusing and attractive Agnes Barber, who had given him the intellectual stimulus that Louie could not. But she, too, was to be lost to him as her long visits to the Haggard family had thrown her together with his brother Jack and now they were engaged.

Haggard wrote *Jess* in nine weeks, completing it by the end of 1885. He had written three novels in twelve months: the first was already celebrated world-wide; the others were to be serialised – *Allan Quatermain* in *Longman's Magazine* and *Jess* in the *Cornhill* – and would later be published in book form. Meanwhile he was filled with volcanic creativity as, after a lifetime of frustration, his ideas erupted in the torrent of fiction. His early dismissal by his family as a dullard; the education accorded to his brothers but denied to him; his despatch to Africa as an unpaid minion; his father's refusal to let him marry the girl of his choice; the political betrayal, as he saw it, of his hero Shepstone in Africa; the consequent failure of his farming enterprise; his unhappiness with the prospect of a career in the divorce courts; and his marriage to a dutiful wife, lacking in the imaginative flair that drove him; his romantic hankering after Lily, now beyond his reach, and the knowledge that perhaps he should have chosen Agnes Barber, who was now about to marry his brother; all this created a surge of story-telling which found response in every reader who had known frustration.

King Solomon's Mines had ensured that Rider Haggard was famous. The law was now relegated to second place and, when he did go to his chambers in an inner courtyard of the Temple, he spent much of his time writing fiction. Yet he was aware that this was not a proper life's work, nor a real achievement for a gentleman. So he talked of going into politics, or some form of public service. With the latter in mind, Andrew Lang took him to dinner at his club to meet the Conservative politician Arthur Balfour, then president of the Local Government Board. Nothing came of this introduction, so restlessness found expression in moving house again. With the means to entertain and invite guests to stay, the house in Fairholme Road was proving too small and they moved half a mile northward to the larger 69 Gunterstone Road. One of a long terrace, its five storeys of grim, grey brick were encrusted with stucco floral reliefs around door, windows and cornices; the room beside the front door became Haggard's study, his desk again set in a bay window facing a cliff of similar houses across the street.

At once he began to write furiously; as he put it, 'in a white heat, almost without rest ... it came faster than my poor aching hand could put it down'.[17] Again the theme was immortal love but the idea for the story had been triggered by earlier memories. One was the horrid doll brought from the back of the toy cupboard at Bradenham to frighten the children; another was said to be the little Egyptian figure with the sweet face in the museum at Didlington. These perhaps suggested the mythology and religions of the ancients and the deification or demonisation of the feminine.

Again Africa enticed and threatened. This time it was not so much his own experiences in the wilds but tantalising stories he had heard. One was of the colossal ruins of Zimbabwe, which he had never seen but which had been visited by particularly daring explorers shortly before his own arrival. Some four hundred miles north-east of Pretoria, across the Drakensberg range, and reached only by the most dangerous of journeys, this was a great stone city without a known history. Then, about half-way to Zimbabwe, was the curious tribe of the Lovedu and, on his travels with Judge Kotzé, Haggard had come to within a hundred miles of them. They, it was said, were ruled by a white queen with magical powers, who was said to be immortal. This was achieved, it was ru-moured, by the queen taking white male travellers as lovers, having any male offspring killed and the females brought up by her mute female attendants so that one of them could secretly replace her when she died. In Haggard's story, the queen was named Ayesha, and also called She-Who-Must-Be-Obeyed. She was visualised by her creator as a symbol of the fragility of human life, the longing for immortality and the mystery of life's purpose, which had obsessed Haggard since childhood. The book was to be called *She*.

Like *King Solomon's Mines*, this was a story of a quest, but was powerfully charged with mystical and sexual under-tones. Aware of the effect of contrast, it began in the familiar cosiness of England; this time, the adventure opened slowly in a Cambridge college, where a don named Holly (ugly but physically strong) becomes guardian to a friend's son, Leo Vincey, who has the looks of a Greek god and can indeed trace his ancestry back to one Kallikrates, a priest of Isis in Ancient Egypt. An inscribed potsherd, bequeathed to Vincey, tells the story of his ancestor's murder by a strange white queen of a savage African people and that his death must be avenged.

Holly, who tells the story, Vincey and their manservant travel to Africa and, after many adventures, are about to be killed by tribesmen when one of their elders reminds them that all white men are to be delivered alive to their queen. They are taken to the hidden cavern-city of Kôr and finally presented to the beautiful Ayesha, first seen wrapped in white gauze like the apparitions conjured up at the séances Haggard had attended in London as a young man. They discover that Vincey is the reincarnation of Kallikrates for whom Ayesha, or She, as her subjects call her, has been waiting for two thousand years and whom she intends to make immortal like herself.

Holly and Vincey are horrified and fascinated by She, who rules her strange domain with extreme cruelty and expresses violently totalitarian views, even suggesting that she might usurp Queen Victoria's throne. Finally she announces that Vincey is to bathe in the pillar of divine fire, 'the Fountain and the Heart of Life', which confers immortality. He hesitates and to encourage him, she strips naked and steps into the flame herself. In the next passage Haggard's imagination excelled itself:

> Oh, how beautiful she looked in the flame! No angel out of heaven could have worn a greater loveliness. Even now my heart faints before the recollection of it, as naked in the naked fire she stood and smiled at our awed faces ... But suddenly – more suddenly than I can tell – an indescribable change came over her countenance ... The smile vanished and in its stead there crept a dry, hard look; the rounded face seemed to grow pinched ... The glorious eyes, too, lost their light and, as I thought, the form its perfect shape and erectness ... Where was that wonderful roundness and beauty? And her face by Heaven! – *her face was growing old before my eyes!* ...
>
> True enough ... Ayesha *was* shrivelling up; the golden snake that encircled her gracious form slipped over her hips and to the ground. Smaller and smaller she grew; her skin changed colour and in place of the perfect whiteness of its lustre it turned dirty brown and yellow, like to an old piece of withered parchment ... Then she seemed to understand what kind of a change was passing over her and she shrieked – ah, she shrieked! – Ayesha rolled on the floor and shrieked. Smaller she grew and smaller yet, till she was no larger than a monkey. Now the skin had puckered into a million wrinkles and on her shapeless face was the stamp of unutterable age ... [18]

Even Haggard himself was uncertain how he came to invent such a parable. Writing to the schoolmaster, who had taught him Classics at

Ipswich and had translated into Greek the inscription on the potsherd in *She*, he explained, 'Of course the whole thing is an effort to trace the probable effects of immortality upon the morally unregenerate. She's awful end is in some sense a parable – for what are Science and Learning and the consciousness of Knowledge and Power in the face of Omnipotence?'[19] He knew he had written a remarkable book and did not understand how he had done it. Had he been guided by some mystical force? Or had it been the welling up of inherited memories of his own Norse ancestors' legends? Certainly he was aware that he was driven in its creation but probably did not consider that the force might be his own subconscious mind and emotions.* Whatever it was, he recognised it as an extraordinary achievement and, when he delivered his completed manuscript to his agent, A. P. Watt, he said with emphasis, 'There is what I shall be remembered by.'[20]

He was right. The literary men, whom he admired, vied with each other in their praise. Andrew Lang, on reading the proofs, declared, 'I think it is one of the most astonishing romances I have ever read. The more impossible it is, the better you do it, till it seems like a story from the literature of another planet.'[21] The historian Sir Walter Besant congratulated Haggard on 'a work which most certainly put you at the head – a long way ahead – of all contemporary imaginative writers. If fiction is best cultivated in the field of pure imagination then you are certainly the first of modern novelists.'[22] The poet and critic Edmund Gosse told Haggard that, reading it overnight, 'it was impossible, while the book was in my hands, to take my eyes from a single page.'[23] As a result, he continued, 'it does not appear to me that I have ever been thrilled and terrified by any literature as I have by ... *She*.'[24]

The serialisation began in the *Graphic* in October, with *Jess* still running in the *Cornhill* while *Allan Quatermain* had just finished in *Longman's Magazine*; the latter story was to be published in book form on the first day of 1887. Longman had placed a first print order of 10,000 copies with the expectation of following it with further orders in batches of 5,000. It was expected to outsell *King Solomon's Mines*, which, in 1886, sold 25,000 copies, a huge sale at that time; and that was only the beginning.

In the summer of that year, Haggard finally felt able to give up the law and took his family to a rented property near Ditchingham House, which

---

* Both Jungian and Freudian psychologists – including Dr Carl Jung himself – were to use *She* to illustrate the concept of the *anima*, the feminine force in mankind.

was still let. There he began another novel set in the present and in Norfolk; a story of conflict between the old gentlemanly order and the *nouveaux riches* with love and fortunes lost and won. In this he could make use of those he had known since childhood, including his father, and himself identify with the hero who gave his name to the title, *Colonel Quaritch, VC*.

A few days after the publication of *She*, Rider Haggard planned to leave London without waiting to read the reviews. Probably the pressures of work and the extravagance of the praise already received made him nervous of anti-climactic criticism which might, perhaps, pick on the book's occasional lapses into slipshod prose, to which Andrew Lang had gently drawn his attention. In any case, he had had an idea for a novel about Cleopatra, which would mean visiting Egypt for the first time. He would not, however, risk taking his young family to a country notorious for its lack of hygiene but would meet his brother Andrew who was serving there.

Egypt, Ancient Egypt, had long enticed him. His mother had talked about it in her romantic way; there had been the Amhersts' private museum at Didlington; its mythology had been touched upon at Lady Caithness's séances; in Africa, there had been after-dinner speculation about the possible influence of Egyptian civilisation on the black tribes of the equatorial regions. Ancient Egyptian literature and art were hauntingly beautiful. Their religion seemed satisfying to him as it had answers to every question and their convictions were reinforced by the colossal scale and brilliant imagery of their religious and funerary art and architecture. Through this art it was possible to identify with them as fellow-humans; they were good-looking, too, and there was eroticism in the lightness and transparency of their clothing when, in the Victorian present, a glimpse of a bare, young, female shoulder, let alone a bosom, was, as they would say, enough to drive a man mad.

It seems that some time in the first half of 1886, while his family was still at Gunterstone Road, Haggard himself had a brush with some shadow of that strange period of the distant past. So far as is known, he made the most cursory record of an incident which may have been the product of his powerfully macabre imaginings. His brother Andrew, seconded to the Egyptian army with the temporary rank of *bimbashi*, or colonel, and knowing of Rider's fascination with Egyptology, had shipped an embalmed, encased mummy to him in West Kensington. On arrival, it was placed upright in his study, where on this particular night he was working late. Next morning, it is said, an agitated Haggard announced that the mummy must leave the house immediately and not remain there for another night; indeed, it must be sent at once to the museum in Norwich Castle. He would give no reason for his sudden decision but, so it was said, that morning the study was in disarray and grey with mummy-dust...*

* Haggard's grandson, Commander Mark Cheyne, heard the story told as if it had taken place at Ditchingham House. But the records of the Castle Museum, Norwich, show that a Ptolomeic mummy of Nesmin was presented to the collection by Colonel Haggard in 1886, when the house was let. Haggard wrote in his diary on 31 March 1917: '...I walked to 69 Gunterstone Road, a house I have not seen for 30 years or more and stared at the outside of the ground-floor room, which was my study. In its window stood my desk, now at Ditchingham, on which I wrote *She* in six weeks. That stuccoed, suburban residence was a queer birthplace for the immortal ... In that room also I had the experience with the mummy.'

CHAPTER FIVE

'Then, in truth, I descended into hell'

RIDER HAGGARD'S VISIT to Egypt at the beginning of 1887 was an escape, a pilgrimage and a recharging of the imagination. He was now a celebrity with *She* a best-seller and both *Jess* and *Allan Quatermain*, already serialised, to be published as books during the coming year. The risk that all highly successful popular novelists run of being savaged by critics he had compounded by writing, shortly before his departure, a controversial article for the *Contemporary Review* entitled *About Fiction*, which was so disparaging of his fellow-novelists that it was bound to provoke hostile reaction.

He chose to travel first to Paris to see the Egyptian collection in the Louvre, then on by train to Brindisi to board a ship for Alexandria. It was a difficult journey; the train broke down in Italy and some of his luggage was lost. But his fellow travellers – including friends of his family; the sister of Sir Henry Bulwer, his first employer; a publisher of plays; and a big-game hunter on his way to join Henry Stanley, the American journalist and explorer, in Equatorial Africa – knew exactly who he was and most other passengers seemed to be reading either *King Solomon's Mines* or *She*. On the dockside at Alexandria, his brother Andrew was waiting to escort him to Cairo, which he saw as the gates of the Ancient World rather than a city of high-ceilinged hotels and dusty bazaars. He was thrilled by the hot, bright sunlight, the hard blue of the sky, the wail of street cries and the presence of the past.

Haggard had been given an introduction to Emile Brugsch, the deputy director of the Department of Antiquities, who thrilled him with his account of a recent discovery. At Deir-el-Behari near the Valley of the Kings in the Theban Hills across the Nile from Luxor, they had found a deep pit where, three thousand years before, priests had hidden scores of royal mummies, taken from their painted tombs to save them from robbers. He described, and Haggard reported, how, on entering 'the long passage where for tens of centuries had slept the mighty dead ... and by the light of torches had read a few of the names upon the coffins . . . he had nearly fainted for joy.'

When the mummies had been removed for shipment by river to Cairo, 'the fellaheen women ran along the banks wailing because their ancient kings were being taken from them. They cast dust upon their hair, still dressed in a hundred plaits, as was that of those far-off mothers of theirs who wailed when these Pharaohs were borne with solemn pomp to the homes they called eternal.' Their lamentations may have also been caused by the loss of revenue to the villages which still lived by tomb-robbing and selling the plunder to archaeologists.

'Poor kings!' continued Haggard's musing, 'who dreamed not of the glass-cases of the Cairo Museum and the gibes of tourists who find the awful majesty of their withered brows a matter for jest and smiles.'[1] He, of course, did not. To Louie, he wrote, 'I looked with feelings of awe and veneration at the dead faces of Seti and Rameses,'[2] and he felt a pleasurable *frisson* when told of the opening of one hitherto undisturbed tomb where the archaeologists saw in the sand on its floor the footprints of the priests who had laid the mummy to rest three thousand years before.

Taken to watch excavations at a necropolis near the Pyramids of Ghiza, he was struck by an inscription commemorating a priest, who 'sleeps in Osiris awaiting resurrection' and remarked that such an epitaph would not be out of place in a Christian cathedral. He was struck by the concept of the *Ka*, the spirit of the departed, which roamed free, but was distressed by the indignity of treating the mummies as curiosities, which he considered 'a great argument in favour of cremation'.[3]

He cruised up the Nile by paddle steamer, going ashore to visit temples and tombs and finally the grandest of all in the Valley of the Kings. Crossing the river from Luxor to the west bank, occupied for millennia by the dead and their keepers, he jolted over the rough roads in a horse-drawn gharry into the bare, brown, sun-seared valley. There, he was taken into the tomb of Seti I, down steeply sloping passages decorated with frescoes of flying vultures into chambers painted with visions of the sky, as flocks of bats flickered above the flames of the guides' torches.

Further up river, near Aswan, he was taken to another necropolis and, squeezing through a door choked almost to the lintel with sand, saw one painted mummy case within and, beyond, innumerable skeletons. It then occurred to him that the original, mummified occupant of the tomb had been joined later by victims of the plague. The hypochondriac in Haggard suddenly remembered that plague germs long outlived their victims and, in sudden panic, shouted to his companions not to follow him and that he was coming out. Then, as he related later, the vibration of his voice dislodged the sand above, which began to pour through cracks in the stone roof. 'Like a flash, I realised that in another few seconds I, too, should be buried. Gathering all my strength, I made a desperate effort and succeeded in reaching the mouth of the hole just before it was too late, for my friends had wandered off to some distance and were quite unaware of my plight.'[4] Just how desperate his plight had been might be linked to the power of his imagination, which had become accustomed to making the most out of any prospect of a tight corner.

Back in Cairo in March, Haggard decided he had 'seen enough for one go' but took up a long-standing invitation to visit Cyprus, where Sir Henry Bulwer was now High Commissioner. Although he stayed at Government House in Nicosia and was taken on fascinating excursions, he hankered after home and missed the calm companionship of his wife.

'I cannot tell you how homesick I am, old girl,' he wrote to Louie. 'Or how I want to see you and the kids again. I will never come on a trip of this kind again without you ... I am very anxious to get to my work again, my head is full of Cleopatra, for which I have got a very strong plot.' He then urged that they return to live at Ditchingham House as soon as possible.

> We seem to be a good deal better off now, in fact there must be a great deal of money due ... I cannot tell you, my dear, what a pleasure it will be to me if I find myself in a position to give you back the home again which you lost by marrying me. I think that the best thing to me about such a measure of success as I have won is that it has relieved my conscience of a great weight. I do not think I had any business to marry you when I did – it was pulling you down in the world. However I think that I have now attained, in name if not fortune, such a position you would not have been likely to exceed if I had not met you ... I dare say you think me a queer chap for writing like this ... [5]

In April, they were reunited in London, he bringing her a present of two molar teeth from an Egyptian mummy. Haggard was even more of a celebrity than before his departure but not entirely in the way he had expected. The publication of *She* had proved the sensational success all expected, out-selling *King Solomon's Mines* within three months. By August, some 43,000 copies had been sold and Haggard's earnings were more than £1,800.* It had stirred up hostile criticism, too, aggravated by the articles he had written for the *Contemporary Review* belittling much current fiction. He had dismissed the eight hundred novels published in Britain each year with the comment 'most of this crude mass of fiction is worthless.' He had attacked the standards of both writers and readers but he had, by implication, extolled his own genre with what seemed like false modesty. 'In the paths and calm retreats of pure imagination', he, whose own imaginings were neither calm nor particularly pure, declared that writers might 'even – if we feel that our wings are strong enough to bear us in that thin air – cross the bounds of the known and, hanging between earth and heaven, gaze with curious eyes into the great profound beyond. There are still subjects that may be handled *there* if the man can be found bold enough to handle them.' When other novels had had their day, he concluded, such writing would appeal 'not to a class, or a nation, or even to an age, but to all time and humanity at large'.[6] Most critics were themselves authors, and not nearly so successful as the newcomer, whom they could and did accuse of attracting readers with sadism and thinly veiled eroticism. Lapses in his prose were picked upon: 'It is as though a subject roughed out by Michelangelo had been executed with an eye to New Bond Street popularity by Gustave Doré,'[7] declared the critic of the *Pall Mall Budget*; the *Church Quarterly Review* entitled its criticism, 'The Culture of the Horrible: Mr Haggard's Stories'[8] and *Court and Society* accused him of writing 'the literature of gross excitements and vulgar display'.[9]

More serious were accusations of plagiarism, mostly from unlikely sources. Unconvincing as they were, this seemed to Haggard to cast doubts on his honour as a gentleman and it hurt him deeply. When Andrew Lang tried to laugh away his anger, he made it worse by seeming to give credence to the charges by writing the doggerel,

> The critics, hating men who're Dabs
> At drawing in the dibs
> Declare that Haggard cribs his crabs,
> And so they crab his cribs.[10]

Always volatile, he was 'rather sickened on the novel writing trade'[11] and even talked of abandoning it, but further enquiries about joining the Colonial Service were fruitless. Yet the pull of story-telling exerted itself again as did his delight in its rewards. Not only had the tenant left

---

* Equivalent to about £93,000 in 1993.

Ditchingham House, so that the Haggards could return whenever they wished, but they moved to a much larger house in London – 24 Redcliffe Square – where they could entertain in style. Also Haggard was elected a member of the Savile Club, the most fashionable literary club in London, and was asked to join a group of writers – which included Lang, Besant and Gosse – at their Saturday lunch parties.

In London, he was vulnerable to his celebrity, particularly after the magazine *Vanity Fair* published a caricature of him by 'Spy' as a tall, thin, elegant young man with a long nose and drooping moustache, entitled 'She'. He was invited to Queen Victoria's Jubilee celebration at Westminster Abbey (although the invitation went astray) and was asked to make speeches and give interviews, to which his excitable mind and manner were well suited: 'Mr Haggard has a way of jumping up suddenly and walking about restlessly for a moment or two, though never interrupting the conversation by doing so.'[12]

To escape from all this – enjoyable to him as it was – and write in peace, Haggard took his family back to Ditchingham in May, 1887. There, he wrote *Cleopatra* in little more than two months and into it he poured his obsession with Ancient Egypt. As in *She*, a powerful, sexually attractive woman was at the heart of the story but he allowed himself to play with concepts of time and reincarnation. There were no contemporary characters in this story, so all could speak in the rolling cadences which perhaps owed as much to memories of his father reading lessons in church from the Old Testament as to any instinctive knowledge of how the ancients talked.

The convoluted story, told by an Egyptian priest, was the popular mixture of lightly draped eroticism and mysticism with sharp touches of cruelty. Cleopatra herself, when seen asleep by the narrator, is reminiscent of She:

> There she lay the fairest thing that man ever saw – fairer than a dream and the web of her dark hair flowed all about her. One white, rounded arm made a pillow for her head . . . Her rich lips were parted in a smile, showing the ivory lines of teeth; and her rosy limbs were draped in so thin a robe of the silk of Cos, held about her by a jewelled girdle, that the white gleam of flesh shone through it.

He has visions of travel through time, space and numinous worlds:

> And, as I gazed, filled with wonder, I was caught upon the Wings of Flame and whirled away! away! faster than the lightning's flash. Down

I fell through depths of empty space set here and there with glittering crowns of stars. Down for ten million miles and ten times ten million, till, at length, I hovered over a place of soft unchanging light, wherein were Temples, Palaces and Abodes such as no man ever saw in the visions of his sleep ...

When finally he himself is condemned to death and awaits the executioners, he writes:

Oh, Cleopatra! Cleopatra, thou Destroyer! if I might tear thy vision from my heart! Of all my griefs, this is the heaviest grief – still I must love thee! Still must I hug this serpent to my heart! Still in my ears must ring that laugh of triumph, the murmur of falling fountain – the song of the nightinga – [13]

The reader's imagination completes the final horror.

Cleopatra was sold for serialisation in the *Illustrated London News*, with publication as a book scheduled for 1889. Haggard had published three other novels in 1888: *Colonel Quaritch VC*; *Maiwa's Revenge*, a hunting story set in Africa with Allan Quatermain as its hero; and *Mr Meeson's Will*, a contemporary novel with a publishing background. Able to produce a novel in two or three months and possessed of extraordinary energy, Haggard was also writing three others, *Allan's Wife*, another Quatermain adventure in Africa; *Beatrice*, another novel of contemporary social life; and *The World's Desire*, an historical romance about Helen of Troy; the first for publication in 1889, the others in the following year.

As his rate of production exceeded the capacity of his publishers and there was a risk of flooding the market, Haggard could again take time off to travel. One expedition was a solitary pilgrimage to Garsington, where he had stayed so happily as a boy. It was wet, depressing weather and his mood became sombre as he remembered his youth: 'You were shaken by the same hopes and fears that shake you now. The same dark mystery hung over you; alas! it only grows darker with the growing years. "Going back" is not without its pleasures but, on the whole, it does not tend to promote cheerfulness of mind.'[14]

Another expedition was to Iceland. Proud of his supposed Danish ancestry and linking this with the daring and bloody history of the Vikings, he had been thinking of writing a novel inspired by their sagas. He had in mind a hero, rejected by his father, exiled from the woman he loves and forced to live by piracy. To give this a more dramatic setting than Denmark, or, indeed, his own native East Anglia, which had been ravaged and then settled by the Danes, he chose Iceland which the Vikings had reached on their great voyages into the Atlantic.

He took passage from Leith in the *Copeland*, a small trading steamer of one thousand tons, with a friend named Ross and, after a rough voyage, reached Reykjavik in time for his thirty-second birthday. His aim was to visit the sites of the sagas and, taking an Icelandic schoolmaster as a guide, set out with a string of shaggy Iceland ponies to carry their baggage. Across the starkly majestic landscape they travelled, between bare mountains, past still lakes and torrents in which they fished and hot geysers in which they cooked fresh joints of lamb. The coming of the short night was particularly memorable:

> The mighty black mountains shutting one in ... A grey gloom creeps across the sky, then the light turns blue and ghostly – everything looks unreal and the loneliness is unutterable. A wild duck, flying like an arrow from the river to the fjord, is the only living thing that can be seen, the brawling of the water the only sound that can be heard. One looks upon the desolate sides of the fells and it becomes easy to understand how the Icelanders learnt their faith in trolls and goblins ...

It was also easy to fall into a melancholic reverie and Haggard did so. Musing on the fate of the characters in the Icelandic sagas, he wrote in his diary:

> Where are they all? Day by day they saw the cold light fall upon those great mountains flecked with snow, every silent pool of the river, every crack and stone ... were familiar to their eyes, but where are they – can it be that they are gone forever? The rattling whistle of the whimbrel echoes overhead, a raven flies croaking from the drift, a wild duck passes swiftly to her nest upon the lake. That is the answer, the only answer given to those who seek what has been in what is ...

But he found spectacular settings for his saga, like the tremendous waterfall divided by rocks so that

> the double arches of water meet and fall in one torrent into the bottomless pool below ... Just where the curve is deepest, a single crag ... juts through the foam. If a man could reach it, he might leap from it some twelve fathoms sheer into the spray-hidden pit beneath – there to

sink or swim. The crag is called Wolf's Fang. From the depth of the chasm, the spray boils up like steam – a glorious thing to see.[15]

Such scenes inspired what was to be his Norse saga, which he would call *Eric Brighteyes*, and he could already hear in his mind's ear the dialogue spoken in much the same biblical measures as did his Ancient Egyptians, Zulus and the inhabitants of Zu-Vendis and Kôr. After a month in this sad place, Haggard and Ross re-embarked in the *Copeland*, which had loaded a cargo of Icelandic ponies, and sailed for Leith. The voyage was to provide a suitably apocalyptic climax to his own saga of that year. It was rough, the weather worsening throughout the week's passage to Thurso. As the little ship plunged in huge seas, the hatches had to be left open to ventilate the holds, where scores of ponies were stalled, and there was the danger that she would fill and founder. Arriving safely off the coast of Scotland, the weather moderated but fog came down; yet the captain decided to continue because the wretched ponies had suffered terribly in the storm and were short of fodder. As the ship steamed blindly ahead, Haggard was on deck and later described what happened:

> Suddenly, the dense mist seemed to roll up in front of us, like the drop-scene at a theatre, and there appeared immediately ahead black cliffs and all about us rocks on which the breakers broke and the water boiled as it can do after a great gale in the Pentland Firth ... There was a cry: the engines were reversed but the current and that terrible tide caught the *Copeland* and dragged her forward.

The ship shuddered and her bottom scraped over rocks and, as the swell sucked away from the shore, her bow was caught fast, while her stern sank back with sixty fathoms of water beneath the keel. There was a rush for the ship's boats but their davits were jammed and the falls tangled. As the hull lurched and ground and the tide swirled, a boat hove in sight and Haggard asked the captain of the *Copeland* if he might hail it. 'Aye, Mr Haggard,' he replied, 'do anything you can to save your lives!' So the loud Haggard voice bellowed for help across the water. Warily, the boatmen pulled closer through white water washing over the rocks, ran alongside and the passengers scrambled aboard.

There were attempts to save the ponies which were cut loose and manhandled out of the hold, some to swim ashore, others to drown; but no humans were lost. Set ashore on the island of Stroma, they stood watching while the tide ebbed and eventually the ship's back broke. Villagers joined them and one, the schoolmaster, approached Haggard, raised his hat and asked, 'The author of *She*, I believe? I am verra glad to meet you.' That afternoon, they chartered a boat to take them to the Scottish mainland, where they were put ashore and taken by cart to Wick. 'During the shipwreck and its imminent dangers my nerves were not stirred,' he wrote later, 'but afterwards of a sudden they gave out. I realised that I had been very near death and all that word means. For some days I did not recover my balance.'[16]

Home by the end of July, he at once wrote an account of the shipwreck for the *Illustrated London News*, then settled down to begin *Eric Bright-eyes*. Nettled by criticism of his occasionally slapdash style, he determined to take more care and the book was completed in four months instead of two. Although he had spent only five weeks in Iceland, Haggard felt an affinity with his characters, confident of their blood in his veins. He had finished writing by the end of the year. Meanwhile, *She* had been adapted as a play and staged at the Gaiety Theatre.

Critics continued to carp, particularly Frank Harris, the editor of the *Fortnightly Review*. 'The taste for novels like Mr Haggard's,' he had written, 'is quite as truly the craving for coarse and violent intoxicants because they coarsely and violently intoxicate.'[17] Such words from so notorious a libertine and braggart as Harris should not have worried Haggard unduly, but the skin of his confidence was thin and he was hurt. The writing of historical novels, through which contemporary Norfolk gentlemen did not wander, suggested more excursions into other ways of life and, in June, 1889, he started work on another African novel in which all the characters were Zulus. Again it was to be a bloodthirsty epic and it was to be titled, after its heroine, *Nada the Lily*.

While staying at their house in Redcliffe Square, Haggard often lunched at the Savile Club in Piccadilly, to which he had belonged for two years. There he could meet not only his new-found literary friends but other writers including Max Beerbohm, Thomas Hardy, Anthony Hope, Henry James, H. G. Wells and, albeit only as a guest, Oscar Wilde. Also introduced to the club by Lang at this time was a young man, ten years Haggard's junior, but with a reputation to match. Rudyard Kipling had already made his name as a writer of light verse and short stories. A plain young man with a square face, heavy, dark moustache and alert eyes behind small round spectacles, his attraction was an inquisitive energy and an imagination as lively as Haggard's but on a tighter rein. Like Haggard, Kipling felt himself to be something of an outsider.

The Savile Club thrived on ideas and conflict and immediately,

Haggard and Kipling were cast as literary rivals. When the latter was coming up for election to the club, one member wrote to a friend, 'Did I tell you of my making the acquaintance of Rudyard Kipling? The Savile was all on the *qui vive* about him when I lunched there ... with Gosse. Rider Haggard appeared really aggrieved at a man with a double-barrelled name, odder than his own, coming up. Literally.' Writing to Robert Louis Stevenson in Samoa, Henry James promised, 'We'll tell you all about Rudyard Kipling – your nascent rival. He has killed one immortal – Rider Haggard.' Others saw them as equal front-runners and *Harper's Magazine* declared dismissively, 'It is a pathetic fact that with such artistic and important books in our reach, the great mass of us prefer to read the Rider Haggards and the Rudyard Kiplings of the day.'[18]

In fact, the two men took an instant liking to each other. Both had felt rejection in childhood, Kipling having been sent to England from India to undergo a mostly unhappy education in exile; both had lived on the frontiers of the Empire in Africa and India; both admired men of action; both wondered about the mysteries of humanity; neither was good-looking or attractive to women but both were celebrities. 'Rider Haggard, to whom I took at once,' Kipling was to remember, 'he being of the stamp adored by children and trusted by men at sight; and he could tell tales, mainly against himself, that broke up the tables.'[19]

So, soon after they were introduced, Haggard invited Kipling to dine at Redcliffe Square; he arrived late, having been slightly hurt in a street accident. At the Savile, they enjoyed swapping ideas for stories and Kipling, knowing of Haggard's love of the macabre, sent him a story about an Egyptian mummy, a curse and a ghastly consequence – a story that he had been tempted to make use of himself – beginning his letter, 'Forgive a junior's impertinence but this thing was plucked up the other day across some drinks and it seemed – but of course you know it.' After telling the story, he ended, 'Were the mummy not in it, I could and would take the thing and play with it. But there is a King in Egypt already and so I bring the body to his feet for what it is worth.'[20]

Haggard's fascination with Egypt – even when writing about Vikings and Zulus – was such that he asked an Egyptologist to design a letter-heading and book-plate of hieroglyphics within a cartouche reading, 'H. Rider Haggard, the son of Ella, lady of the house, makes an oblation to Thoth, the Lord of Writing, who dwells in the Moon.' His mother had first inspired his interest in Egyptian mythology and, when *Cleopatra* was published in June, 1889, he dedicated it to her in the hope that it would remind her of 'the old and mysterious Egypt in whose lost glories you are so deeply interested'.[21]

Ella was now aged seventy, in failing health and her eyesight was poor, but she was able to read the dedication and, well aware of the savaging he had suffered from the critics, replied, 'It certainly redounds greatly to you, dearest Rider, whatever the critics may say and I have no doubt they will do their worst. But I think posterity will do justice to your production.'[22] But in December, she was dying and he was summoned to Bradenham. He looked down upon what he was to describe as 'the gentle sweetness which characterised her face in youth, grew ever with her years and may be said to have reached its most complete development upon her bed of death ... '[23]

She died on 9 December and was buried beside the village church, then under snow. Her son was grief-stricken. She had always been the calm centre of his life; from her imagination, his had grown. Although he had not seen much of her since he left home for Africa more than a decade before, she had always seemed close.

> Indeed [he was to write], she seems to be much nearer to me now that she is dead than she was while she still lived. It is as though our intimacy and mutual understanding has grown in a way as real as it is mysterious ... No night goes by that I do not think of her and pray that we may meet again to part no more.[24]

As a memorial he published a book of her religious verse, with a memoir by himself, called *Life and Its Author*.

Like him, she expressed human bewilderment as to the purpose of life:

> Oh human mind! entangled in the maze,
> Perplexed of these our philosophic days,
> Each path of thought thou dost pursue,
> Each path reject – unfound the mystic clue.
> Then whither fly?

Science seemed to present a confusing challenge to religious faith and had to be tamed:

> Or – what though Science, with her tragic hand,
> Strong Nature's Forces train to your command;
> Though tyrant's Steam, now curbed and conquered slave,
> Propel her Master over land and wave;
> Or though – more wond'rous still – th' Electric Spark

> Span, at a word, yon Ocean, wild and dark,
> And in Thoughts interchange, where lost to sight,
> Divided Souls and Continents unite.[25]

The answer to her puzzlement was Christian faith, which he was increasingly to rely upon as the final defence against despair. After her death, he found in the drawer of her writing table, waveringly written in pencil:

> Lo! in the shadowy valley where He stands:
> My soul pale sliding down Earth's icy slope
> Descends to meet Him with beseeching hands
> Trembling with Fear – and yet upraised in Hope.[26]

His own hope and his principal comfort was his son, Jock. Now aged eight, the boy was extraordinarily like his grandmother with soft eyes, a wide mouth curved like a cupid's bow and 'a nature of singular sweetness'.[27] Haggard was fond of his two little daughters and of his practical, if unimaginative, wife, but the boy was reflective and affectionate and his father saw him not only as his heir, who would carry their name through the twentieth century, but as the next step in founding a Haggard dynasty of strong, brave men with lively minds.

It was to Jock and the others that Haggard now returned. They would live, he decided, at Ditchingham, and would probably let their house in London. He would become a literary squire spurning the money-makers and carping critics in London, just visiting his friends at his club if he felt so inclined. On his own country estate, an inefficient tenant farmer was leaving the farm – 'The heart had been dragged out of it and very little put into it in return',[28] complained Haggard – so that he could now become a gentleman-farmer on a small scale, letting twenty-six acres and farming a hundred and twenty himself. 'Mustard Pot Hall' would have to be redecorated and made splendid with oak panelling.

Just as their immediate future seemed settled, Haggard once again heard the sirens sing and this time the enticement was to Mexico. He had been increasingly fascinated by the Aztec civilisation and its strange parallels with Egypt: the elaborate art and architecture, which even included pyramids, and the bizarre religious ceremonial, with the added piquancy of human sacrifice, which would, he thought, provide a splendid setting for a novel.

He had heard a story which whetted his appetite for adventure as much as anything related by archaeologists in Egypt. A year earlier, he had met a certain John Gladwyn Jebb, a tough, intelligent Englishman who, like himself, seemed to have been cut out for the role of Empire-builder. Jebb was, however, in commerce and, now living in Mexico, had recounted to Haggard his meeting in Mexico City with a Cuban geologist, who had told him a strange story. While prospecting on the shores of Lake Tezcuco, the geologist had been told by a Mexican, who could be seen by his features to have been descended from the Aztecs, about Montezuma's treasure.

When the first Spanish invasion of Mexico ended in disaster and the expulsion of the invaders from the capital after the death of Montezuma, they had fled the city loaded with booty. On what became known as the *Noche Triste*, they had tried to fight their way to safety across the causeway from the island in the lake on which the capital stood. But the loot weighed them down, most of it having to be abandoned and many of the looters killed. Knowing that the Spaniards would return, the Aztecs decided to hide the treasure, including 'eighteen large jars of gold, either in the form of ornaments or dust, several jars full of precious stones, much arms and armour, also of gold', and a great golden head of the Emperor Montezuma with emerald eyes. Stonemasons worked fast to build a secret cache at the bottom of a pit sixty feet deep. When it had been sealed and covered, the hiding-place was marked with the planting of two trees.

Shown the supposed site – marked by two huge and ancient trees – the Cuban had obtained permission from the landowner to prospect there for sulphur. Digging by the trees, they had found at a depth of sixty feet a great stone carved with the symbol of an owl. Blowing this apart with dynamite, they entered a tunnel which led to steps at the top of which lay a bronze spearhead and, beyond, a wall of some very hard material fused by heat. While preparing to blast a way through, they heard that the land had been sold, so they filled in the excavation, declared that no sulphur had been found and left. The Cuban had then asked Jebb for his help. Well connected and popular, the Englishman had been granted permission to dig for antiquities on the site and organised the expedition, which he now invited Haggard to join. After much enjoyable planning and speculation, it was decided that, as Louie and Jebb's wife were friends, both couples should go to Mexico. A further piece of serendipity was that the Jebbs asked if, on their return, they could take over the house in Redcliffe Square.

The Haggards spent a happy Christmas at Ditchingham. Sad as Rider was at the death of his mother, he accepted such bereavement – after a relatively long life, fulfilled by motherhood – as inevitable and the will of God. He was comforted by his own children and, above all, by Jock. Now nine, he was exactly the boy his father had hoped he would become. He was manly, riding ponies, climbing trees, making a start at golf by putting on the lawn and had once offered to fight anyone who belittled his father. He was also imaginative and had charmed his father when, at the age of four, he had looked up at a full moon and said, 'Look, Dad, there is God's lamp!'

Haggard loved his son so deeply that, as the time for departure drew nearer, he was subject to the irrational fear that, when he left for Mexico, he and Jock would never meet again. Specifically, he imagined that he himself would die on his journey and so obsessive did this dread become that he secretly put his financial affairs in order and, sealing the relevant documents in a strong-box, deposited them at Gosling's Bank. He was comforted, however, by the knowledge that the boy would be well cared for during his parents' absence. Edmund Gosse had a son, Philip, of about the same age and had invited Jock to stay with his family at their house in London, 29 Delamere Terrace, overlooking the Regent's Canal in Maida Vale. Even so, when the parting came there was a terrible finality about it. 'With a cheerful face I kissed him,' recalled Haggard, 'I remember how he flung his arms around my neck. In a cheerful voice I blessed him and bade him farewell, promising to write. Then he went through the door and it was finished. I think I wept.'[29]

Haggard and his wife sailed for New York in the liner *Etruria*, arriving on 10 January 1891, to a celebrity's welcome, for he had been famous since *King Solomon's Mines* had been published there six years before, followed by *She*. Interviewed by American reporters, he replied to their blizzard of trivial questions with courtesy and an occasional touch of veiled sarcasm: 'Do you make your plots before you write your stories, or do you write your stories first?' 'Undoubtedly I make the plots before I finish the stories.' But the *New York Times* report included a description of the famous author under interrogation:

In the parlor of the Victoria Hotel last night, from 7 to 7.30, a tall, lank, middle-aged man was fidgeting about in an alleged easy chair, tying his legs into bowknots and doing everything with his hands that the hands of a naturally awkward man ever did do when he was in a state of nervousness … He is a tall man, probably six feet high, somewhat loosely put together, with a slight stoop of the shoulders. He has dark hair but the delicate moustache which adorns his lip is quite light in colour. A long pointed nose gives his face a thinnish appearance but a careful look at him shows that he has a full forehead and that his eyes are well apart. He has an agreeable manner and a pleasant smile. When he shakes hands he gives a quick nervous grip and he simultaneously gives a pull sufficiently strong to take a man who has not good understanding quite off his feet. [Then the interviews over] Mr Haggard did not urge his torturers to remain after they showed their readiness to leave.[30]

From New York they travelled by train to New Orleans and then Mexico City, where they stayed at the Jebbs' house. Excursions began at once. Haggard, with the beginnings of a story about Mexico at the time of Montezuma already in his mind, found exactly the setting he relished. In an echo of 'Sheba's Breasts', the twin mountains in *King Solomon's Mines*, Mexico City was guarded by two huge volcanoes, Popocatapetl ('The Hill that Smokes') and Ixtaccihuatl ('The Sleeping Woman'). The former, he noted,

when I first saw her as the sun rose over the mountains of Tenoctitlan (as the Aztecs call the city of Mexico), I could see nothing but the gigantic shape of a woman fashioned in snow, lying like a corpse upon her lofty bier, whose hair streamed down the mountainside. But when the sunbeams caught her also she seemed to start out in majesty from a veil of rosy mist – a wonderful and thrilling sight.[31]

Excursions began at once to acclimatise themselves. They rode out into the hills, looking at archaeological sites, the sacrificial pyramids on the summits of which living victims had had their hearts cut out, and the brilliant displays of multi-coloured birds and flowering plants. Haggard began collecting seeds and roots for the greenhouses at Ditchingham, an edge of risk added to the search by the danger from snakes.

Yet he was still haunted by foreboding and could not relax and enjoy these fresh experiences. They were due to leave for the shores of Lake Tezcuco on 9 February but the day before, a Sunday, his fears were realised. As he wrote later:

My presentiments had returned to me with terrible strength and persistence. One Sunday morning in the Jebbs' house in Mexico City, as we were preparing to go to church, they were fulfilled. Mrs Jebb called us to their bedroom. She had a paper in her hand. 'Something is wrong with one of your children,' she said brokenly. 'Which?' I asked, aware that this meant death, no less, and waited. 'Jock,' was the reply and the dreadful telegram, our first intimation of his illness, was read. It said that he had 'passed away peacefully' some few hours before . . . Then in truth I descended into hell.

When Jock had arrived at the Gosses' house he, young Philip and his sister had enjoyed themselves watching boys sliding on the ice of the Regent's Canal below their window and then were themselves taken skating on the Round Pond in Kensington Gardens. But Jock had been infectious with measles and all three soon succumbed. They seemed to be making good recoveries when Jock suffered a sudden relapse. Removed to a sick-room away from the others, he deteriorated fast. There was nothing the doctors could do; and he died. Nobody was sure what had killed him but it was put down to a 'perforated gastric ulcer', which was unlikely, and later, meningitis. When the Gosses sent the fateful telegram they kept the news from their own children.

> He was my darling [mourned his father], for him I would gladly have laid down my life . . . I can see the room now. Jebb weeping by the unmade bed, the used basins – all, all. And in the midst of it myself – with a broken heart! . . . I staggered from the room; I wrote a cable directing that the burial should take place by the chancel door of Ditchingham Church . . . Afterwards I took up a Bible and opened it at hazard. The words that my eyes fell on were: 'Suffer little children to come unto me, and forbid them not.' The strange chance seemed to cheer me a little. That afternoon I went for a walk in the great avenue. Never shall I forget that walk among the gay and fashionable Mexicans. I did not know until then what a man can endure and live.

Dazed and half-expecting to wake from a nightmare, Haggard decided to abandon the treasure hunt but not to return to London, or Norfolk, immediately. He and Jebb would travel, visiting a silver mine in which the latter had an interest, arranging to meet their wives later in New York. They did so, often travelling by mule, or canoe, through magnificent scenery and danger from bandits. Haggard recorded it all in his memory – the lawless towns, the giant tarantulas, the wall before which the Emperor Maximilian had been shot in 1867 and even the stranger who amazed him by claiming that 'in the future we would telegraph through the air without the use of any connecting wires' – but it was noted without emotion for his mind churned with anguish.

As a theist, he could only assume that this was punishment for his sins. But would he ever meet his son again? Thoughts of the immortality of the spirit and reincarnation chased each other through his mind. His mother had clung to her Christian faith, so he must do the same. 'If it is true, as I believe,' he later confided in memoirs to be published only after his own death, 'then surely my spirit will find his spirit, though it must search from world to world. If, with all Earth's suffering millions, I am deluded, then let the same everlasting darkness be our bed and canopy.'[32]

At last the journeys ended in New York, and Rider and Louie sailed for Liverpool and home, arriving at Ditchingham just before what would have been Jock's tenth birthday. Their two little daughters were dressed in black and beside the chancel door of the church was the earth of a freshly dug grave. Louie, with her customary stoicism, held her grief in check, calmly taking over command of the household. But Haggard was still in a state of shock. He had been ill with influenza yet was determined to write and drove himself to begin the novel set in Mexico that he had planned. It was to be called *Montezuma's Daughter* and the hero was to be a traveller from Ditchingham, whose young son is murdered. While he remained outwardly calm, Haggard poured his grief into the fiction, putting his own unspoken words into the mouth of his traveller from Ditchingham when he heard the terrible news:

In that moment I think my heart broke – at least I know that nothing has had the power to move me greatly since, though this memory moves me day by day and hour by hour, till I die and go to seek my son ... There is no hope but faith, there is no comfort save in the truth that love which might have withered on the Earth grows fastest in the tomb, to flower gloriously in heaven; that no love can be perfect till God sanctifies it and completes it with his seal of Death. I threw myself down ... and wept such tears as a man may weep but once in his life days.[33]

When the earth over Jock's grave had settled, his father had a marble plinth and cross set above it, inscribed with words he had chosen from the Book of Samuel, 'I shall go unto him, but he shall not return to me.'

CHAPTER SIX

'The jangle of imaginary spurs'

❧

IT WAS AS if Rider Haggard's past and his future – his mother and his son – had been wiped out. In reflection of this, Jock's letters and school reports were locked away, his books shifted to top shelves in the library, his toys stowed in the attic and it was made known to family and friends that, after the initial receipt and acknowledgement of condolences, he was not to be a subject of conversation.

> Jock was dead and so he must not be mentioned [recalled one of Haggard's nephews]. To come on a book or a toy that had once belonged to my young cousin ... was to strike a hush over the room such as might almost have been observed towards a relative who had been hanged for murder. There was a guilty silence. Jock haunted the house the more obtrusively because everyone pretended they could not see him.[1]

The stricken father suffered in mind and body. Sunk in deep depression, he went down with repeated bouts of influenza and digestive problems. His wife, more resilient, felt that permanent mourning was negative and unproductive, so recovered more quickly, showing irritation with the gloom imposed on their house by her husband.

Throughout that summer he tried to lose himself in writing *Montezuma's Daughter* but only succeeded in finding himself again for, in essence, it was curiously autobiographical. Its hero, Thomas Wingfield from Ditchingham, is forbidden to marry the girl of his choice, travels abroad and makes a fortune and then to Mexico, where he marries Montezuma's daughter. His wife and children – including his son – die of plague; he marries again but his children – including his favourite son – are murdered. He returns to Norfolk to find his first sweetheart:

> Now I could see the woman's shape in the moonlight; it was tall and stately and clad in a white robe. Presently she lifted her head to watch the flitter of a bat and the moonlight lit upon her face. It was the face of

Lily ... my lost love, beautiful as of yore, though grown older and stamped with the seal of some great sorrow.

They marry at St Mary's Church at Ditchingham, where, of course, Haggard had been married and Jock had been buried.

There in the quiet light of the June evening I knelt in the chancel upon the rushes that strewed the grave of my father and my mother and sent my spirit up towards them in the place of their eternal rest and to the God who guards them. A great calm came upon me as I knelt thus ...[2]

The writing of this story was doubtless therapeutic but it did not revive Haggard's enthusiasm for writing more fiction, even after *Eric Brighteyes* was successfully published. Even a local historian's discovery that, unknown to Haggard, there had been a real Thomas Wingfield living in Ditchingham at the time when the novel was set, did not inspire a sequel.

Yet his livelihood was the writing of fiction and he was the most popular novelist in the country. His Zulu novel, *Nada the Lily*, was to be published in the following spring, *Montezuma's Daughter* a year later and now his publishers, Longman, had in mind a sequel to *She*, in which the same adventurers find another lost civilisation in Africa. But he could not, as yet, bring himself to start writing again.

At home he had created an extraordinary atmosphere, reflecting his exotic tastes and his roaming thoughts. There was no other house like it – not even Didlington Hall with its private museum – and the visitor could instantly recognise it as the home of Rider Haggard. Ditchingham House had been built at the end of the eighteenth century but its interior was Victorian and imperial. It was the Victorian fashion for a gentleman's house to be over-furnished and cluttered with booty from the Empire but this clutter and booty was unique since everything prompted a story from its owner. This cabinet had belonged to Lady Smith of Ladysmith and had forty secret drawers of which only half could be found. This officer's monocle and this brass cartridge-case had been picked up on the battlefield of Isandhlwana but, as could be seen, the pistol had misfired, costing its owner his life. That cedar rod might have been the one Moses cast before Pharaoh. This desk had belonged to Charles Dickens. That gold ring had been worn by Queen Taia, 'the feminine Henry VIII of Egypt and one of the most fascinating and beautiful women who ever lived'.[3]

The heavy doors had been made for the Queen's yacht *Victoria and Albert* and the dark oak panelling, recently installed by Haggard, was hung with Zulu assegais, Arab swords, a giant pair of buffalo horns, framed illustrations for *She* by Maurice Greiffenhagen, portraits of past and present members of the Haggard and Margitson families. There was a bronze Etruscan jar, Ancient Egyptian bows, a jade idol from Mexico, a whip of hippopotamus hide, a huge bronze head of Sappho, a redwood stool made for Zulu royalty. There was a painted portrait from an Egyptian mummy-case with an extraordinarily calm expression. This was an Icelandic silver chalice. That was the knobkerrie which once belonged to Haggard's Zulu servant, now used as a walking-stick. Here, an ebony dining-table inlaid with ivory portraits of Roman emperors. Everything prompted Haggard to speak the line he loved to write, that, even as he told the tale, he held the very object it concerned in his hand.

The study was shared with a tame rat, Jack, and by his desk were cupboards for fishing rods and guns with a thousand cartridges in the drawers. Outside, three greenhouses sheltered giant ferns, brought by canoe and mule out of Mexico, and orchids from Natal together with grapes, figs and peaches. Roses grew around the croquet lawn in the acre of flower garden, and in the spread of grass and parkland trees in front of the house a lily-pond had been dug and planted. In spring, drifts of daffodils flowered beneath the fine trees. Haggard himself was as active outdoors as indoors, assisted by five gardeners and labourers in the garden and grounds while seven servants were under Louie's orders in the house.

No balm could have been more soothing to the unabated pain of Haggard's grief than the surroundings of his home. The garden and the greenhouses offered constant interest, activity and pleasure to the eye and four hundred yards to the south of the house spread what he described as the 'most quietly and consistently beautiful' view he had ever seen. This was of the Waveney valley, where the original bank of what had once been a tidal estuary, now shelved steeply nearly a hundred feet to the water level. The escarpment had once been known as the Earl's Vineyard, having been planted with vines by the Earl Bigod in the Middle Ages; later it became the Bath Hills, named after an eighteenth-century bath-house on the river bank. Now, as then, it looked out across water-meadows to the river and Bungay Common beyond.

For the most part of the year, the plain below is golden with gorse [Haggard wrote], but it is not on this alone that the sight depends for beauty, or on the green of the meadows and the winding river edged with lush marshes that in spring are spotted by yellow marigolds and purple with myriads of cuckoo flowers. They all contribute to it, as do the grazing cattle, the gabled distant roofs and the church spires but I think the prospect owes its peculiar charm to the constant changes of light which sweep across its depths. At every season of the year, at every hour of the day, it is beautiful but always with a different beauty.[4]

That was the landscape he preferred to the wild terrain of topless peaks and bottomless gorges, caverns and precipices, deserts and waterfalls and ruined cities seen by his mind's eye and from which he seemed to be returning. The fervid dreams he shared so profitably with his millions of readers could not satisfy, or help ease his grief for his lost son. But conjuring life and growth from the land around him could help and the cycle of life, growth and death could at least share a pattern with that of mankind.

Haggard's confidence began to return. Although his son's name could still not be mentioned in his hearing, he became outwardly more cheerful and the pallor and the sad, sunken eyes gave way to the robust looks of the countryman. The loud, carrying Haggard voice and laugh could again be heard from the next field, or outside the house from within. He began to grow a beard which jutted from the small chin, imparting the dash he had always cultivated and did so with such success that he was described as 'a Norseman in looks' and, when dining at the Garrick Club in London, as having 'a cavalry face and the jangle of imaginary spurs'.[5] He played his part in country life as a magistrate and as a churchwarden of St Mary's, where he would read the lessons with same theatrical relish as had his father at Bradenham. Morning prayers were said daily at Ditchingham House before breakfast, where the family and their guests would assemble in the front hall, the servants would file in and all would seat themselves on high-backed chairs set against the walls; Haggard himself would read a passage from the Bible, then all would kneel on the seats of their chairs while he led the prayers.

Professing his mother's faith in Christianity, Haggard saw it as the highest rung in a spiritual ladder. 'I have a respect for Thor and Odin,' he declared with only a slight touch of humour. 'I venerate Isis and always feel inclined to bow to the moon!'[6] He kept an open mind about spiritualism and reincarnation, having the idea that his knowledge of Ancient Egyptian life must come from first-hand experience in a former existence. His superstition, or, as he saw it, his open-minded curiosity, was engaged when the Jebbs reported strange happenings at the Haggards' former house in Redcliffe Square, where they now lived. They had been beset by a poltergeist, phantom footsteps and an inexplicable chill wind which blew indoors. Jebb put it down to the presence of an idol of a hideous dwarf, reputedly from a place of human sacrifice, which they had brought home from Mexico. Feeling some responsibility for her old house, Louie went to stay with them. Resilient and pragmatic as she was, she remained resolutely in her room for two disturbed nights but, on the third,

> the horror and terror, the sense of unmitigated evil that descended on her, was so frightful that she lay amid an ever-increasing racket of knocks and bangs absolutely unable to move, until all the clothes were torn off her bed and she rose and fled to the Jebbs' bedroom where she spent the rest of the night.[7]

The idol, like Haggard's mummy in Gunterstone Road, was banished by being presented to the British Museum. Soon afterwards, Gladwyn Jebb, whose business interests had been failing, took his family back to Mexico, where, after another expedition to mines in the wilds, he sickened and died.

Meanwhile Haggard had been writing his latest romance, as he called those novels drawn wholly from the imagination, yet, since the deaths of his mother and Jock, he no longer wrote with relish. It was as if he had perfected no more than a money-making formula. He had engaged a secretary, Ida Hector, with a new-fangled typewriter, which she had recently been trained to master, and he would dictate his stories to her. He had moved his study from the ground floor of Ditchingham House to the former billiards room on the first floor, reached by a private staircase and commanding a view of the garden. Thither he and Miss Hector would retire while downstairs his booming voice could be heard, echoing in the stair-well, as it embarked on another welter of adventure, blood-shed and the supernatural.

> ... at the western extremity of the temple [the great voice rumbled through the house], a huge statue towered seventy or eighty feet into the air, hewn, to all appearance, from a mass of living rock. Behind this colossus ... the sheer mountain rose, precipice upon precipice, to the foot of a white peak clad in eternal snow ... This fearful colossus was fashioned in the shape of a huge dwarf of hideous countenance, seated with bent arms outstretched ... as though to bear the weight of the sky ... Long before the brilliant rays of the moon lit the amphitheatre they

struck upon the huge head of the dwarf idol and there, in this giddy perch ... sat Juanna herself enthroned in an ivory chair. She had been divested of her black cloak and was clad in a robe of snowy linen cut low upon her breast ... She sat quite still, her eyes set wide in horror ...

The new book was *The People of the Mist*, in which another English gentleman with 'the mind of a Norseman, or an Aztec',[8] dispossessed of his inheritance and forbidden to marry the girl of his choice, travels to Africa, finds a lost city and rescues Juanna, the captive maiden. After desperate adventures and much blood-letting, he returns home to be knighted and become lord lieutenant of his county. Haggard sent the typescript to Andrew Lang, as was his custom, but was offended when his friend criticised it for 'too much gore', adding that 'the murder of the children may stodge the reader'. Although he probably recognised the truth of this, Haggard never again sought Lang's advice on his novels and their friendship began to cool. While his profitable fantasies became a commercial operation, his attention was concentrated on the real world of his family, his garden and his farm. This cheering fecundity came to full flower when, soon after William Haggard's death, Louie told him that she was pregnant. She was not particularly maternal but was determined to help her husband through his grief for Jock and hoped to give him another son.

The baby was born on 9 December 1892, exactly three years after the death of Ella Haggard. When the doctor emerged from Louie's bedroom, Haggard looked up questioningly.

'A very jolly little girl,' announced the physician.

'Is she – quite strong? Nothing wrong with her?'

'Nothing whatever.'

'Well, after all, that is all that matters.'[9]

Haggard tried to keep his disappointment to himself within the family but wrote to his old friend Agnes, who had married his brother Jack, 'I dare say you will have seen in *The Times* that the event has come off resulting in a girl, as a boy happened to be wanted. However, she is a dear little baby ... so it would be ungrateful to grumble. Indeed I am so fond of children that I would much rather have a girl than nothing at all.'[10] The infant was named Lilias Rider Haggard. Disappointed as he was, he consoled himself that no second son could compete for his affection with Jock. In any case, the birth of the baby had added to his confidence and strengthened his grasp on the life around him. It softened the finality of the death of his father early in 1893. William Haggard had been ill with jaundice and when Rider visited Bradenham in March, he found the old squire unnaturally quiet, shrunken and sharp-featured. So it came as no surprise when, a few weeks later, he was again called to his family's home. On arrival, he was told his father had died the day before, 21 April. His last words had been, 'If I am to get better, God will be with me – if I die, He will also be with me. God is always present, is He not? He is in this room.'

Rider walked alone in the garden and through the familiar woods. The estate would be inherited by his eldest brother, William, a diplomat, but it was unlikely that he would want to become a farmer. He himself would like to sell the Ditchingham estate and buy his old home, where he had such deep emotional roots, but Louie loved her home, too, enjoyed her circle of friends in the sociable neighbourhood of Bungay and found Bradenham remote and lonely. Before leaving, Rider stood in silence beside his father's body: 'He looked fine and peaceful in death: he was a very handsome and, in many ways, a remarkable man. I never knew anyone who resembled him in the least or who was the possessor of half his energy. God rest him!'[11] He had loved the Jovian squire despite cause to the contrary. His father had denied him the education and career given to his brothers and had prevented him from marrying the woman of his choice. His father had, initially, at least, shown scant recognition of his son's achievements. He had damped and frustrated his ambition and initiative so that these had emerged from his imagination as fiction rather than through his actions as the successful colonial administrator, lawyer or soldier he might have become. That he had been a success as a novelist and was now rich and famous was entirely of his own making. Yet William Haggard had had an appetite for enjoyment and sudden surges of generosity. He was on a larger scale, in sharper focus and more heightened colours than most men, as was the son who recognised this. Magnanimous as were Rider's feelings towards him, his death had removed an impediment. Now he could be his own man.

Squire Haggard was laid in the churchyard next to the gentle Ella and their son returned to his own domain at the far side of the county with a new air of authority about him. This had been further enhanced when, early in 1892, he had been invited to stand for Parliament as candidate for the safe Conservative seat at King's Lynn. At the time he had not felt free enough of his preoccupation with grief to accept. But the possibility of a new career in politics appealed to his emerging independence of mind and, when he was again approached at the beginning of 1894, he accepted. Had this been his decision two years earlier, he would have been, by then, a well-known member of Parliament but the new opportunity was no sinecure. He was invited to stand by the Conservatives as a 'Unionist and Agricultural' candidate in the forthcoming general election in the large but thinly populated constituency of East Norfolk and was unanimously adopted in March, 1895. This would be the way back into reality after so long an excursion into worlds of his own creation.

Haggard's own interest in politics had begun when he had hoisted the Union Jack over Pretoria at the annexation in 1877, which he had seen as the organic and morally right growth of the British Empire. When it had been lowered four years later at the retrocession, he had seen this as an abdication. He saw the mission of the British as the improvement of mankind, no less. As he made his fictional *alter ego*, Allan Quatermain, say of this,

> For most of the years of my life I have handled the raw material, the virgin ore, not the finished ornament that is smelted out of it – if, indeed, it is finished yet, which I greatly doubt. I daresay that a time may come when the perfected generations – if Civilisation, as we understand it, really has a future and any such be allowed to enjoy their hour on the World – will look back to us as crude, half-developed creatures whose only merit was that we handed on the flame of life.[12]

Having been brought up during the heated debate over Darwin's theory of evolution, he assumed that the white races were higher on the evolutionary ladder than the black but that did not make them superior human beings, only more sophisticated.

> I cannot believe that the Almighty, who made both white and black, gave to one race the right or mission of exterminating, or even of robbing or maltreating, the other and calling the process the advance of civilisation [he wrote]. It seems to me that on only one condition, if at all, have we the right to take the black man's land; and that is that we provide them with an equal and a just Government, and allow no maltreatment of them, either as individuals or tribes, but, on the contrary, do our best to elevate them and wean them from savage customs. Otherwise the practice is surely indefensible.[13]

In Natal and the Transvaal, he had been able to take part in this process. Now that he lived in the eastern counties of England, he felt it was his duty to maintain the health of the Empire's most vital organism. This, in Norfolk, meant the agriculture upon which its economy was based and which Haggard, as a gentleman-farmer, believed he understood. But he did not understand Conservative policy, or chose not to, for his own policies were a robust and individualistic compound of Tory protectionism and radical reform that came close to socialism.

In his adoption speech at Norwich on 16 March, he declared that duty should be imposed upon imports of wheat and barley in order to save Norfolk farmers from undercutting by foreign competitors. He also maintained that the resulting revenue 'should be devoted to a most truly democratic end, to the end of an Old Age Pension Scheme'.[14] Cheap rail transport for farm produce should be subsidised by the Government.

His plan to protect the Norfolk farmers was as popular as he expected it to be but there was vociferous opposition from an unexpected quarter. As the election campaign began, the candidate had to make many journeys across the flat Broadlands of Norfolk by wherry, the shallow-draught sailing-barges traditionally used for transport along rivers and canals and across the wide broads, and he was quickly made aware of the wherrymen's views, for it was they who carried inland the grain landed at the Norfolk seaports.

Electioneering in rural Norfolk could be rumbustious, having changed little since the eighteenth century and now the franchise was far wider. Then it had been Whigs and Tories; now it was Liberals and Tories. His predecessor, Sir Edward Birkbeck, had been defeated by the Liberal, a Mr R. J. Price – 'a gentleman unconnected with the county' – by four hundred and forty votes. Although Haggard regarded the constituency as 'one of the most difficult in the kingdom from the Conservative point of view',[15] it was winnable and victory seemed 'about the most important thing in the whole world'.[16] He was optimistic, writing to a sister-in-law that he had had 'a *very* good reception' in one village but adding, 'There is a *chance* of winning the seat but my adversary is a tough customer.'[17]

As in the past, electioneering involved much entertaining of the electorate. In order to induce the voters of East Norfolk to listen to political speeches, they were often delivered at smoking concerts arranged by the candidates' agents. The main attraction at Haggard's was his old friend from Natal, Arthur Cochrane, who had a talent for singing comic songs – particularly one called 'The Baby on the Shore' – heard in the music-halls. Haggard, accompanied by a resolute Louie and her friend Jessie Hartcup, would join the jollities in parish halls and tavern parlours thick with tobacco smoke, while Arthur sang his jaunty little songs until the mood seemed relaxed enough for the candidate to say a few words on behalf of the Conservative Party, or, to be more exact, expound his own slightly eccentric views.

'Staunch Conservative though I am,' he told one meeting, 'I may tell you also that, if I am returned to Parliament and a Conservative Government comes into power and refuses to do justice to agriculturists, I shall vote against it.'[18] Heckling he had expected and thought he would be able to shout it down. But there was jostling and the threat of violence, too. One meeting at Horsford was reported in the *Norfolk Chronicle* to have been 'interrupted continually by an organised gang of youths and eventually broke up in disorder',[19] and another at North Walsham also had to be abandoned. His meeting at Horsham St Faith was broken up and he was pelted with eggs at Coltishall. He, Louie and Cochrane became accustomed to emerging from a parish hall or village school to 'face the booing without, which was sometimes accompanied by hustling and stone-throwing'.[20]

It was not only the local press that reported and commented upon his campaign. His candidature interested London editors not only because of his fame as an author but because he had also taken to making political speeches in London. In one he had teased them by a joking demand that the authors of newspaper paragraphs should be taxed more heavily than the authors of novels because they made more money. The national and foreign press began following his campaign with mixed opinions. The *Cable*'s correspondent wrote that Haggard 'with a vivid sense of the needs of agriculturalists ... combines the power to compel attention to his views and ... has the faculty of exciting enthusiasm, which, joined to originality and eloquence, is irresistible, even in the House of Commons'.[21]

However, the *Saturday Review* stated that

The dissatisfied gentry, who cheered Mr Rider Haggard's childish panaceas for their ills, forget that, if they make little or no money off their land, they possess compensation denied to other victims of the universal hard times. The very ownership of land in England gives them a social prestige not to be estimated by any measure of weight or coinage. Their names are in the county books; tugged forelocks and obsequious tradesmen's hats salute them at every turn; the village dogs gasp with admiration at their gaiters when they walk abroad. All these advantages, rooted in the placid natures of a kindly peasantry, Mr Haggard shares with his fellow squires. He had other advantages peculiar to himself, based upon the amiability of a vastly larger, though not less simple, popular constituency outside East Norfolk. He should content himself with these and leave the weary task of politics to others.[22]

But much of the peasantry in East Norfolk was neither placid nor friendly. The Liberals – or, rather, anybody opposed to the Conservatives – found a leader and, as Haggard saw it, rabble-rouser in Lord Wode-house, the son of a great Norfolk landowner, Lord Kimberley, who led a campaign of vilification against both Joseph Chamberlain, the Liberal who had gone over to the Conservatives, and the local candidate, declaring that the former had been 'peeling off his principles' and that 'Judas was a great deal more respectable than Mr Chamberlain and so was Barrabas.' Haggard, for his part, was said to be an exploitative employer – allegedly paying his farm workers only nine shillings a week – and had been guilty of atrocities in South Africa, including the murder of women and children.

So by polling day on 19 July an over-excited, sometimes hysterical, mood had overwhelmed the traditional placidity of East Norfolk. It was an alarming ordeal for the Haggards, although Rider's hopes of victory were high as he and Louie, accompanied by their neighbours, Mr and Mrs Hartcup, set out on a final tour.

> The contest was a keen one [reported *The Times* next morning], but the close of the poll left the Unionists with strong hopes that Mr Rider Haggard had been returned ... During the day, Mr Rider Haggard and party made a tour of the constituency on a drag* and in places met with very rough treatment. Mrs Hartcup, who was on the drag, had her head cut open by a stone. At Stalham, a very rough reception awaited the party, which had to take refuge in an hotel, where they were besieged by the mob.[23]

This report was 'in no way exaggerated' Haggard wrote in a long letter to the newspaper:

> Mrs Hartcup still lies ill from the effects of the blow from a stone, which had it struck her one inch higher would possibly have cost her her life ... The scene both at Ludham and Stalham and the hideous

* A large, strongly built, open coach.

ferocity of the mob can scarcely be described in words. No one who had not witnessed it would believe that such an unprovoked outburst of everything that is vile in human nature could possibly occur within 120 miles of London.

What made it worse was that he now knew that he had been defeated, albeit by only a hundred and ninety-eight votes, halving the Liberal majority, and believed that, but for his agent's failure to ensure that all his supporters received polling cards, he would have won.

Why have I failed [his letter asked]? I say unhesitatingly, first, because of the numerous falsehoods ... spread about me and my supposed conduct towards agricultural labourers in my employ, and, secondly, because a number of my meetings were broken up by organised gangs of roughs, whose threatening demeanour alarmed the minds of peaceable electors. The third and perhaps the chief cause of our defeat was that several of the polling places, notably those at Ludham, Stalham and, I believe, in the notorious district of St Faith, were terrorised and dominated by mobs of roughs collected there to frighten my adherents among the labouring classes ... At none of these places did the authorities seem to have considered it necessary to provide police protection. At least I can vouch that at Ludham about two hundred ruffians were expected to flee at the rebuke of one constable, and at Stalham an inspector and two constables, all of whom, I believe, were ... injured, were considered sufficient to cope with the angry passions of a mob of 500 or 600 men collected from the country round and, I have been told, Norwich.[24]

Haggard described what had happened at Stalham – in what came to be called the Battle of Stalham Bridge – to a reporter from the *Pall Mall Gazette*. On reaching the village and the waiting mob, he said:

All I know is that they swayed the coach backwards and forwards in their efforts to turn it over and that when the three poor policemen attempted to protect us and drew their truncheons, they were set upon in most cowardly fashion. I caught sight of one of them bleeding at the wrist and hands. We got our party safely in to the Swan Hotel, despatched our telegram to North Walsham and Yarmouth and waited for three hours while the mob surged and raved in front of the house ... At last came the welcome message that a relief party from North Walsham and a force from Norwich, armed with cutlasses, were on the way to our relief. It was just about midnight that the North Walsham party appeared. I believe there was a slight fight at the outset but almost directly our assailants fled ... I had to beg our friends not to retaliate, or they would have followed up the scoundrels and there would have been a midnight fight with consequences not nice to contemplate.[25]

Haggard was shocked and angry. He, too, had been hurt by the stone-throwing: 'We were all struck more or less severely,' he told *The Times*. The election campaign had cost him personally £2,000 and had ended by denying him a seat at Westminster and providing him with a more violent experience than any that he had had in Africa, where he had just been 'accused ... of having committed atrocities'.[26] His humiliation was aggravated by a mocking report in the *New York Times* that 'Rider Haggard's tempestuous boo-hooing about the way that the rustics chiv-vied him and his swell turnout in Norfolk lanes might have been funny if it had not been angering to see a grown man so little able to take a beating with a decent grace.'[27]

He was particularly outraged that his successful opponent, Price, should have declared that reports of the riot had been 'grossly exaggerated' and that the mob at Stalham had been 'for the most part thorough good fellows'.[28] The fact that Lord Wodehouse and a drover were both charged with assault and fined soon afterwards did little to assuage his anger. His enthusiasm had curdled. He was not mollified even when Arthur Balfour, the Conservative and Unionist leader of the House of Commons, wrote to commiserate that his treatment in East Norfolk had been 'a scandal to the name of freedom ... soiled by the disgraceful scenes of which you and your friends were made the victims' and was 'very sorry that ... you have failed to join the great Unionist Army, which has been sent up to Westminster. You will have better luck, I am sure, next time.'[29]

He had already decided that there would never be another time, explaining:

Now I understand I was never a real Tory – that, in short, as a party man I am the most miserable failure. As a politician I should have been useless from any whip's point of view. He would – well, have struck me off his list as neither hot nor cold, and a dangerous and undesirable individual who, refusing to swallow the shibboleths of his tribe with shut eyes, actually dared to think for himself and to possess that hateful thing, 'a crossbench mind' ... [30]

To tell the truth [he concluded] the whole business disgusts me with its atmosphere of falsehood, or at least of prevarication, and its humiliating quest for support. In short, it turned one who in all essentials would have been a moderate Liberal into an Imperialist.[31]

The political adventure had, however, sharpened his appetite for the realities from which he had escaped through his imagination. 'I was utterly weary of a retired life,' as he put it, 'and of the writing of books, from which I sought eagerly for some avenue of escape.'[32] His one spell of practical experience had been in Africa so he was excited by an offer from a well-to-do friend, William Wills, of a partnership in the company publishing the weekly *African Review* and the prospect of making money by speculation in African trade.

So, despite the warning of his brothers, who knew that the Haggards had no flair for handling money, he moved back to London and travelled daily to an office in the City, dressed in the uniform of black frock coat, striped trousers and top hat. He did not enjoy commerce, which he had been brought up to despise, unless it was combined with some vigorous, or creative activity like farming and writing. But he did enjoy a renewed involvement with African affairs, particularly since, had he been elected to Parliament, he had planned to make it a special interest. Then, at the end of the year, news came from the Transvaal that fired his blood.

On 29 December 1895, a cavalcade of British horsemen – gentlemen-adventurers and nearly five hundred troopers of the British South Africa Company's police force – had invaded Boer territory, heading for the new gold-rush city of Johannesburg. Led by an acquaintance from his South African days named Leander Starr Jameson, its objective was to join a rebellion against the republic by the foreign majority, the *Uitlanders*, who had been drawn there by the discovery of a massive gold reef on the Rand in 1886 and had settled in Johannesburg but were denied representation in government. Jameson, a doctor who had become administrator of the new colony of Rhodesia – founded by the visionary imperialist, Cecil Rhodes, the prime minister of Cape Colony, who supported the adventure – was trying to force the hand of history. The Transvaal had recently been linked by railway through the Portuguese territory to the sea and so no longer relied on British permission to export and import. Above all, Jameson and Rhodes suspected that the Boers would try to bring about German expansion from East Africa into South Africa.

What became known as Jameson's Raid ended in farce and almost in tragedy. The *Uitlanders* did not rise; after skirmishes, the raiders were rounded up by armed Boers and, on their surrender, narrowly escaped summary execution. As news reached London, Haggard was relieved that he was not a Member of Parliament trying to defend Jameson, which, he admitted, would have been 'neither a pleasant nor an easy task'.[33]

However he did so at length in the correspondence columns of *The Times*. Admitting that the raiders' 'heroic effort' might have been 'an international crime and an act of rebellion against the authority of the Queen', he pleaded that 'they undertook it believing that they might save their countrymen and women from attack and possibly from massacre.' He glorified the fiasco, writing,

> For three days they pushed forward through the burning heat of the African midsummer to hurl themselves at last upon a strong position held by more than twice their number of brave, unwearied men. Repulsed from thence ... still they struggled on ... without food, without rest, fighting hard and losing heavily by the way. At length, their ammunition exhausted and reeling in their saddles with fatigue, they yielded to a force which now outnumbered their own fourfold and there, within a few miles of the city they came to save, the net of doom closed round them. Dr Jameson may be a 'rebel' and therefore worthy of reprobation, or even of punishment, yet I think that, now when we know the blood-stirring story of his failure, but few of us who have ever had the honour of shaking him by the hand will cease to remember the fact with pride.

While others had been embarrassed by Jameson's breach of international manners, Haggard saw it as justified, blaming the *Uitlanders* for failing to respond to his call to arms, suggesting that those in Johannesburg would 'not easily forget that it has been christened "Judasburg"'. His letter continued, somewhat disingenuously:

> We make no inordinate demands. We do not seek to re-annex the Transvaal ... All that we ask of that country is that it should bow to the undoubted suzerainty of the Queen ... We are the paramount Power in South Africa and we have been paramount for generations ... they themselves were our subjects until it pleased Mr Gladstone to grant them a limited independence. We destroyed their enemies, the Zulus ... Here lies their true road to honour and safety, and not by way of unlawful alliance with Germany ... [34]

For fear of German expansion from their embryonic colonial empire in East Africa underlay British fears for South Africa.

Haggard was flattered to be regarded as an authority on African affairs, particularly when his views were quoted by *The Times* in a leading article. He had been elected a member of the Athenaeum Club and was as familiar there as at the Savile and other clubs, with, Edmund Gosse noted, his 'loud laugh and goggle eyes and the joke repeated two or three times for fear you have not perceived it'.[35] Yet despite his sometimes overwhelming presence, he was neither confident nor content in the City, feeling out of his depth in finance. When Wills decided to leave for a long stay in South Africa, he himself decided to return to occupations and surroundings he knew and the partnership was dissolved.

There was no need for him to dabble in commerce, for the writing of novels had become a profitable routine, although they had lost some of their zest since the death of Jock. They were serialised in magazines before publication and, since *The People of the Mist*, he had written another contemporary novel, *Joan Haste*; another story about a lost city, *Heart of the World*; and an African adventure called *The Wizard*. This activity he could continue at Ditchingham and, in the spring of 1896, he returned to Norfolk to resume his life as a literary gentleman-farmer.

He was just taking up the reins of country life again when a shadow from the past fell across his path. After twenty years, the long-lost love, Lily, returned to his life. Her own, during that time, had been disastrous for her rich husband, Francis Archer, a stockbroker, the sole trustee of her family fortune, had embezzled all within his grasp. Declared bankrupt, he had fled to Africa, abandoning his wife and three sons. Penniless, she turned to Rider Haggard for help and he, with Louie's magnanimous agreement, came to her rescue. It was a gesture worthy of the English gentlemen in his novels. He agreed to maintain not only Lily and her sons but her impoverished sisters as well, finding a house for them in Aldeburgh on the Suffolk coast.* There was no question of a resumption of the early relationship but the memory of it was, in itself, enough for Haggard; he enshrined in his imagination, not only what-might-have-been but, perhaps, what-might-be-to-come for, of course, love was immortal.

* The Red House, later occupied by Sir Benjamin Britten and Sir Peter Pears.

CHAPTER SEVEN

'Nothing less than a national danger'

THE IDEA OF Rider Haggard, the creator of Kôr, Zu-Vendis and King Solomon's Mines, down on the farm was comic to most of those who read his novels. 'A curious spectacle,' wrote one literary critic, 'as curious, say, as She peeling potatoes at the back door.'[1] Indeed, the humorous magazine *Punch* published a skit about 'Allan Quatermain's farm' in Norfolk:

> Today Sir Henry Curtis took his turn at minding the ostriches. Despite the gloomy predictions of the neighbouring farmers, they thrive uncommonly well in Norfolk ... Umslopogaas was employed in exercising the alligators ...
>
> The voice of some unseen speaker said softly, 'Macumazahn!' 'Hullo,' said I, thinking it was Umslopogaas – for, of course, none of our Norfolk labourers address me by my native name. 'Hush!' said the voice – in which I now recognised an undesirable sweetness ... 'Speak not but look yonder beside the hedge.'
>
> Instinctively, I obeyed. A curious white mist hung over the spot. Even as I spoke, it rolled away and there, in all the brilliance of her eternal beauty, stood *She-Who-Must-Be Obeyed*!
>
> 'Gracious goodness!' I gasped, 'What the dickens are you doing here on a respectable English farm? Why, you died for good in that last chapter years ago!'

So it continues until She demands in vain that Quatermain leave Norfolk and return with her to Africa.

"'You dare to refuse me? Then ... watch your peas – and take warning, oh Macumazahn!" Even as she spoke, she vanished into air.'[2]

It was no joke to Haggard, of course, who had been brought up among farmers and had become one himself. His earnings from fiction an annual income from advances, royalties and serialisation estimated at upwards of £3,000* had enabled him, despite the present depression in agriculture, to expand his estate from the some two hundred acres that Louisa had inherited. He now farmed three hundred and sixty-five acres, two-thirds at Ditchingham and one-third at Bedingham about five miles away.

In Haggard's youth, farmers had been prosperous with foreign wars and the discovery of gold in South Africa, Australia and California keeping prices high and more than two million British farmers and their workers in employment. In retrospect, it seemed to have been an idyllic time for landowners, squires, gentlemen-farmers, yeoman-farmers, tenant farmers and agricultural labourers, sharing the rewards of hard work, the jollities of the seasons celebrated at climactic harvest suppers. All that had now changed. Foreign competitors and the new-found American ability to harvest the great plains and export their crops by train and steamer to Europe, had combined with bad weather and disease in crops and livestock to bring about a depression that laid waste that happy pastoral scene by the time he had returned from his years in Africa. When he abandoned hopes of Westminster and the City of London and returned to the land in 1896, the slump was at its worst and he realised that he could only continue to farm at a loss.

He could, of course, continue to write successfully and was already working on another African novel; this time about the Boers, showing surprising insight into their points of view. But during his first year of full-time farming he decided that that was to be his next subject. He would keep a journal and commonplace book of the coming year, recording the work of the farm, the changing seasons reflected in the trees and plants, birds and animals, and his own musings. Haggard could be verbose but never dull and would harness his pen to a year in the life of his land. He would look back, as was his custom, because, for him, every scene was crowded with ghosts.

There are few things which give rise to reflections more melancholy – since the fate of those bygone worthies is the same that awaits us all – than the contemplation of any ground to which we chance to be attached and see and walk day by day [he wrote in one of his morbid moods]. How many dead eyes week by week, as ours do, have dwelt upon the swell of yonder rise, or the dip of the little valley? How many

* Worth about £150,000 at the time of writing.

dead hands have tilled that fallow, or mown that pasture? ... And the land itself? Scarcely changed, I believe.[3]

He would begin writing on 1 January 1898, finish on 31 December and call his book simply *A Farmer's Year*. Not surprisingly he described his intention with a characteristic allusion:

> In Ancient Egypt, the gentlemen-farmers of the Fifth and Sixth Dynasties, whilst yet alive, caused their future sepulchres to be adorned with representations of such scenes of daily life and husbandry as to them were most pleasant and familiar ... Whilst considering them, it occurred to me that [in] this book, by means of methods of my own age, I ... follow the examples of the authors of these rock-hewn manuscripts who lived some fifty centuries ago.[4]

On the appointed day he began, 'Never within my recollection have we experienced so mild and open a winter as that of the year which died yesterday ... '[5] The month continued with his notes on a mad hare, Bungay compost, first lambs, old-age pensions and the migration of labourers from the land. His scope was eclectic, covering the art of ploughing, the comparative sensitivity to pain in men and animals, dowsing, English snakes, interviewing a lunatic in church, drying wet hay, rural elections, the humming of gnats, fear of the dark, the vitality of seed, the effect of weather on temperament, sheep-dipping, old methods of cottage-building, the sudden fall of elm boughs, the cunning of dogs, the rising of the harvest moon...

He speculated, for example, on the possible uses of dock leaves: 'One British variety of dock produces four times as much tannin as does oak bark ... If the tannin is good, behold a new industry!'[6] He compared the mating ritual of turkeys with square-dancing and the cry of the startled corncrake with ventriloquism. He deplored the end of the farm labourer's career when, all too often, he must 'sink to the workhouse': 'Is this a necessary end? I think not'[7]; he recommended some form of national insurance to provide pensions. A magnificent sunset seemed apocalyptic to him:

> A very beautiful evening sky ... heavy heaps of cloud floating in a depth of intensest blue ... the light of the sinking sun, thrown upwards in fan-like rays from behind another plumed and hearse-like bank of clouds ... while far away the thunder boomed like the deep tones of a Dead March swelling from some vast organ in the heavens to celebrate a demon's obsequies.[8]

At the beginning of September, when General Kitchener defeated the forces of the Mahdi and added the Sudan to the African territories under the suzerainty of the Queen, he was speculating that 'the advent of cycles makes people suffer more from the exertion of walking than they were wont to do. All summer long one has been accustomed to roll from spot to spot upon a bicycle . . . I believe that soon it will be difficult to induce the children to . . . put one foot before the other.'[9]

His discursiveness seemed artless, sometimes thoughtful, sometimes charming with occasional bursts of empurpled prose. There was an underlying seriousness, however, as in his concern over the drift of young men from the land:

> They crowd to the towns to seek a living there, sometimes to succeed, sometimes to sink to misery, or to the earning of bread by hanging about the dockyard gates in the hope of a casual job. The labourer is leaving the land principally, if not entirely, because the land can no longer pay him what he considers a just reward for his toil . . . But what is the remedy? I suggest that perhaps it may be found in the re-creation of the extinct yeoman class . . .

The means he suggested for achieving this were daring, almost socialist, in concept.

> If they have a stake of ownership in the land, men will not leave it . . . By way of a beginning . . . why does not the Government empower any suitable authority, such as the County Councils, or the Board of Agriculture, to buy up the glebe lands at a fair valuation and resell them on easy terms to suitable applicants to be farmed as smallholdings?[10]

This proposal to nationalise and then distribute church land was not well received by his Conservative friends, who were relieved that this maverick squire had not been elected to the House of Commons.

The population problems of rural Norfolk were not his only concern. The Empire was just as close to his heart and in May, between notes on thatching haystacks and an egg-eating turkey, he described how an old farm labourer had told him about his son in South Africa: 'He gets on won'erful well, he du. Began as a mason working on a bridge and is his own master now, so I understand, with lots of land, cattle, black men and bacca plants.' Haggard glowed with the thought of this 'fine instance of the contrast between the old country and the new and of the good fortune of those who are bold enough to break their ties and seek their fate in the Colonies.'[11] As he saw it, rural England should be the mainspring of the great global enterprise for spreading prosperity and civilisation, the British Empire.

When *A Farmer's Year* was published in September, 1899, it was received with gratifying praise from the critics as fresh and thought-provoking. Less than a fortnight later came news that Haggard had long been expecting: war had broken out again between the British and the Boers in South Africa. The Transvaal had been joined by the Orange Free State to challenge British domination and had taken the initiative in the confrontation. Their leader, President Kruger, had delivered an ultimatum demanding the halting of military preparations in Natal and, when that was rejected, declared war, so relieving the British of the need to do so.

Although he had not been to South Africa for eighteen years, Haggard was thought to be well informed on the crisis. He wrote more letters to the newspapers, made speeches and his early book about Cetewayo was republished under the new title of *The First Boer War*. But, while he had expected this, the unexpected also tied his thoughts to Africa. Lily wrote to him saying that her husband had asked her and their youngest son to join him in exile there and that she had agreed to do so. It was an ache in the old wound: there was no evidence that Haggard had the slightest hope of becoming more than friends with his old love – the very idea would have been a breach of his code – but she represented the promise and emotions of his youth. When she wrote to thank him for his 'friendship and never failing kindness', hoping that 'we may meet again in (for me) happier circumstances', he wrote under her signature '*Finis!*'[12]

Another loss followed. His brother Bazett had returned from Samoa, where he had been working as land commissioner since he parted from his wife, Julia. There he had made friends with the expatriate Robert Louis Stevenson, and was popular but not taken seriously; his world was said to 'revolve round his native county, Norfolk, whence sprang all that was finest in the British race, particularly the Haggard brothers'.[13] Now, dispirited and ill, he had come home to die, hoping that his successful brother would help provide for his four sons; Rider Haggard was generous in taking the next generation under his wing.

There was much else to occupy his mind. During his year's immersion in farming, he had continued with the production of fiction. But the plots that jostled for priority were not all the familiar compounds of mystery

and imagination. One, fired by his new involvement in the real world of
choices and decisions, was highly topical. While in Mexico he had been
shocked by the scale of the smallpox epidemic. Fearful of outbreaks in
Europe – and even in England – he became an advocate of vaccination,
which was facing opposition and indifference among the British, and he
determined to write a novel to present the need for it in dramatic form.
Doctor Therne was not a commercial success but it established Haggard
as an altruistic crusader in worthy social causes.

It was a brave book to write because both the Government and the
public were against vaccination – as was Haggard's central character, Dr
Therne – and the consequences of their opposition were potentially
disastrous. *The Lancet*, the journal of the medical profession, com-
mended 'Mr Haggard's courage in thus entering the lists against the
Anti-Vaccination party ... He has risked losing many readers and creating a fanatical opposition ... for the sake of telling the truth.'[14]

Meanwhile the pattern of Haggard's friendships and family life was
shifting. Rudyard Kipling had gone to the United States, married an
American, Caroline Balestier, and had been living for four years in
Vermont, where a daughter had been born. His books and verse, written
with a sensitivity and style that Haggard could not match, had made him
the most celebrated writer in the British Empire. But some of the in-
spirations for *The Jungle Book* came after reading *Nada the Lily*, when,
as Kipling admitted, 'the pen took charge and I watched it begin to write
stories ... which later grew into *The Jungle Books*.'[15]

The Kiplings had returned in 1896 and he and Haggard resumed their
friendship, often meeting at the Savile Club and at literary gatherings.
Next year, Queen Victoria's Jubilee was celebrated and Kipling was
commissioned to write a commemorative verse for *The Times*. He had
just returned from a visit to the Channel Squadron of the Royal Navy and
had been impressed, writing to Haggard,

> Any nation save ourselves, with a fleet such as we have at present,
> would go out swiftly to trample the guts out of the rest of the world;
> and the fact that we do not seems to show that even if we aren't very
> civilised, we're about the one power with a glimmering of civilisation
> in us.

The potential of that strength worried him and he struggled to express
this in the verse, asking Haggard for comment and explaining in American slang, 'What I wanted to say was "Don't gas but be ready to give

people snuff."'' But he had, he wrote, 'only covered the first part of the notion.'[16] What he had written was the great hymn to retrospection, couched in richly sonorous language recalling Haggard at his most apocalyptic, only more finely tuned. It was *Recessional*:

> God of our fathers, known of old –
> Lord of our far-flung battle-line –
> Beneath whose awful Hand we hold
> Dominion over palm and pine –
> Lord God of Hosts be with us yet,
> Lest we forget, lest we forget! . . .
>
> Far call'd our navies melt away –
> On dune and headland sinks the fire
> Lo, all our pomp of yesterday
> Is one with Nineveh and Tyre!
> Judge of the Nations, spare us yet!
> Lest we forget, lest we forget!
>
> If, drunk with sight of power, we loose
> Wild tongues that have not Thee in awe –
> Such boasting as the Gentiles use
> Or lesser breeds without the Law –
> Lord God of Hosts, be with us yet,
> Lest we forget, lest we forget!

It was the warning of the slave in the chariot holding the triumphal laurel wreath over the Roman emperor's head, whispering in his ear, 'Remember, Caesar, thou art mortal.' It was a warning which his friend had pondered in Africa when the honourable proconsuls, Shepstone and Osborn, had been replaced by men who seemed less noble than they. The verse cemented the two friends' view of the Empire as an evolutionary process that was as spiritual as practical, self-questioning but, when necessary, wearing a knuckle-duster under the kid glove. Speaking at a dinner attended by both men, Haggard put it forcefully: 'I do not believe in the divine right of kings, but I do believe . . . in the divine right of a great civilising people – that is, in their divine mission.'[17]

They found that they had more in common when, in 1899, Kipling's adored seven-year-old daughter Josephine suddenly died of fever. Both now suffered grief that they knew would be with them for the rest of their lives – although Kipling had the consolation of a son, John, now aged two – and, as a result, they felt a deeper understanding. Neither was married to the love of his life; each valued the company of other men for the ethos of the Empire, despite the talk of Queen and Motherland, was masculine.

There was a shared interest in South Africa, where the Kiplings decided to spend the winters. The war with the Boers had gone badly for the British, who had suffered a succession of defeats by an enemy who disdained parade-ground tactics and was a master of fieldcraft and marksmanship. Kipling sailed in the first month of the new century for Cape Town, where he settled his family and himself travelled northwards to see something of the war. He was treated like visiting royalty, addressing the troops, reciting his verse in military hospitals, even spending several weeks working as a journalist on a soldiers' newspaper; he was taken to watch a minor action in progress before returning to Cape Town to collect his family and sail for England. As a propaganda exercise, Kipling's visit had been good for the soldiers' morale but not for the reputations of the generals and their political masters; he had been appalled by the lack of training for this sort of war and he said so loudly on his return.

Haggard might have been expected to emulate, or, at least, to envy his excursion and the lionising. But English agriculture was now his favoured campaign and, when the editor of *The Times* invited him to become his war correspondent, he declined on the grounds that, at the age of forty-four, he was too old. 'A great subject lay to my hand,' he wrote, 'that of the state of the English agriculture and of our rural population.'[18] Yet he was aware that his ideal of a rural squirearchy supported by a powerfully reinforced tier of yeoman-farmers would not find support in any political party. The number of farm labourers in the country had fallen by more than a third in twenty years so something had to be done to halt the flow of countrymen into the towns. He was convinced that the only solution was to give far more of them a stake in land – including some of the Church of England's glebe land – which would have to be nationalised and then redistributed.

What place is there in politics for a man like myself [he asked], who has the most earnest sympathies with the poor and who desires to advance their lot in every reasonable way, but who loathes and detests the Radical method of attempting to set class against class and of aiming all their artillery at the middle section of society – the real prop of the race – for the reason that it is Conservative in its instincts and votes against them at the polls? Again, what would be thought of one who, posing as a member of the Tory party, yet earnestly advocated the division of land amongst about ten times as many as hold it at present, thereby spoiling a great many great estates and often interfering with the interests and pleasures of those who shoot and hunt, or who seek this road to social success? Assuredly for such a one there is no standing-room upon any of our political platforms. 'Away with him!' would be the cry.[19]

Hitherto, Haggard's experiences of farming had been confined to his family's estate at Bradenham, Ditchingham and Bedingham, but now it was to spread a little farther afield. Always aware of the need to watch his children's health – and knowing that Ditchingham House had had an unhealthy reputation since three young sisters had died there early in the nineteenth century through drinking water from a contaminated well – he determined that they should continue to have regular, bracing seaside holidays. Instead of taking lodgings, he could now afford to buy a house by the sea and he chose one nearby at Kessingland, on the Suffolk coast just south of Lowestoft.

Cliff Grange, which he re-named Kessingland Grange, stood on a low cliff of sand and shingle on a flat and undistinguished coast. It had been converted from two coastguard cottages into a rambling, two-storey house, of which his daughter Lilias was to write 'with all its wandering passages, queer cubby-holes and unexpected rooms, it was like some large, stationary ship, which perhaps gave Rider the idea of naming every bedroom (by the time he had finished with building there were seventeen of them) after a British admiral.' The many-windowed house was, she continued, 'filled with clear, shadowless light and the smell and the sound of the sea'. The three girls adored it, knowing 'the creak of every door, the tick of every clock, the smell of every room ... It was enchanted ground.'[20] Like 'Mustard Pot Hall', it soon filled up with Zulu shields and assegais, Landseer prints, relics of Nelson, and framed illustrations to their father's novels by Maurice Greiffenhagen. Haggard himself delighted in this setting for thinking 'thoughts to the accompaniment of the roaring waves'[21] but nowadays his thoughts were less of lost cities, beautiful white queens and immortality and more of practicalities. Here, as inland, there were problems, including one affecting Kessingland Grange itself. It was in danger of being washed away by the sea.

As an East Anglian, Haggard knew what the sea could do to a coastline: how it would scour away sand dunes; how sand-spits would grow into the sea from the mouths of rivers and then break into islands; how the power of the tides could seem capricious and was irresistible. At other points along the coast of Norfolk and Suffolk, whole villages had been swallowed by the sea, most spectacularly at Dunwich. Along the stretch of dunes between Lowestoft and Aldeburgh, there was nothing to stop the sea, particularly when wind and tide summoned up a surge. Kessingland Grange stood at the most easterly point in its ten acres of land, fifteen yards from the edge of the low, crumbling, sandy cliff and it was obvious that it would not need many tidal surges, driven by a north-east wind, to undermine it.

The defence of his house turned Haggard into a practical King Canute. A sea wall would be too expensive to build and could itself be breached, or undermined, as could wicker fascines filled with earth. So he had the cliff sloped at the cost of some of his precious margin of level land and decided to plant it with some binding plant. There were various types of ground-cover plants and grass that would grow in salt and sand and he finally chose marram grass which grew over coastal dunes in spiky clumps and spread rapidly. So he planted the marram on the *glacis* of sand facing the invading seas and awaited the outcome. As the grass began to spread its roots, it did indeed seem to bind the wind-blown sand and, to his delight, the level of the slope actually began to rise.

Behind its defences, he planted a vegetable garden, had a well dug and a windmill erected to pump the water. He himself liked to occupy the room named 'Nelson' and think, write and gaze out to sea, listening to the wind and the surf and the happy sounds of children. Pleasant as this was, Haggard had become restless as the century came to its end and hankered after another spell of travelling abroad. Plans to visit Persia having been deterred by a cholera epidemic, he decided to take his family to Florence and then continued – with only his young nephew, Ella's son, Arthur Green, as his secretary and companion – on a tour of Cyprus and the Levant.

They left on the first stage of the journey in the first month of the new century, expecting a pleasant cultural saunter across Europe which Haggard would record in the discursive travel book he had in mind. It did not transpire as expected.

'Moderate' was the report of the Channel weather at Charing Cross, which as the station-master explained mysteriously, might mean a good deal [Haggard recorded]. In fact we did find it blowing a gale, for the spray drives right over the train on to the unhappy passengers as they splash towards the boat quivering and livid ... with anticipatory qualms.

The qualms were justified and not only at sea. Haggard, who liked to glorify the discomforts of trek and camp, loathed grand hotels and he wrote:

> If I were asked to devise a place of punishment for sinners ... a first-class Continental hotel is the purgatorial spot to which I would commit them ... Thither they should travel once a month (with a family) in the *wagon-lit* of a *train de luxe* with all the steam-pipes turned on to one of those foreign, gorgeous hostelries, where every decoration strikes you like a blow, surrounded by hard servility on fire for unearned fees, fed with messes such as the soul loathes and quaking beneath the advancing shadow of a monstrous bill.[22]

Via Paris, Basle and Milan, they reached Florence to find it far from the benign, sun-warmed Renaissance city of their expectations. They were staying with his brother Jack's wife, the former Agnes Barber, who during his absence on business in the Pacific had rented a house there for herself and her four children. It was old, vast and gloomy with stone floors, overlooking on one side an overgrown garden which had once been a nuns' cemetery and, on the other, across a narrow lane to a church from which wafted chanting and whiffs of incense. The city was in the grip of a harsh winter. He almost felt at home for it was scoured by

> piercing gales – *tramontane* is the local name – which reminded me of winds I have felt blowing straight off the pack ice in northern latitudes ... fogs that would have done no discredit to London in November and rain whereof the tropics might be proud. When the *tramontane* in its glory leaps and howls along the dusky streets of Florence, then indeed does the traveller think with a repentant affection of the very bleakest spot he knows upon England's eastern shores, yes, even in the bitterest day of March. Is there anything in the wind line quite so deadly cold?[23]

There was an epidemic of influenza.

> One meets a great many funerals in Florence, all of them after nightfall. Very common is it, as the visitor walks down some narrow street, to hear a measured tread behind and look round to see the brethren of *Misericordia* at their work of mercy. These are they who, drawn from

every rank of society, for more than five centuries have laid out the dead, or carried the sick of Florence to where they might be succoured ... Their robes are black from head to foot, covering the wearer, all but his hands and feet, so that nothing of him can be seen save perhaps his eyes as they glitter through the little openings in the hood ... Six of them go together three in front and three behind and between them is the stretcher, also arched over with black cloth. These stretchers are apt to excite a somewhat morbid curiosity ... Watching many of them I learned at last to know, by the way the crossed straps pressed upon the shoulders of the bearer and the fashion in which these stepped and set their feet upon the ground, whether or no they were empty or laden; also by any little movements of the cover, or the lack of them, whether the occupant, if there should be one, was alive or dead ... Their work is holy, though perhaps the ambulances of a London hospital would do better.[24]

But he did keep a practical farmer's eye on the Tuscan countryside, particularly the vineyards, concluding that the rewards of wine-production were so meagre that he 'should not recommend it to young men seeking new lands in which to farm'.[25] His ruminations and note-taking were interrupted by what he saw as impending disaster when his three daughters went down with influenza and he convinced himself that Lilias would die. His worries became so irritating to Louie that, as soon as the child was better, she urged her husband to continue his planned tour with only young Arthur Green as company.

'Rome!' he noted after some days there. 'What is the chance visitor who sees it for the first time to say of the Imperial City? Silence is best.' That, of course, he found impossible to keep, particularly after a visit to the Colosseum. His imagination ran riot at the thought of the parade of the gladiators through the arena: 'The contrast between the living men, splendid lusty animals, the muscles swelling on their limbs, the fire of flight in their keen eyes, the harness clanking as they walked, and the limp, gashed, senseless corpses which presently slaves dragged ... by iron hooks fixed in their flesh ... to the last oblivion.'
He was equally moved by the Christian catacombs:

What a life must these poor innocents have led, who crowded into those darksome burrows, to worship while they lived and to sleep when life had left them, often enough by the fangs of a wild beast, the sword of a gladiator, or the torment of the tarred skin and the slowly burning fire. Truly these were faithful unto death and, as we are taught and hope, their reward is not lacking.

Despite his professed Christian faith, he was continually taunted with doubts, usually concluding that human beings were not supposed to show curiosity in such matters.

Haggard, himself struggling against influenza, was tortured with feverish nightmares one of which was that he had to demonstrate 'one hundred different methods of folding an india-rubber bath in five seconds of time and fifty different methods of emptying the same without spilling a drop under pain of being thrown living from the top of the Bargello tower in Florence'.

At Naples, he wandered through Pompeii with the local guidebook, which described with a ghoulish relish, worthy of himself, the plaster cast made from the impressions of victims' bodies in the lava ('A young woman fallen upon her face ... the shift which she was covered of brought near her head in the act of defence, or fright and caused all her beautiful naked body to be seen'). He was thrilled to see a stone fountain worn by Roman drinkers' hands and felt that the ruined city 'strikes the imagination because it offers more to the imagination; Vesuvius ought to strike it more'. Otherwise he noted the unusual Neapolitan method of harnessing cab-horses, the begging by 'practically the entire population' and the piratical extortions of the boatmen, who would row passengers out to their steamers, then stop and demand more money before putting them aboard. 'In Naples,' he noted, 'I should in future always carry a pistol to show if necessary.'[26]

By this time, he had realised that it had been a mistake to bring his nephew as his secretary 'in the heyday of his very fascinating and festive youth'. The young man had brought a typewriter with him but, recorded his uncle, 'all he did with it was to drop it on my toes out of the rack of a railway train'.[27] At Naples, his duty had been to forward their luggage for shipment to Cyprus and Haggard asked if he had been given a receipt for this. 'Rather,' he replied, 'do you suppose that I am green enough to come without it?' When confronted with the news that he had had it sent to Reggio instead of Brindisi, he raised his dripping head from the wash-basin 'staring at vacancy as though he had seen a ghost'.

'My friend,' said his uncle sternly, 'do you understand what you have done? Has it occurred to you that this exceedingly thick and uncomfortable brown suit, with three flannel shirts and a leather medicine-case ...

are all we possess to travel with to Cyprus, where, such is the hospitable nature of its inhabitants, we shall probably be asked out to dinner every night?'

'We've got some cigarettes and a revolver and you can have my dinner-jacket,' replied the youth and Haggard noted with martyred resignation, 'I took the dinner-jacket at once; it was several sizes too small for me but better than nothing. Then I expressed my feelings in language as temperate as I could command.'[28] The tones were, no doubt, those of his father, the squire.

Cyprus, which he described as being about the same size as Norfolk and Suffolk and also as 'a Cinderella among our colonies', intrigued him. 'With a little more care – and capital – she might again become what she was of old, the Garden of the Mediterranean, a land of corn and wine and, in fact as well as figuratively, a mine of wealth.'[29] The future agricultural possibilities of the island fascinated him as much as its turbulent past. He delved into the practicalities of farming while looking for traces of past Egyptians, Greeks, Romans, Phoenicians, Venetians and Turks.

In Salamis, he had a sudden idea for the plot of a novel and jotted it in his notebook:

A man disappointed in love comes to live as a hermit in Cyprus – farming. He has quarrelled with his fiancée. He reads about the place. He finds the tomb of a queen. Fumes overpower him and he falls asleep there. He sees his past life when he was King of Salamis. A lady appears in it. She wears the face of his modern love. Things draw on to their marriage. He marries her and the curtain falls. He awakes knowing he has dreamed but there is a ring in his hand and he remembers that in his dream the bride said – Give it me again when we meet again.

A few weeks later he hears that some visitors have reached the town. Drawn by an impulse he revisits the tomb and there he finds the woman he was once engaged to – or the bride of his dream whose garment she wears. It is the living woman who stretches out her hand to him. Mechanically he takes the ring from his finger and puts in into hers.

'So it is true,' she says. He asks what. 'My dream of a month ago that brought me here.' But she will never tell him what the dream was![30]

Strolling through the Venetian ruins of Famagusta, he picked up cannon-balls fired during the Turkish siege of 1571 and noted that the atrocities committed in Cyprus by the Turks were 'too dreadful to dwell on'[31] but characteristically did so. Also characteristically, young Arthur whispered that he had something important to say. '"Speak up," I answered, wondering, with an inward groan, whether he had engaged himself in marriage to the barmaid of the Nicosia Club.'[32] He had not, as it happened, but he had decided to abandon his idea of ordination in the Church of England.

Thence they continued, via Beirut, to what was known throughout Christendom as the Holy Land. Much of this exploration was on horseback, sometimes with armed Bedouin guards and he was able to relate the landscape and the towns to memories of his father's readings of lessons from the Bible. Jerusalem stirred his imagination as he walked across the site of King Solomon's temple. 'What has it not seen?' he pencilled in his notebook, 'Titus – Solomon – siege on siege – slaughter on slaughter – Our Lord driving out the money-changers – Crusaders – Turks – and what is left for it to see?'

Deep beneath it, he found in the ancient quarries an echo of the subterranean landscapes he had described in his fiction and he noted:

Here in those vast and awful chasms filled with darkness and silence and as yet unexplored in all their recesses one can understand how it happened that no sound was heard in the preparation of the stone... The place is wonderfully awesome... its heat and stillness are oppressive to a degree and I was glad when with melting tapers we panted back up the steep slope to the point of light that marked the entrance. What tragedies may not these vaults have witnessed during the siege?[33]

Visits to the scenes of the New Testament inspired reverence rather than the resonant responses aroused by the temples and tombs of Egypt.

A daily consideration of sites and scenes connected with the mighty career of Jesus Christ [he wrote], in itself tends to overwhelm the spirit. Many abandon the task, other have not the qualities necessary to its attempt. Still, for those who can overcome these obstacles, who, above all, can sweep away doubt's strangling web ... a sojourn in the Holy Land is one of the highest and most excellent educations... No man... can say that he understands the whole mystery of our religion. The veiled face of Truth, the secret meaning of things spiritual, are hidden from his purblind eyes. Stare and study as he will, at best still he sees as in a glassy darkly ... [34]

They returned by sea to Marseilles and thence via Paris, where they were shocked to see that 'the book stalls were laden with caricatures of Her Majesty of a nature offensive to her subjects'; for the Boer War had, in foreign eyes, cast the British as oppressors of innocent Dutch farmers. Because of his nephew's inefficiency, Haggard had written none of the travel articles for *The Times* that had been commissioned but had gathered background material for two historical novels – *Pearl Maiden* about the sack of Jerusalem and *The Brethren* about the Crusades, to be published in 1903 and 1904 respectively – and quickly wrote the book about his travels, *A Winter Pilgrimage*. This did not end on a note of spiritual exaltation but with the adventures of the tortoise, named Capernaum after the place of its capture. Lost in the confusion of embarkation at Port Said, this creature turned up in his labelled basket at Ditchingham railway station a couple of months later. 'Now he inhabits the garden,' Haggard concluded his story, 'but disliking our climate, which forces him to spend so much of his time under ground, continually attempts to return to the Sea of Galilee via the stable-yard and the orchard.'[35]

News from South Africa depressed him for, although the British now had some three hundred thousand troops in the field, the war dragged on. Even those who had been enthusiastic in asserting British paramountcy were sickened by the herding of many thousands of Boer families into what were called concentration camps, where they were soon stricken with disease and hunger. Such was the disenchantment, that when the editor of the *Daily Express* invited Haggard to tour South Africa immediately the war ended and write a series of articles, the latter persuaded him that this would not interest his readers, sated with war news.

However, Haggard had an alternative to offer. He wanted to emulate a Georgian agricultural reformer named Arthur Young who had toured the country reporting on the state of English farming. He would do likewise, seeking ways out of the current depression, and he managed to persuade the editor to commission a series of fifty articles. As this seemed to be almost on the scale of the Domesday Book, Haggard invited his old friend from Natal and the East Norfolk election campaign, Arthur Cochrane, to accompany him on the tour of the English counties.

It was an appropriate moment to take a fresh look at the state of England at the beginning of the new century. Then, on 22 January 1901, the seemingly immortal white queen of the polychromatic Empire, Queen Victoria, died. The new king, Edward VII, brought with him the comforting nineteenth-century whiff of cigar smoke but everywhere else there was talk of change. The war in South Africa might rumble on but it was clearly nearing its end with a pyrrhic victory for the British, who would still have to contend with the probability of a growing Boer majority in the territories. Future challenges lay elsewhere for there was now real industrial, and so political, rivalry from Germany, France and Russia; also, looming ever larger on the Atlantic horizon, the United States of America.

Early in that year, Haggard and Cochrane set out. This journey was not in search of inspiration from crumbling relics of past glories and horrors to inspire further fiction, for he was about to explore realities. Wiltshire was their first destination and Haggard recorded in discursive, journalistic style:

> Yonder, to our right, stands a grey old hall backed by a wood-crowned hill, with purple-budded trees broken here and there with masses of sombre yet shining fir. In front of its windows the Avon, its gentle stream embanked by marshy bottoms, lined everywhere with water from brimming dykes, which now gleams and now turns black as the storm-clouds come and go and the squalls hiss through the red growths of the pollard willows. On either side are the Wiltshire Downs, rolling away endlessly like the veldt of Southern Africa.[36]

Then he was in a farmhouse hearing how the value of the seven hundred surrounding acres had fallen by £20,000 in eighty years. Although the tenant farmer's rent had been reduced from an annual £800 to £250, he was lucky if the land earned him £100 and he had made more when he was paying the higher rent. He found labour almost impossible to obtain and when Haggard pointed out a lad working in the farmyard, he replied, 'Aye, he is the last left and he will be off soon.'[37] They went on to discuss crops and prices; Haggard asking the questions and Cochrane recording all in a notebook.

On they travelled to Hampshire and then across to the Channel Islands, back to Sussex and Kent, then down to Devon. Haggard's articles began to be published in April and their itinerary seemed more attuned to the news paper readers' need for variety than any cohesive agricultural theme, but they were readable and accurate. Statistics and interviews with farmers were mingled with descriptions of the country-side and there were occasional odd experiences when staying overnight in unexpected places. In one landowner's castle, Cochrane had to sleep in a four-poster bed with black hangings and black funereal plumes at its corners in a room hung with grim family portraits and a black coal-box shaped like a coffin. It was, he was sure, literally the death-bed of the castle where its former owners had lain in state. Next morning, when Haggard collected him, they were unable to find their way through the stone corridors to the breakfast-room.

As he progressed, Haggard's original views on the decline of English farming were confirmed. The exodus from the land would, he believed, affect the character and health of the whole nation. Despite a rising population, the number of men working in agriculture had fallen by half during the second part of the nineteenth century and he quoted the Bishop of Ripon as saying that 'this migration was nothing less than a national danger ... something of the sort happened in France before the Revolution and in the Roman Empire before its fall.'[38]

The solution, he declared, was the revival of small holdings and, to prompt this, loans should be made available on generous terms for those wishing to buy their own land, so renewing their forebears' love for, and loyalty to, the soil. He urged that agricultural taxes be eased and imports of foreign foodstuffs curbed. As transport of produce was one of the farmer's principal problems, he called for the Post Office to arrange its cheap transport by rail and road and that new light railways should be built in agricultural areas. He concluded:

> If our Country is to decline from its present high position, the principal cause of its fall will be our national neglect to maintain the population on the land. If high civilisation necessitates a flight from the villages, then it is of a truth that broad road which leads to the destruction of advanced peoples.[39]

Rural England was published in two volumes in November, 1902, shortly after the fourth Colonial Conference had called for imperial preference in trade. A reforming mood had arisen since the end of what was known as the Second Boer War (the first having been that which had culminated in the Battle of Majuba Hill) and Haggard was in tune with it. The Boers had accepted British sovereignty but had been promised representative government and financial aid; they had lost some four thousand men killed in action against six thousand British amongst them his brother Alfred's son Gerald, while both sides had lost heavily from disease.

The book was well received – although a minority of critics thought

Haggard over-pessimistic – and he was now accepted as a major authority on agriculture, the *Quarterly Review* commenting, 'We cannot recall an instance, except that of Mr Haggard, in which a distinguished writer has beaten his inkstand into a ploughshare.'[40]

Welcome comment came from Rudyard Kipling, who had bought a manor house at Burwash, in Sussex, called Bateman's, with a view to farming its land – not much more than a smallholding – himself.

> I have been reading *Rural England* with deep joy [he wrote]. I take off my hat to you deeply and profoundly because it is a magnum opus and altogether fascinating and warning and chock full of instructions ... I – alas! – hold land now ... an old house and a 25-acre farm of good hop land and fruit and a mill (water) that dates from 1196. The farm is let down and neglected ... Now you see why your book touches me ...[41]

The book was discussed – and usually praised – by Cabinet ministers and at Westminster there was a feeling that Haggard's loud call for reform had broken the log-jam of apathy and that Government action would now begin. When Lord Onslow, the Minister of Agriculture, wrote to him explaining that the Government had not been 'supine' but that Parliamentary procedure and financial stringency delayed any reforms the Government had in mind, Haggard ended his letter of reply, 'It is my sense of the urgent necessity of these reforms that has induced a humble person like myself to write big books, take long journeys, make speeches, indite letters to newspapers, etc – all gratis work, of course – in the intervals of getting my livelihood by other means.'[42]

At last, the cast of characters who populated and sold his novels – the gentlemen-adventurers, the white queens and the Zulu kings, the wicked sorcerers and the diaphanously draped handmaidens, the jilted lovers and the sensate mummies – seemed to troop back into a toy cupboard from which they could be summoned whenever another book was required. Meanwhile, their creator was again living in the world of non-fiction.

CHAPTER EIGHT

'Planting folk on the land'

AWARE THAT HIS talent as a novelist, upon which his income depended, needed constant inspiration, Haggard decided to resume the travels abroad which had been interrupted by his two-year commitment to *Rural England*. So, at the beginning of 1904, he took his eldest daughter Angela on a visit to Egypt, his most luxuriant source of invention. They travelled by sea and soon wished they had not for the ship struck the worst weather her captain had known for twenty years.

Always keen to capture dramatic scenes and sensations, Haggard pencilled notes in his pocket-book:

> Rolling very heavy during the night. Some cabins flooded. The rush of the combers – ceaseless – pitiless – mighty ... The tempest howling like a thing alive – the scudding level hail and rain – the spray torn from the surges and whirled up and round. Then the outbreak of the sun and the water falling from the hurricane deck and rigging sparkling like diamonds and falls back into the sea from the side of the ship as she wallows in the gale-driven seas.[1]

The wind-gauges were blown out, the fore-hatch stove in, the engines overheated and, even after they finally entered the Mediterranean, the storm roared on. When the ship crawled into Marseilles, some passengers abandoned their plans and went ashore but the stoic Haggards stayed aboard. The ship nearly foundered off Crete and on the coast of Africa was caught in a sandstorm, which covered her in mud. When she finally docked at Port Said, Haggard, who had already been shipwrecked once, confessed, 'never was I more glad to find myself on land again'[2] and the ship's engineer was carried ashore, apparently driven mad.

After that, their journey up the Nile was like an opium dream. Haggard delighted in sharing with his daughter the sumptuous sights, which began at Cairo, where he wrote in his pocket-book:

> The Nile can look very solemn ... In the distance, fading into night, the

crest of a mighty Pyramid. To the right, dense groves of palms. To the left, wide desert backed far away by the white cliffs of hills. Above, the purple sky, faintly suffused with pink; beneath, the wide, gleaming river and, floating on it like settling birds, the white-winged boats.[3]

But Haggard did not feel comfortable in modern Egypt – 'The very smiling dragoman would cut our throats'[4] – but relaxed in the company of the Ancient Egyptians and those devoted to their study. So the happiest days of their tour began when they had travelled up the Nile Valley by train to Luxor. Here he found a fellow Norfolkman in charge of excavations in the Valley of the Kings across the river. This was Howard Carter, the son of a minor artist from the market town of Swaffham, a few miles to the west of Bradenham, who had also been bewitched by the Egyptian antiquities at Didlington Hall. Indeed, the Amhersts had become his patrons and he had come to Egypt as the official artist with an archaeological expedition. Now aged thirty, Carter was directing an excavation financed by an American millionaire to search for undisturbed royal tombs in the great necropolis among the hot, tawny Theban Hills. The two men took to one another at once; Haggard, who felt that 'the place had a strange fascination for me',[5] understood exactly what Carter meant when he declared that he felt 'a religious feeling' in the Valley of the Kings so profound 'that it appears almost imbued with a life of its own'.[6]

In March, 1902, Carter believed he was on the threshold of an important discovery and escorted his new friend round the excavations.

Dull windy day [noted Haggard]. Crossed Nile – rock tombs of Kings. Saw those of Seti, Rameses III and Amenhotep II. All now lit by electricity! The unwrapped body of Amenhotep lies in its sarcophagus – calmly asleep with an electric light blazing on his still majestic face … Such is the end of royalty, a poor, hideous dishevelled corpse.[7] [They were shown more mummies] Mr Howard Carter believes the 3 bodies in tomb of Amenhotep II are those of Queen Hatshepsut, her daughter and an unknown king or prince … He agrees about the scandal of removing … the dead and approves of my trying to ventilate it.[8]

The ancient dead should be left where they were in this 'wonderful and weird place, this Valley of the Kings with its rugged, naked cliffs shattered by sun and time. Another proof of the genius of the Egyptians that they should have chosen such a great spot so strangely suitable – for the burial of their great.' So he, like Carter, was shocked to see mummies left outside the entrances to the tombs before removal to the museums, or as rubbish. 'The piteous mockery of it – carted away, stripped, made a show of! even in their everlasting habitations ... ' He felt guilt, too, when an Egyptian guide pointed to labourers clearing rubble from a tomb: 'The guide Abdullah said, "All this owing to English ... " Soon the 3 thousand year sleep of its occupant will end.'[9] Later he wrote:

> How should we like our own bodies to be treated in such a fashion? ... If one puts the question to those engaged in excavation, the answer is a shrug of the shoulders and a remark to the effect that they died a long while ago. But what is time to the dead? To them, waking or sleeping, ten thousand years and a nap after dinner must be one and the same thing.[10]

They travelled further up the Nile to see the great river-bank temple of Abu Simbel but Haggard's most fulfilling moments were when he sat at ease on the terrace of his hotel at Luxor, gazing across the Nile to the west bank that was dedicated to the dead and those attending on them – priests and embalmers in the past; guides and archaeologists in the present – and let his imagination roam.

One evening he sat alone at a table by the railings of the terrace and noted the sequence of sunset and nightfall:

> The extraordinary swiftness of the sunset beyond the Western Hills. A great glowing ball, it sinks almost visibly upon their low brown ridge and so while one looks it is gone. The E. side of the hills is veiled in shadows but on the placid waters of the Nile a glow still lingers and the opposing mass of rugged cliff hides the sepulchres of so many mighty kings, stands up scarred and grim as it did upon the day the first Pharaoh looked upon them ... A grey mist rises on the lowlands between the further bank and the hills, clinging round the dense green of the trees. From the town on the left rises the constant clamour of the noisy Fellaheen. Three Soudanese with their tangled mat-like hair stroll past on the path beneath. A year or two ago they may have been fighting us – now they want to sell shell necklaces. A blind boy thrusts his sightless orbs against the bars – calls attention to his physical deficiencies and remarks that the Englishman is his "father and his mother".
>
> A Nile boat glides by – its long, sloping pennon-like sail looking like a bird against the sky of pink-flushed primrose. The wind has failed with the sun – the oars splash swiftly in the water. A frog begins to

croak. The firmament flares up, then grows grey and seems to die – and high in its vast arch the first star appears. It is night.[11]

At the end of their tour Haggard felt that Ancient Egypt was his second homeland: 'I confess I know more of her kings, her queens and her social conditions than I do of those of early England.'[12] He had collected inspiration and background material for four future books – a contemporary novel, *The Way of the Spirit*; an historical romance, *Morning Star*; an Egyptian adventure, *Smith and the Pharaohs*; and *Queen Sheba's Ring*, to be published, after serialisation, some time hence – together with an immediate series of articles for the *Daily Mail*. They returned home via Spain, visiting the cities of Andalusia and giving Haggard the idea for yet another historical novel, *Fair Margaret*.

Back at Ditchingham, he resumed his squirearchical family life with gusto. His daughters were proving lively companions – his dead son remained a subject barred from conversation – and Lilias recorded his daily routine: 'Before breakfast and after morning prayers, which the whole household was expected to attend (and indeed it was no penance to hear Rider read the Bible), he went round the orchid houses and garden. After breakfast, the morning was devoted to letters and general business to do with the estate.'

At lunch and dinner,

> the long table in the dining-room, which Rider had had made of solid oak from his own design with extending ends, had seldom less than ten or twelve ranged down its sides ... Across the polished wood, the old silver, which it was his joy to collect, and the six candles in their branched candlesticks, flowed the endless tide of family chatter and chaff, known as 'Ditchingham Stories' and discussion on every subject between heaven and hell ... Fools he never suffered gladly, nor those he would dismiss swiftly with, "Small beer, my dear, small beer".[13]

He took any opportunity to tell guests of his own adventures and, when pleased with some joke, or sally he would loudly crow, 'What hey! What hey!'[14]

Having devoted the afternoon to the farms and garden, he would dictate his books to Miss Hector in his study after tea and, if there were no guests, after dinner. This was now in what had been the high-ceilinged billiards room, where his desk faced leaded casement windows and, beyond, the garden, trees and the fall of the land into the Waveney Valley.

The family assembled in this room for an hour's talk before bedtime, which, in his case, was seldom before one o'clock in the morning.

One visiting journalist described him at the time as

Tall, large-framed, straight and strong-shouldered, dark and bearded, altogether a commanding figure; a representative of the best type of English country gentleman ... Observe ... his physical and mental restlessness, his eyes that seem to be wandering through eternity and at the same time taking keen and minute note of immediate surroundings and proceedings, the quick transition of his moods, his rapidity of thought and directness of utterance, sometimes having the appearance of bluntness or even brusqueness, and especially when ... the deeps within him are stirred and he pours out a stream of words impelled by burning and long-settled conviction ... and you feel the impact of his eager, tense, nervous personality.[15]

To the impressed visitor, the convictions might well have seemed long-settled but, except in imperial and agricultural matters, this was seldom the case. His ideas were in a constant state of flux, surging and sucking between rocks of doubt rather than conviction. He had hopes, some of which he would express as religious faith but even in those sketchily charted seas, he was always waiting for a fresh squall that would carry him safely to the shore where he hoped Jock and his mother were waiting. Meanwhile, he concentrated his massive energy and his capacity for thought on practical activities that would advance his family and their estate, England, the British Empire and his lucrative writing, in that order of priority.

Yet, in the midst of his campaign for agricultural reform and his busy family life, he experienced something that reversed one of his beliefs. One of the greatest pleasures had been shooting, whether big game in Africa, game birds in Norfolk or just strolling over his land in winter with a gun under his arm. He was not callous and, as a good shot, was careful to kill as cleanly as he could but had never suffered any qualms about the killing of animals for sport, food or both. 'The Animal Kingdom' was different from humanity, he believed, in that animals lacked the divine spark, having life but lacking immortal souls. Yet he was fond of horses and dogs and, when favourites among the latter died, he usually accorded them burial in a little graveyard in the garden; one such, Spice, which had been with him in Africa, had been given his own inscribed memorial at Bradenham.

At this time his favourite gun-dog was an old black retriever named Bob – 'a most amiable and intelligent beast' – which belonged to his daughter Angela and lived with the others in kennels by the stables. On the night of Saturday 9 July 1904, Haggard went to bed and in the early hours of the Sunday morning suffered a nightmare from which he was woken by his wife calling to him from her bed. As he described it:

> I dreamed that ... Bob ... was lying on its side among brushwood, or rough growth of some sort, by water. In my vision, the dog was trying to speak to me in words, and, failing, transmitted to my mind in an undefined fashion the knowledge that it was dying. Then everything vanished and I woke to hear my wife asking me why on earth I was making those horrible and weird noises. I replied that I had had a nightmare about a fearful struggle and that I had dreamed that old Bob was in a dreadful way and was trying to talk to me and to tell me about it.

He repeated the story at breakfast, then was caught up in the Sunday activities of matins at St Mary's and lunch, so that it was not until the evening that Lilias, who often fed the dogs, reported that Bob, last seen late on Saturday evening, was missing. A search was made but it was not until the following Thursday that the dog was found, dead and floating against a weir in the Waveney more than a mile from the house. Later, he heard that Bob had been struck by a train on an open-work bridge between Ditchingham and Bungay and that this must have happened late on Saturday night. Dried bloodstains showed that he must have been knocked off the bridge, mortally hurt, into the shallows of the river, 'undergoing, I imagine,' he noted, 'much the same sensations as I did in my dream and in very similar surroundings to those that I saw therein – namely, among scrubby growth at the edge of water'.

The implications of the dream were, he thought, profound.

> I am forced to conclude [he wrote in a letter to *The Times*], that the dog Bob, between whom and myself there existed a mutual attachment, either at the moment of his death ... or, as seems more probable, about three hours after that event, did succeed in calling my attention to its actual or recent plight by placing whatever portion of my being is capable of receiving such impulses when enchained by sleep, into its own terrible position.

He followed this with a more detailed account written for the *Journal of the Society for Psychical Research*. The dream and its aftermath caused a stir and Haggard received numbers of letters from strangers reporting similar experiences. He himself was 'at first frightened and upset' but, as the implications became apparent, it seemed to show that, as he put it, 'the spirit even of a dog can live on when its mortal frame is destroyed and physical death has happened. If a dog – then how much more a man!'[16]

His first action in consequence was to stop shooting. So, when the season began in late summer, he would accompany the guns, carrying only a shooting-stick. He did not try to persuade his guests to follow his example and stressed that he would happily shoot for food, if that was necessary, or, of course, for self-protection. He did, however, continue to fish, even if guiltily, assuring himself that salmon or trout were not so responsive to pain as hot-blooded creatures and that, anyway, Christ had consorted with fishermen.

After more rumination, Haggard wrote to Sir Oliver Lodge, the physicist and pioneer of research into radio waves, who was also studying the possibilities of communication with the dead, sending him some of the letters resulting from his experience. He sought assurance that some other evidence of personal survival of death had been discovered.

By scientific experience, I have myself become absolutely convinced of persistence of existence [replied Sir Oliver], and I regard death as an important episode – the reverse of birth – but neither of these episodes is really initial or final. One is the assumption of connexion with matter, the other is the abandoning of that connexion.

If it be further asked whether, after we have abandoned matter, we can, by indirect means, occasionally continue to act upon it – on the matter of the inorganic world, or the matter of our friends' brains, for instance – I am inclined to answer, though now more doubtfully, that in my judgement the evidence points to the existence of some indistinct and undeveloped power of this sort. The simplest and best-developed variety of this continued interaction with matter is on the side of telepathy. This is experimentally found existent between the living, and I have reason to believe that this is the one mode of communication which survives the transition ... but, as to details, the whole subject has yet to be explored.[17]

Sir Oliver's own doubts, slight as they might be, were a spur to further exploration for Haggard, although he liked to warn others against dabbling too deeply in the occult. His early experience with spiritualism had been unsettling and unsatisfying and he declared:

Mysticism in moderation adds a certain zest to life and helps to lift it above the level of the commonplace. But it is at best a dangerous sea to travel before the time. The swimmer therein will do well to keep near to this world's sound and friendly shore lest the lights he sees from the crest of those bewildering phantom waves should madden or blind him and he sinks, never to rise again. It is not good to listen for too long to the calling of those voices wild and sweet.[18]

Yet he could not resist wading in himself. He had written a contemporary novel, *Stella Fregelius*, in which the spirit of the hero's dead lover returns to come between him and his wife. Indeed so closely did it reflect Haggard's own romanticised longing for the Lily of his youth that he had taken the typescript with him to Florence to show to his confidante, Agnes Haggard, in case she felt that he had made this all too obvious; it was, however, published in 1904.

Kipling was another with whom he could talk frankly and that autumn he visited him at Bateman's for the first time and, as he put it, 'we jawed ourselves hoarse on all things in heaven and earth'.[19] He found the old house 'most charming ... all panelled with old stone arched doorways and he has furnished it according ... '[20] It was the first of many visits – balanced by the Kiplings' visits to Ditchingham – when the two men, easy in each other's company, let their talk range wherever it led.

He also sent Kipling an advance copy of his sequel to *A Farmer's Year*, entitled *A Gardener's Year*, based on the gardening diary he had kept at Ditchingham throughout 1903. It was not so discursive as its farming companion and was written for the serious gardener, so Kipling, who now knew Haggard well enough to make frank comment, replied, 'everything in the book delights my sympathetic soul except your or-chids. I want to know more about the new lawns ... tree cutting and orchard works and you waste whole pages on *Muscisimilifloribunda Venezuelianinis* and such like. But I suppose you have fellow maniacs in this ploy.'[21]

Haggard was now feeling comfortably established as an authority on all things rural; and coastal, for his experiment with marram grass on the dunes at Kessingland had already raised their level five feet, so holding back the sea. He was invited to address appropriate gatherings and, in the autumn of 1904, one of these speeches was entitled, 'The Garden City in Relation to Agriculture', garden suburbs being the current fashion. He praised the new Letchworth Garden City and the benefits of country, or semi-rural, life: 'Towns are all very well but you want strong, steady, equal-minded men, who can only be bred on the land'; and he deplored land being used as 'convenient preserves in which so many hundreds and thousands of pheasants can be shot ... If it be devoted to sport alone, it cannot grow food and it certainly cannot grow men and women.' He again mourned the exodus from the countryside, called for many more smallholdings with 'people's banks' to finance them, new farm cottages at low rents and cheap rail transport to carry produce to the towns.

'I have become an agricultural bore,' he declared. 'When I have entered a room before now, I have heard people say, "Here comes Rider Haggard, for goodness sake do not mention the word agriculture."' Always hoping for quick and tangible results he felt a failure without them and announced in conclusion, 'Well, what has been the end of it all? Failure. I have failed.'[22] It was too soon for such pessimism. His campaign had been more effective than he realised and it had already taken effect in Westminster and Whitehall.

Despite Haggard's long agricultural interlude he had managed to write a sequel to *She*, entitled *Ayesha, the Return of She*. But She was not quite what she had been and nor were the questing Holly and Vincey (the latter no longer the young Greek god; now, although middle-aged and heavily bearded, he was 'refined and full of thought, sombre almost ... Clear as crystal, steady as stars, shone his large grey eyes'). She, when rediscovered in Central Asia, is still the wizened creature last seen at Kôr but, for Vincey's sake, she bathes in another Sacred Flame and resumes her 'ethereal beauty'. She is no longer the wild, erotic, amoral creature they had known for there is now 'a gentle radiance on her brow'.[23] Her original wickedness has been inherited by *another* immortal white queen, her rival for supremacy. After various adventures, Vincey is unable to resist snatching a kiss, although he must have assumed that it would be instantly fatal. So Ayesha bears the corpse of the most recently ended incarnation of her lover into the heart of the volcano, which presumably will revive them both for another bout.

Although the novel was to be serialised in the *Windsor Magazine* and an initial print order for twenty-five thousand copies was made, it was of curiosity value rather than a success in its own right. Next he was commissioned, for an advance payment of only a third of the amount he had commanded in his first tremendous years as a novelist, to write another African adventure story, which he eventually named *Benita*. it was a tangible sign of his shift from fantasy into fact.

Just then, a fair wind from another direction caught his sails. In January, 1905, he received a letter from Alfred Lyttelton, the Secretary of State for the Colonies, proposing an exciting challenge. The Government was becoming increasingly concerned with poverty and unemployment in the overcrowded cities and they and colonial administrations in the Empire were equally worried about under-population in the great empty spaces of Canada, Australia, New Zealand and South Africa where, despite the victorious conclusion of the Boer War, the Afrikaners seemed bound to become the dominant white race. Haggard's advice had already been sought by the administrators of the new African territory of Rhodesia, which was short of British settlers. There had been a slump in migration from the British Isles; an annual total of more than two hundred thousand in the middle of the last century had fallen to about fifty thousand by the end of it. Now the numbers had slightly increased but most of these headed for the United States and less than thirty per cent chose British territory for settlement.

The Government was concerned and Lyttelton, who had heard of Haggard's theories about population problems in rural England, made him an offer that he knew would strike a response.

The Rhodes trustees have agreed to give a sum of £300 (inclusive of all expenses) to defray the expense of sending a Commissioner to the United States to inspect and report on the 'Labour Colonies' established ... by the Salvation Army [he wrote]. It is thought that if, on enquiry, this system is found to be financially sound and to be of a real benefit to the poorer classes, it might prove a useful model for some analogous system from the United Kingdom to the Colonies.

He invited Haggard to become the Commissioner, a task 'for which your experience as an observer both of men and agricultural affairs so eminently qualifies you'. There would be no payment beyond expenses but, Lyttelton stressed, the reward would be in performing public service and, as a representative of the Government, he would report directly to himself at the Colonial Office. This was the final temptation: that he would represent his country just as had his heroes Shepstone and Osborn; in any case, he did not need more money.

He quickly accepted and soon afterwards called on Lyttelton in Whitehall. His arrival there was, as he said, 'curiously emblematic':

I missed the right entrance to the Colonial Office and finally obtained admission through a little back door ... After a cessation of twenty-six years, was I not once again entering the official service of my country through a back door by means of this unexpected commission with which I was now honoured?[24]

Kipling, who was spending the winter at Cape Town and had read a newspaper report of Haggard's appointment, wrote encouragingly, 'What is the telegram about your going out to America to study Salvation Army methods of planting folk on the land with a view to applying 'em to this part of the world? If it is true, hurry up and turn the current this way. We want *picked* men, breeding women worse.'[25]

Before leaving for the United States, Haggard was to have an interview with General William Booth, the founder and commander of the Salvation Army and visit the prototype 'labour colony' in Essex. Already his attitude to the Salvation Army differed from that of most of his fellow members of the executive class, who regarded it as worthy and its work amongst the poor as admirable, but also as a naive and rather comic example of religious fundamentalism.

Booth was a Methodist minister who, believing in the appeal of military showmanship – ranks, uniforms and brass bands – had, in 1878, transformed his mission in the East End of London with that ethos and those trappings. Spurned by the middle and upper classes in the Church of England, who regarded Methodism as a creed for the lower orders, the Salvation Army attracted instant attention and support throughout industrial Britain, its soldiers soon familiar on street corners and village greens. Its military bands, its bonneted girls shaking tambourines, its officers' thunderous sermons offered excitement and redemption. The mission spread rapidly outside Britain and particularly in the United States where, surviving a *putsch* by some of its own senior officers, General Booth remained its Commander-in-Chief.

Haggard, familiar with the rather touching sight of little Salvation Army bands playing outside crowded London gin-palaces, had shared that patronising view and, indeed, summed up a popular attitude thus:

The Salvation Army is a body of people dressed up in semi-military uniform ... those of whom are women in unbecoming poke-bonnets, who go about making a noise in the name of God and frightening horses with brass bands. It is under the arbitrary rule of an old gentleman named Booth, who called himself a General and whose principal trade assets consist in a handsome and unusual face and an inexhaustible flow of language, which he generally delivers from a

white motorcar, wherever he finds that he can attract the most attention. He is a clever actor, in his way, and I am told that he has made a
large fortune out of the business... [26]

Then, while working on his research for *Rural England*, he had met and
interviewed Booth. The two had much in common, not least a certain
theatricality. Booth, then aged seventy-two, looked, with his bright eyes,
hooked nose and streaming white hair and beard, like an Old Testament
prophet. Like Haggard, he talked in practical generalities and with
imaginative originality. Booth, too, was an author and his book about
urban poverty, entitled in Haggardian style, *In Darkest England*, was as
famous as anything the other had written. Both men had a Jewish strain
in their ancestry and both were excited by military punctilio and parade.
Both were physically striking and Booth, splendid in his frogged uniform
of dark red and blue, remarked to Haggard, 'Ah! but you would look
grand in my uniform!'[27] Admiration was mutual.

At their interview two years earlier, Haggard had begun by explaining
his worries about the growing lack of young men on the land. Booth
explained:

> They read the newspapers; they come up to the towns by excursion
> trains; they see the glitter and the glare ... The boys see the toil of their
> father and mother ... and nothing before them at the end but the
> probability of pauperism ... The young fellows say, 'No, I should
> sooner go and struggle and die in the towns in the attempt to get
> something better.'

He also blamed 'the newspapers and periodicals and the glory of war ...
and the railways and telegraphs and penny postage ... All these things are
against your keeping a man on the land.'

Smallholdings were the answer, they agreed, and both mentioned the
development of such farming in Denmark as their example, much to the
satisfaction of Haggard, who liked to draw attention to his supposed
Viking ancestry. There was no argument over the requirements and
Booth declared, 'Put a man down on five hundred acres of land and he
will perhaps have to slave and toil and probably get into the Bankruptcy
Court, but put a man on ten acres and help him on to his feet and you
make him a happy man.' He would be capable of the work involved and
be his own master so that he would not face the possibility of a domineering employer, a point illustrated by Booth remarking that he had
heard farmers 'talk to their horses and pat them on the neck and speak to

them like a gentleman, and talk to Tom, Dick or Harry as if he were a beast'.

But, he continued, before 'scalliwags and the poor homeless'[28] could be transplanted from town to country, they would have to be trained and that was why the Salvation Army had started training camps in England and America. It was one of these, at Hadleigh, on the coast of Essex, thirty-nine miles from London, that Haggard was now to inspect.

It was February, and the flat northern shores of the Thames estuary were bleak and swept by cold winds blowing unimpeded across the plains of Europe from Russia. The land itself was 'poor and cold in character', he was to write in his report, 'most of it ... wretched pasture of an utterly innutritious nature, much of which the tenants do not even take the trouble to keep clear of brambles and other noxious growths'.[29] Here, in 1890, the Salvation Army had purchased three derelict farms covering three thousand acres to establish the Hadleigh Colony for training men in general farming, stock and poultry rearing, fruit-growing and brick-making. There were now some seven hundred inhabitants: men under training and their instructors, Salvation Army officers and their families.

Commissioner Haggard – as he was now known – was received like an inspecting general and behaved like one. He knew that the Salvation Army called its assembly halls 'citadels' but this was even more like a military establishment, administered under discipline. He was briefed on the finances, both the capital outlay and the wages paid to inmates, which, in addition to board and lodging, averaged three shillings a week but could rise to fifteen. He was shown the dairy, the greenhouses, the egg-incubators, the brick yards, the mess-hall at meal time, the dormitories and the Inebriates' Home.

He interviewed several of the men under training but although these exchanges were again those of an inspecting officer and a private on parade, Haggard recorded them in their entirety in his report.

He asked one, 'How long have you been here?'

'Four and a half years, sir.'

'What were you before you came?'

'Sanitary engineer.'

'Went astray, I suppose?'

'Yes.'

'Not astray now? Doing all right?'

'Yes.'

'You are superintendent of the laundry?'

'Yes.'

Of another, he asked, 'Where do you come from?'

'London, sir.'

'What were you doing there?'

'Only walking about the streets.'

'Why were you walking about the streets? Have you a mother?'

'Yes.'

'Could not your mother support you?'

'No.'

'You were getting a living the best way you could and then the Salvation Army found you and you were sent to this Colony by a lady?'

'Yes.'

'How long have you been here now?'

'Four months, sir.'

He asked a third, 'What were you before you came to the Colony?'

'Brushmaker in London, sir.'

'Did you fall out of work?'

'Yes.'

'Got in a bad way?'

'I did, in London and around the country.'

'The Salvation Army picked you up?'

'They did.'

'And you are now a cook here? What do you look forward to doing ultimately? Going to be a cook?'

'I want to go to Canada in the spring.'[30]

That seemed satisfactory, but Haggard's aim was to attract farm workers to the land in England; only when 'the heart and brain' of the Empire, as he liked to put it, had been restored to health could the rest be considered, although emigration was what the Government seemed to have primarily in mind. Flattered as Haggard was to be going to the United States as a Commissioner, he was not a *Royal* Commissioner and this was to be seen as the first clue to a Machiavellian plot by the Government.

Another General Election was pending and the Unionist Coalition in power was smarting from criticism concerning the lack of action over the country's agricultural slump and urban poverty, which had been kept in the public eye by two celebrated critics, Rider Haggard and General Booth, respectively. The proposed scheme might effectively dispose of them both. To involve Haggard in agricultural training for the urban poor and send him to America to study the Salvation Army's labour colonies, should distract him from his campaign for more smallholdings, which had attracted much attention and popular support but which seemed to the ruling politicians dangerously radical and prohibitively expensive. His mission was also to gratify General Booth, whose attack on government inactivity in relieving poverty had drawn blood. As Haggard's mission was to be funded by the Rhodes Trust, he was not a *Royal* Commissioner and the Government needed not act upon whatever recommendations he made; all that should be necessary would be vague official enthusiasm until the General Election had been held and the matter could safely be dropped.

Unaware of such deviousness and gratified by his new and seemingly important position of trust, Rider Haggard – accompanied by his daughter Angela, now aged twenty-two, as his secretary – sailed on 22 February 1905 for New York in the liner *Teutonic* as a representative of his country.

CHAPTER NINE

'What an England we could make'

WHEN THE *TEUTONIC* docked at New York, newspaper reporters again swarmed aboard to interview the famous author but he was in no mood to talk about fiction. 'If he still has a She,' wrote one, 'he has put a Salvation Army bonnet on her.'

Questions about the novels met with gruff responses: 'Mr Haggard made interviewing difficult as long as the talk clung to literature' and he was quoted as replying, 'Oh, I don't want to talk about literature!' One journalist reported, 'He seemed to be actually bored by allusions to his books.' He became brusque when asked how he wrote his books, replying that he was writing nothing at the moment; not quite truthfully because he had been at work on *Benita* during the voyage. 'One can't do two things at once,' he snapped. 'My mind is all on the Commission.' Only when asked about that did he 'talk without prodding' and 'then the coldness, the indifference, the reserve – whatever you wish to call the typical English manner with strangers – fell away from Mr Haggard like a mask. He grew earnest, enthusiastic, cogent; but always without self-praise, or over-confidence.' So the reporters settled down to a different sort of interview with a social reformer and they enjoyed his 'breezy, poseless, highly English manner ... He lounges very low in his chair and puffs affectionately at a homely old pipe ... when he got to the practical side of life he began to warm up and talk without prodding ... The Rider Haggard of the new crusade is another man from the jaunty romancer of a decade ago.'[1]

When the reports were published, Haggard and his daughter were ashore, staying at the Waldorf Hotel and their telephone began to ring as editors ordered their reporters to exploit the new angle. Soon afterwards, Angela woke her father at two o'clock in the morning complaining, 'Oh, Dad, *do* come here! There is a lunatic on the telephone who says he wants me to come out walking in the streets.'[2] It was a reporter inviting

Haggard and his daughter to watch his newspaper distributing food to the homeless poor of New York.

First they travelled to Philadelphia to see allotment vegetable gardens, which local philanthropists had given to the poor, and to lunch with a literary society. Then they continued to Washington, where the re-election of President Theodore Roosevelt was still being celebrated. Haggard was also a celebrity in the United States and had, on arrival, been welcomed by the Secretary of State, John Milton Hay, as a prelimi-nary to meeting the President himself and, on 9 March, he was invited to the White House.

President Theodore Roosevelt was of Dutch descent, had sympathy for the Boer cause and, as he was known for his forceful opinions and manner, these might well have collided with those of the English im-perialist. Yet Roosevelt was an imperialist himself in the American cause and the two had much else in common. He was a crusader after Haggard's own heart, having rooted out corruption in the New York police and, on succeeding the assassinated President McKinley, inspired the "trust-busting" campaign against monopolies. During the war with Spain over Cuba he had raised and led his own force of 'Rough Riders', irregulars akin to Haggard's Pretoria Horse. He was concerned with the poor and had enforced laws governing the employment of women and children. He had been a rancher in North Dakota and still hankered after an outdoor life. Above all the two men shared the view expressed by Roosevelt that 'the great virtue of my radicalism lies in the fact that I am perfectly ready, if necessary to be radical on the conservative side.'[3]

They took to each other at once, these two disparate types: the Englishman ('very tall and on his very broad shoulders, his large enough head sits small in the manner of the 'Farnese Hercules',[4] as one fanciful New York reporter wrote of him); and, two years younger, the American ('a short, stout man with a fair, fresh complexion and rows of very even teeth, which he shows in the entirety every time he smiles', as Haggard described him). He found the President 'frank and earnest, nor does he mince words and opinions'; they also had a mutual friend in Kipling.

Opening their exchange, Roosevelt waved a hand towards his crowded anteroom, where Haggard had seen several Indian chiefs "with long black hair, copper-coloured skins and strongly marked features", and told his guest that what he saw was the aftermath of a presidential election in a democratic country. Then he asked about the state of affairs in South Africa, adding that he himself was of Dutch descent. After listening to Haggard, he replied that he had great sympathy with the Boers but, even so, hoped that they would now learn English and become dominant in a South Africa ruled by the British. 'He, at least, was not working against us in the South African war,' noted his guest.

The talk turned to agriculture and the need to keep countrymen from the enticements of the cities. 'I found that his views and mine were identical on this subject,' Haggard recorded, 'as he recognised the inevitable deterioration of the race which must ensue if the land-dwellers were to become city-dwellers.' Roosevelt was worried by some high breeding rates, citing the French-Canadians who were 'crowding out the British-born folk' and who 'settle upon the land and have large families, whereas the English-Canadians draw to the cities'.

Soon afterwards, Haggard and his daughter were invited to lunch at the White House. As it happened, they had already accepted another luncheon invitation for that day, so they attended both, leaving the first early with the excuse that they had an appointment with the President. Roosevelt proved a relaxed and entertaining host, explaining that he was about to receive an official visit from the Swiss ambassador, who would 'stand in a fine uniform and read a lot of rot to me in French, while I shall stand opposite to him and read a lot of rot in English. And that's what they call the high ceremonies of diplomacy!'

After lunch, as Roosevelt led his guests into his drawing-room, he said, 'It is an odd thing, Mr Haggard, that you and I, brought up in different countries and following such different pursuits, should have identical ideas and aims. I have been reading your book, *Rural England*, and I tell you that what you think, I think, and what you want to do, I want to do. We are one man in the matter.'[5] He followed this meeting with a note to Haggard at his hotel, saying how delighted he was to meet them both, adding,'When you get through your investigation of the Salvation Army colonies will you let me know what you find the facts to be? I am immensely interested in the subject.'[6]

Thus encouraged, and after an equally heartening interview with the Secretary for Agriculture, James Wilson, Haggard set out on his tour of inspection. It was to be a coast-to-coast journey by rail, made miserable by the steam-heated sleeping-cars, in which, said Haggard, 'Americans seem to prefer to be stewed alive.'[7] Yet he kept an eye open for detail to jot in his notebook: 'Nightfall on the Texas veldt. The lurid sunset. The rising storm cloud. The jagged lightning – thunder and the dashing rain and the huge dancing hail.'[8] He was to visit three Salvation Army colonies: Fort Romie near San Francisco, Fort Amity in Colorado and Fort Herrick in Ohio, the latter specialising in the rehabilitation of alcoholics. He was also to visit Salt Lake City to see the smallholdings organised by the Mormons, before heading north into Canada to study the possibilities for the settlement of migrants there and to consult the Government in Ottawa.

In a Californian valley and in the light, bracing climate of Colorado, Haggard met a different case of unfortunates from General Booth's 'scalliwags and the homeless poor', the 'hoboes', 'dead-beats' and 'born-tireds' as well as the respectable 'poor whites' of America. He was punctilious in his investigations, recording the scale and composition of each colony and its economics. Usually smallholdings were sold to settlers cheaply with the help of loans repayable on easy terms when the land became productive.

In Canada, where he visited Toronto and Ottawa, he found his own enthusiasm echoed by the Government and the Prime Minister, Sir Wilfred Laurier, caught up in his enthusiasm, crowned his efforts with the offer of two hundred and forty thousand acres of virgin land as a gift for the settlement of British immigrants. Treated as a statesman, he responded as such, discarding his public image as an inventive novelist.

He said as much to the Canadian Club in Ottawa in a long speech which reflected not only his views on himself and his mission but the much wider view of the British Empire and the world. Of himself, he said:

> The time comes to every writer ... when he has an inspiration and does something which he knows to be better than he ever did before ... He creates something and knows that that thing which he has created will live and that it will even go glittering down the generations. He knows, perhaps, that he has cut his name fairly deep upon the iron leaves of the Book of Time ... and for a while he is content ... Then, perhaps, he begins to understand ... that that was not his real inspiration ... And he turns, let us say, to the dull masses of misery that pervade the globe ... and he thinks: Is there nothing that I, humble as I am, can do to help to alleviate that misery? ... These things have some application, certainly in my own humble case ... It is a hard thing, in the first place, to live down the reputation of being a writer of fiction ... Still, humbly, imperfectly, I did attempt it. I have not done much. Yet I have done something. They listen to me now a bit. If they had not listened to me, I

should not be here in my present position today as Commissioner from the Government of Great Britain.

He turned to the drift of population from the land into the cities, both in England and North America, and the pioneer work of the Salvation Army's colonies. Then his horizons widened and he predicted the future.

If the Western nations allow this sort of thing to go on, allow their population to crowd into the cities, then, I say, the career of the Western nations is going to be short ... Gentlemen, children are not bred in the cities. There will come a time when the children bred there are too few – it is coming now ... On the land alone will the supply of children be available that is necessary to carry on our white races. And if they are not carried on in sufficient numbers, what of it?

It was then that his vision moved into apocalyptic depth and focus.

Of course, you have all heard of what they call the Yellow Peril and many people have laughed at it as a bogey. Is it a bogey? Does Russia, for instance, consider that Japan is a mere nightmare? I think not; I think Russia has very definite and distinct ideas as to the prowess of Japan today. Japan is a small nation. Forty years ago the Japanese dressed themselves up in scale armour, like lobsters, and fought with bows and arrows. Look at them today, knocking Russia around the ring.

Imagine the state of affairs when, not little Japan, but, let us say, great China with her 400,000,000 people, has also made great strides towards civilisation ... Imagine these 400,000,000 of stolid, strong, patient, untiring, land-bred men having nowhere to live, having not earth upon which to stand, and seeking a home. And imagine them casting their eyes around for worlds to conquer and seeing an island continent half-vacant ... [He spoke, of course, of Australia.] Imagine them saying ... we will seek the earth; we will take the earth; we will keep the earth. Then imagine the scanty peoples spread thinly over these territories saying: 'But we will pass a law to keep you out.' They answer: 'We will come in nevertheless, we will walk through your paper law.' And those who hold the ground say: 'You shall not come in; we will shoot you; we will keep you out by force of arms.' And their answer is: 'Keep us out if you can; we have arms as well as you; we will come; we will occupy; we will take; we will keep.' Is that a bogey – a mere dream of the night? I tell you it is nothing of the sort. It is the thing which will happen within one hundred years unless ... the people are moved from the cities back to the land.[9]

Salvation, he declared, was possible and when he had returned to London and presented the plan he had devised for the re-settlement of population on the land, a beginning could be made.

Despite this enthusiasm and energy, it had not been an easy tour. There had been interminable rail journeys, during which he had compiled his notes and drafted his report. In Colorado, when he and Angela had been taken to see irrigation works on the Colorado river, they had narrowly escaped drowning in flood-water. On the final stretch of the rail journey, Angela had gone down with influenza. Worst of all was a cruel letter from his brother Andrew who, having failed to make a success of his military career, or to emulate his brother's success as a novelist,* was living in Maine; he had been invited by Rider to see him in New York before he sailed for England:

As to coming down to New York to see you sailing away home again after your rapid and triumphal progress – and leaving me behind, well, my dear Rider, it would be too absolutely distressing and I could not stand it [he wrote]. To be alone on the wharf in New York, with no friends, no glory, no excitement, no money, while seeing the smoke from your funnels disappearing ... The cry is why did I ever leave the Army? Did I blame you for leaving Sir Henry Bulwer for Shepstone, Shepstone for the High Court, the High Court for Ostriches, Ostriches for the Bar and the Divorce Courts, the Bar for Literature? ... Because *I* have been less fortunate than my rich and successful brother in my change of occupation, *I* must be reproached for leaving the Army.[10]

Despite this sudden upsurge of resentment within his family, which was neither the first nor the last, his confidence was such that he could face it with magnanimity; on this occasion, Haggard sent his brother some money and eventually received a letter of gratitude. On the return voyage across the Atlantic in the liner *Majestic*, he completed his report to the Secretary of State for the Colonies, confident that it would be accorded the highest priority and probably be acted upon promptly. On arrival but before going ashore, he wrote to Lyttelton, assuring him that the report, which was about to be typed, would be on his desk in a few days.

* Despite having served gallantly in several African campaigns, Andrew Haggard had proved too temperamental for further promotion. After leaving the Army, he had written several novels and was now turning to history and biography.

Assuming the Colonial Secretary to be avid for news of his mission, he assured him that he had formed a favourable opinion of what he had seen.

He wrote triumphantly that the Canadian Government had '*given* me 240,000 acres of land outright (to be selected *wherever one likes*) and a promise of as much more as is wanted. This is really very handsome.' He stressed that the Salvation Army had put no religious pressure on its settlers and that Sir Wilfred Laurier had agreed with him that there would be no better organisation than that to administer future settlements. Finally, he mentioned that he had a 'most interesting interview'[11] with President Roosevelt in Washington.

Haggard returned to Ditchingham as a man of international affairs: an acquaintance of the President of the United States; one who had been accorded the highest honours in Canada; one whose work was probably only beginning. Once his report had been discussed by the Cabinet and debated in the House of Commons, the next stage would be not only for his recommendations to be implemented in Canada but for him to make similar journeys of enquiry to South Africa, Australia and New Zealand. In May, he wrote to Lord Rosebery,* the chairman of the Rhodes Trust, that he had 'ventured to suggest that a Commissioner should be sent to South Africa and especially to Rhodesia ... I have great hope that the tobacco industry in Rhodesia gives an opening to the smallholder. I think also that your Lordship will agree with me that a British population is desirable in that county.'[12] Indeed, he was so confident of being given such an assignment that, in refusing a speaking engagement for October, he wrote to the Bishop of Salisbury that, 'for aught I know, I may be sent abroad again.'[13]

A few weeks later, slightly put out that he had not been summoned sooner but assuming that it was because of lengthy discussion in the Cabinet, he called on the Colonial Secretary in Whitehall. Lyttelton received him as an equal and amiably assured him that his report, which he held in his hand, was to be published as a government 'Blue Book' in a month's time. When Haggard asked if he was satisfied with it, he replied, 'Satisfied? I think it is splendid.' Then he added 'I wish the Prime Minister would take it up. But *Arthur†* *won't read it – you know, Arthur won't read it!*'[14] Haggard was appalled. It had never struck him that the mission that had absorbed him for the past five months had been an irrelevance;

*Former Prime Minister, 1894–96.
† Arthur Balfour was Prime Minister 1902–5.

that his assignment was serving its purpose by silencing one critic and placating another; and that parliamentary debate and filibustering could delay any conclusion until after the General Election. Lyttelton said soothingly that the report would be debated in both Houses of Parliament in June; then he shortly brought the meeting to a close.

Shocked and humiliated as he was, Haggard determined to press for the maximum attention. He persuaded Longman to print an illustrated edition of his report a few weeks after its publication as a Blue Book. As soon as he received advance copies, he sent one to President Roosevelt with a covering letter urging that 'the scheme I have evolved, namely, that the public credit and the waste forces of Benevolence can be made use of to palliate the gigantic evil of the over-crowded cities and to populate the deserted, or unoccupied, land is one which may be put into operation upon a large scale to the great benefit of humanity.'[15] To his delight, the President replied, 'I agree absolutely with your purpose and with the general outline of your plan' but that it 'should not be left to mere charity and that it should be conducted on strict business principles.' It was, he wrote, 'one of the great problems of our present day' that was 'quite as important for the United States as to Great Britain'.[16]

The Blue Book was published on 19 June and to Haggard's surprise and delight was well received by the press, which had so often mocked or attacked him, with unanimous praise. In a leading article, *The Times* congratulated him on completing 'with commendable despatch, a work of great interest' and hoped that he would continue his enquiries and 'tell us how his plan can be carried out in England, dear land'. The *Daily Telegraph* regarded his report as 'the most important and the least read of his varied literary achievements' and the *Morning Post* hailed it as 'profoundly interesting' and urged its 'fullest consideration'. The *Daily Express* claimed that 'a vista of hope and encouragement is opened by Mr Haggard' and the *Daily Mirror* demanded, 'The sooner we begin the better.'[17] Such praise and exhortation were echoed by some six dozen British newspapers and periodicals.

Haggard was further encouraged by the reaction of the Rhodes Trustees and he wrote to a friend that the report had been 'extraordinarily well received throughout the country. I saw Gerald Balfour* yesterday and Lord Rosebery ... They are both *very* favourably inclined.'[18] Yet when it was debated in both Houses of Parliament that June, it was

---

* President of the Board of Trade, 1900–1905.

referred to a Departmental Committee, which as one brutally frank Conservative agent told Haggard, would 'knock the bottom out of it'. When it eventually was considered, the Committee felt that the settlement scheme would be too expensive and, in any case, would be administered by the Salvation Army, which was considered cranky and by no means as respectable as the Church of England. It decided that intending emigrants should make their own arrangements through various existing agencies. They concluded, 'Though we fully recognize the zeal and ability that Mr Rider Haggard has shown ... we could not recommend that this particular scheme be adopted.' So, in 1906, Haggard's report and recommendations for action were consigned to the parliamentary scrap-heap.

> For me personally this issue was painful [he wrote]. I had worked hard and in all honestness, and, like many better men, I had found myself thrown over. After all the Colonial Secretary's declarations as to the value of my work, I never even received a letter of thanks from the Government, or even, for that matter, a copy of the Report and Evidence of the Committee, which I had to buy like any other member of the public. All that I got was the privilege of paying the bill for, of course, the small sum allowed by the Rhodes Trustees did not suffice to meet the expenses of my tour in a high official position through that very expensive country, the United States.

There had been little satisfaction in the fall of Balfour's Government in December, 1905, and its replacement by the Radicals, since they were no more enthusiastic about his ideas than their opponents had been. It had been 'a fiasco', he concluded. 'My report was destroyed; the divided recommendations of the Departmental Committee, such as they were, were never acted on: in short, all came to nothing ... Well, I tried my best ... and failed.'

His strenuous tour and subsequent work, combined with emotional stress, had damaged Haggard's health and, early in 1906, he underwent an unspecified operation, 'which the effects of my long journey made necessary'. Yet he was resilient and determined and his mission had given him a taste of authority and a hankering after power. He had hopes that the new Government might employ him, particularly after, early in 1906, *The Review of Reviews* declared that 'There is no more capable agricultural commissioner than Mr Rider Haggard' and that he should be despatched forthwith to tour the Continent and report on farming

Into Africa: Rider Haggard (aged twenty), in camp near Pretoria in May, 1877, seated at the feet of Sir Theophilus Shepstone and his staff. Shepstone is seated, centre; to his right, standing, Melmoth Osborn; F. B. Fynney, the interpreter, seated, right.

In Norfolk: Squire Haggard, with his mother, his wife, his son Jock, his daughters Angela and the infant Dorothy, at Ditchingham House in 1884.

The lost love: Lily Jackson in middle age.

'Fresh as a rose and as sound as a bell': Louisa Haggard in her prime.

The father: William Meybohm Rider
Haggard (1817–93) of Bradenham Hall.

The son: Jock (christened Arthur)
Haggard, born in Natal, 1881.

The friend: Rudyard Kipling
in the study he sometimes
shared with Rider Haggard.

The little Egyptian figure (left) in the museum at Didlington Hall, which may have helped the inspiration of the immortal She, here painted by Maurice Greiffenhagen.

A NORFOLK MAN FOR NORFOLK.

H RIDER HAGGARD

SEEKS YOUR

VOTE

AND

INTEREST

PROSPERITY TO THE PLOUGH.

Electioneering: Rider Haggard's handbill in the East Norfolk campaign of 1895.

Campaigning: Rider Haggard riding a coach through Great Yarmouth during the stormy general election.

The proud patriarch: Rider Haggard with his second daughter Dorothy ('Dolly') at Ditchingham, circa 1908.

The enthusiast at full-tilt: the inscribed photograph which Theodore Roosevelt gave Rider Haggard in 1916.

Copyright 1907 by Cheridinet   Washington, D.C.

To Sir Rider Haggard
from
Theodore Roosevelt
July 21st 1916

The horse tried to jump one of
its wings — and I *had* to haul
his head!

In the Hall of Osiris. Sir Rider Haggard, aged sixty-seven, in the temple at Abydos during his final visit to Egypt in 1924.

practices and reforms which might be applied to Britain. Nothing transpired but reading that the administration planned to form a Royal Commission on Coast Erosion, he wrote to his old acquaintance David Lloyd George,* who was now President of the Board of Trade, telling him about his success in planting marram grass on the sands at Kessing-land, which had significantly raised their level. As a result, he was invited to join and readily accepted. The task before the Commissioners might be less urgent than that of urban poverty and colonial settlement, but it had an advantage in that it was Government-inspired and thus a Royal Commission, so he became a *Royal* Commissioner.

'I worked hard on that Royal Commission,' he was to write, adding, 'I do not suppose there is a groin or an eroded beach on the shores of the United Kingdom that I have not seen and thoughtfully considered... also a fine variety of inland swamps which it was thought possible to re-claim.'[19] For him, it was not a chore because he had an almost mystical feeling for the land, particularly when it was his own, or he could imagine it having been tilled by his ancestors.

He had a deep sense, as he walked over his land, of the generations that had worked it before him [his nephew Godfrey Haggard was to write]. He regarded himself as one in an unbroken line of succession. He had a genuine feeling of kinship, as he drained a plot of marshy ground, or wrestled with a piece of heavy soil, towards his nameless predecessors, who had coped, each in their own way, with the same hard, unyielding task.[20]

Even when the land, or coastal marsh or dune, had not been owned by Haggards, a sense of kinship remained.

Like farming itself, the study of coastal erosion could be tedious labour, particularly when combined with his other principal tasks of proof-reading and letter-writing; he was to write to a Norfolk neighbour, 'I am run off my rather ancient legs: coast erosion, coast erosion, coast erosion! Proofs, proofs, proofs! Bores, bores, bores!'[21] It might not be an exciting subject but it was quietly satisfying and at least he was a *Royal* Commissioner.

But, after a year, it was found that erosion itself was not a problem that could fully occupy a Royal Commission; so, meeting Lloyd George at a dinner party, Haggard suggested to him that afforestation and the state

* Having met Haggard at Cricieth in 1884, Lloyd George wrote to his brother in 1897, from the House of Commons, saying they had met again at lunch.

of the nation's ancient forests might be added to their responsibilities. This was done and Haggard began to hatch a scheme for the use of the unemployed in reclaiming land and planting it with trees. Now he could put his knowledge of unemployment to some use as chairman of the Unemployed Labour and Reclamation Committee.

He continued writing his novels, almost mechanically now, to provide an income, for the Royal Commissioners were paid only their expenses. In 1905, *Ayesha*, the sequel to *She*, had been published to mixed reviews. He sent a copy to Andrew Lang and was put out by his first reaction, which was to joke that he was too old for it because 'one no longer has the joyous credulity of forty, and even *your* imagination is out of the fifth form. However, plenty of boys are about and I hope they will be victims of the enchantress.' He was somewhat mollified, however, when Lang sent a teasing postscript next day: 'It is all right: I am thrilled: so much obliged. I thought I was too old, but the Eternal Boy is still on the job.'[22]

Kipling was a more comfortable critic and when Haggard sent him his next book, *The Way of the Spirit*, an Egyptian adventure, early in 1906, he read it twice, praised it with 'I did as I have done with many of your books – simply surrendered myself to the joy of reading and read on.' Gently questioning a point in the plot, he politely added, 'Do you think I'm right?' and 'I'm a little curious on the subject.'[23] He had approved of Haggard's ideas for agricultural reform and resettlement, writing, 'I am slowly discovering England ... as you say it has no grub and no trained men except a few days' supply of each ... The man-question is serious. I entirely agree with you about the town-bred person.' Later he wrote admiringly of Haggard's agricultural ideas, stressing their shared opinion of politicians: 'What an England we could make if we could only get 1/2 of your programme put through. Forgive me if I seem a pessimist. They are all such a set of flagrant and persistent liars ... I shall be enormously pleased tho' if they develop any sparks of decency or gratitude towards you.'[24]

The two men were grateful for each other's friendship, since neither made close friends easily. Not only did they feel they could discuss 'everything in heaven above or earth beneath,' as Haggard put it, but that, 'We do not fidget each other.' At Bateman's and at Ditchingham, each welcomed the other into his study, which was forbidden to others while work was in progress. Kipling told Haggard that 'he could work as well when I was sitting in the room as though he were alone, whereas generally the presence of another person while he was writing would drive him almost mad.'[25] Kipling himself wrote that 'Between us we could even hatch out tales together – a most exacting test of sympathy.' After one visit to Bateman's, Haggard noted in his diary, 'On Sunday and Monday, I sat in his study while he worked and after a while he got up and remarked to me that my presence did not bother him a bit; he supposed because we were two of a trade. He told me that I was the only literary person with whom he could associate at all.'[26]

The first of Haggard's books with which Kipling helped was another African novel, *The Ghost Kings*, for which they compiled the plot jointly, each writing alternate passages of the synopsis on the same sheets of foolscap. When Haggard was sketching the plot for *Red Eve*, an historical novel set at the time of the Black Death, he asked Kipling to help him name the character that symbolised death and he jotted down two dozen possible names, including Morgue, Adam, Koth, Kef, and Tarkoth, before Murgh was finally chosen.

Both men relished the exercise of the imagination and the construction of a plot, although Kipling was the more dedicated to finer details of style. Their compatibility depended more on the shared realisation that story-telling involved the surface of their consciousness and that both were striving after answers to other questions. 'Both of us believe that there are higher aims in life than the weaving of stories well or ill,' wrote Haggard to Kipling, 'and according to our separate occasions strive to fulfil this faith.'[27]

Another, less intimate, friend, who believed that his faith had provided the final answer, was William Booth of the Salvation Army. The failure of their campaign to win government support for farming colonies had, of course, disappointed them both. Yet Booth was an optimist and, determined to capitalise on his friendship with Haggard, invited him to write a book about the work of the Salvation Army for a substantial fee. At first Haggard refused because he neither had time nor would he accept money from the charity. Then he had second thoughts and agreed to do so without payment, except for his expenses.

For three months he toured English cities, visiting the Army's 'citadels' and their out-stations, shelters and orphanages in the slums. The result was, in effect, journalism bound together in a book entitled *Regeneration*. He interviewed, albeit somewhat distantly, derelicts rescued from the streets, amongst them a veteran of the American civil war, an unemployed flower-painter, an impoverished Indian school-teacher and a destitute German student. He talked with released convicts, unmarried mothers and several saved from suicide. Salvation Army officers told him what faced the destitutes; 'They wander about, die off and so on.'[28]

One thundery summer night he visited a refuge for reformed prostitutes and accompanied two Salvation Army 'lasses' on a patrol of Leicester Square.

> It was a strange scene [he wrote]. The air was hot and heavy, the sky filled with black and lowering clouds already laced with lightnings. The music-halls and restaurants had given out their crowds, the midnight mart was open. Everywhere were women, all finely dressed, most of them painted, as could be seen in the glare of the electric light, some of them more or less excited by drink ... Mixed up with these were the bargainers, men of every degree, the most of them with faces unpleasant to consider ... I noticed one young girl whose looks would have drawn attention anywhere, whispering an address from beneath an enormous feathered hat to the driver of a taxi-cab, while her companion, a pleasant-looking, fresh-coloured boy, for he was scarcely more, entered the vehicle, a self-satisfied air upon his face. She sprang in also and the cab with its occupants glided away out of my ken for ever.
>
> Here and there, stalwart, quiet policemen requested loiterers to move on and the loiterers obeyed and re-formed in groups behind them; here and there a respectable woman pushed her way through the throng, gathering up her skirts as she did so and glancing covertly at this unaccustomed company out of the corners of her eyes. While watching all these sights we lost touch of the Salvation Army ladies, who wormed their way through the crowd as easily and quickly as a snake does through undergrowth ... Big drops began to fall, the thunder growled and in a moment the concourse commenced to melt. Five minutes later the rain was falling fast and the streets had emptied.[29]

Haggard was susceptible to the pathos of what were referred to as 'the wages of sin' and 'the worm in the bud' for good reason. Not long before, the love of his early life, Lily, the embodiment of feminine virtue in his eyes, had returned to England from Africa because her husband had died. She had a dreadful story to tell him. Her husband had died of syphilis, having infected her. Again Haggard – with the agreement of Louie – came to her aid, but it could only be financial for her condition was incurable.

What followed was a ghastly reflection of the disintegration of She and also of the novel he was currently writing about the Black Death, which was set on the Suffolk coast, where Lily lay dying at Aldeburgh.

In April, 1909, Haggard made the journey from Ditchingham to her bedside for the last time, and alone. Soon afterwards she died – aged fifty-five – leaving him bereft, not of a lover but of the unfulfilled hopes of his youth, now finally dead. Louie accompanied him to the funeral but not in the memories that came upon him after thirty-five years. As he followed the coffin down the aisle towards the west door and the graveyard beyond, 'the arch of this door reminded me of something, at the moment I could not remember what. Then it came back to me. It was exactly like that other arch through which I had followed her to her carriage on the night when first we met.'[30]

Lily's death had been expected but that of his first grandchild was not. His daughter Angela had married her cousin Tom Haggard, the son of his elder brother Bazett, and Haggard had hoped that her first child would be a boy, who would carry on the family name. It was a girl they named Diana, but she lived only for seven months. Angela discovered that she could bear no more children so, later, they adopted a baby girl and named her after Haggard's Zulu heroine, Nada.

Mortality hung heavily over the life of the family. Early that year, Haggard wrote to his sister Ella that he had been supervising the construction of a family vault beneath the chancel of Ditchingham church with space on its shelves for twenty urns of cremated ashes. 'Digging your own grave is not a cheerful occupation,' he told her, 'and that is what I have been doing during the last week. Also, I could not help reflecting that the next time I went down into that vault it would probably be in a compacter form.'[31]

Rider Haggard was shrouded in melancholy. His imagination was still inventive but he had relegated the writing of fiction to a money-making process in favour of the practicalities of agricultural, social and imperial reform. But now that seemed becalmed and none of his recommendations acted upon. His marriage was, by the standards of which he had dreamed, lacklustre. He and Louie were compatible enough; she was quietly companionable and capable but could not share his imaginings and seldom expressed her emotions, except in irritability. He loved his three daughters and became so desperately worried when Lilias went down with a high temperature that he wrote a four-page letter about it to another Norfolk squire: 'The child seems bright and well but there is the temperature and while that remains it may mean anything ... Children are certainly a dreadful responsibility.'[32]

He was stoic, however, and kept busy, delivering speeches whenever invited to do so. When the report on afforestation by the Royal Commission was published as a Blue Book, he again sent a copy to President Roosevelt. Haggard had been gratified to read that he had taken up his own ideas about under-population with his 'race suicide' campaign and so congratulated him on 'the great work you have done since we met at Washington four years ago'.[33] Roosevelt thanked him for the report, adding that he was 'particularly glad to get it at this time as I hope to call an international conference, which will deal with the questions you touch', adding that he had been 'working along the lines with which I know you have sympathy'.[34] Gratifying as that was, it was followed within a month by the news in March that Roosevelt had relinquished the Presidency and been succeeded by William H. Taft. Everything Haggard touched seemed to turn to ashes.

Yet there was one shaft of light in that gloomy year. In the autumn, the House of Commons considered and passed the Development Bill, which was based on the agricultural reforms for which Haggard had called, allowing for loans and grants to be made by the Government for farming, afforestation, rural industries and transport. It was a new beginning and he felt able, that November, to deliver an optimistic speech at the Bungay Farmers' Club dinner in Suffolk. At the beginning of the century, he said, British agriculture had reached its greatest depth of depression in living memory but now it was once more on an upward trend. Great prosperity might not yet be within reach but now with 'science being yoked to the plough' they might 'once more attain to something like the best'.[35]

Haggard was regarded with some suspicion by the more prosperous farmers. All his talk of breaking up big estates into smallholdings – however much he stressed that the land would be bought at market prices – smacked of socialism. It was known that he had attended a lecture by George Bernard Shaw to the Fabian Society in London. He had also given evidence to the Select Committee on the Housing of the Working Classes Amendment Bill. He had sent a copy of *The Poor and the Land* to the socialist Sidney Webb, who, with his wife Beatrice, also sat on reformist Royal Commissions, and he had replied:

Perhaps we may make the conditions of life in the English country more attractive than at present. Have you considered the startling idea of a *Legal* Minimum Wage for farm laborers [sic]? What would happen if no farmer was allowed (under penalty of fine and imprisonment) to employ any laborer for any shorter time than twelve months ... and not for a wage less than £1 a week all the year round?[36]

This suggested to the more ardent Conservatives in East Anglia that Squire Haggard might be dangerously close to becoming a traitor to his class.

The hopeful news for farmers did little to lighten the sombre scene for, he believed, the old world was dying. Even the inner keep of his civilisation, the British Empire, was in danger. All were aware of the growth of rival industrial giants, notably Germany and the United States, but he himself feared the dynamic people of the Far East. In 1910, as if in sympathy, King Edward VII, the courteous old roué, himself died. Happening to meet one of the King's doctors while dining at Claridge's Hotel, Haggard was told that his patient had not realised how ill he was and had smoked a cigar on the day he died. Contrary to rumour, the King had not been distracted with worry over political problems 'because he was not that sort of person'; he died because his heart was 'worn out', having 'warmed both hands at the fire of life'.[37]

One of the battered rocks left by the receding Victorian and Edwardian tide was Haggard himself: famous, slightly shocking novelist; agricultural and social reformer; imperialist and man of opinions. It was not only upon his own particular subjects that his advice or support was sought. One such supplicant was Solomon Cohen, the secretary of the Young Men's Zionist Association in Liverpool, who saw a parallel between Haggard's aspirations and their own.

The object of the Zionist movement is to secure a publicly recognised and legally secure home for the Jewish People in Palestine [he wrote]. The withdrawal of large Jewish masses in course of time and by means of a well ordered emigration from the countries of persecution would prevent the excesses against the Jews which are, from time to time, committed to the horror of the civilised world.

Cohen reminded Haggard that he had written of his visit to Jerusalem and his first sight of the Wailing Wall, 'Why do they wail when a few of their financiers could buy up the country?' He continued,

Well, Sir, the financiers appear to be too busy making their fortunes ... Instead of wailing, Zionism is a call to the Jewish people for self-help, for *work* in the direction of their hopes and the upbuilding of national life. It is an appeal to the heroic spirit of the Jew and has already achieved the moral victory, of straightening the backs of the bent and infusing into the Jewish Youth the spirit of a great ideal to live for, and work for, amid the materialism of the age.[38]

Haggard himself might have written that and it stirred his blood, which was, of course, partly Jewish. There was an anti-Semitic miasma in English society, mostly of wariness against the foreign, the parvenu and those who lived by trade. He seems to have seen the Jews as an heroic race that had been dispossessed by being too clever and ambitious for their own good; his admiration for the early tribal leaders was reduced by his dislike of any modern man who made money by its manipulation; and he had paid little attention to their more recent history of persecution which had left them landless. Thus he liked to refer to his paternal grand-mother's family as Russian – since they had been living in Russia – rather than Jewish. Yet he was so stirred by Cohen's letter that he telegraphed his reply: 'YOUR MOVEMENT HAS MY HEARTY SYMPATHY. THE JEWS BELONG TO PALESTINE AND PALESTINE SHOULD BELONG TO THE JEWS. WHY DO NOT YOUR RICH MEN LEAD THEM FROM THEIR LANDS OF BONDAGE BACK TO THEIR APPOINTED HOME?'[39]

Sometimes his short-fused imagination took fire from the news of the day. The most ominous threat to Great Britain was coming from a vigorous and aggressive Germany and he looked over the North Sea from the windows of Kessingland Grange imagining German battleships on the horizon. Haggard did not see himself as alarmist but once his imagination had created a scenario, he liked to present it in practical, definite terms. So, in February, 1910, when he was invited to address a meeting at Loddon in support of the formation of a Norfolk branch of the Red Cross League, he chose to alarm his bucolic audience with a warning of impending invasion. During the next twenty years, he told them, there was a twenty to thirty per cent chance of an invasion of the British Isles being attempted and a six to eight per cent chance of it succeeding. 'I am not a scaremonger,'[40] he declared, but that, of course, made the danger seem even more real. Yet some of his prophecies in South Africa had been fulfilled and, pessimist that he was, he was aware of the gaping abyss awaiting all that he wished to protect.

CHAPTER TEN

'What we can imagine must be realisable'

On 22 June 1911, King George V was crowned in Westminster Abbey. It was Rider Haggard's fifty-fifth birthday and, conscious that this coincided with the beginning of a new and dangerous time, he jotted in his notebook, 'Coronation. What struck me among the elect at the Athenaeum. Not a word of poor Edward, whom we saw carried past a year ago. How much more so among the vulgar. Sic transit – quite natural and yet – after all that flood of gush.'[1]

At fifty-five, Haggard was now the self-confident man of affairs, able to talk of politics or economics with authority and of his fiction-writing as an amusing way of making money. Indeed he was able to write what he liked without worrying whether it might offend those who had once commanded his awe. This became apparent in a short novel he wrote called *The Mahatma and the Hare*, which affronted his rural friends.

Since his curious dream about the death of his dog and his consequent rejection of blood sports he had had another dream about a hare which spoke of the horror to which it had been subjected by sportsmen. In his fantasy, Haggard described the meeting between a hunted hare and a holy man, with the former explaining how it had been persecuted by 'a first-rate, all-round sportsman', who 'spent most of the year killing the lower animals such as me'. The climax came at the gates of heaven when a voice asked, 'Who has suffered most? Let that one first taste of peace!' and then commands, 'Draw near, thou hare!'[2]

The novella was a commercial failure for, as he said, it had

no great public vogue, largely this is because so many of the papers neglected it as though it were something improper. Their reason was, I think, that they feared to give offence to that great section of their readers who, directly or indirectly, are interested in sport ... our habit of killing other creatures for amusement.[3]

155

His increased confidence was reflected in his bearing and his nephew, Godfrey Haggard, was to describe him at this time:

> He was long and loose-limbed, with sparkling, rather piercing blue eyes, a big nose over a sensitive mouth and a small beard which had turned grey. His hair was untidy. He wore his tie knotted through a gold ring (which once had graced the hand of Pharaoh) and he avoided a crease to his trousers. His clothes rather hung than sat upon him; I think he had them made what is called 'easy fitting'. He looked like somebody and people, when I walked with him in London, turned round to stare at him.[4]

His vision had widened beyond the bounds of the Empire. Denmark had long intrigued him, both as his ancestral home and as an agricultural country where smallholders were reported to thrive. So, in the autumn of 1910 he had spent two months there with the nineteen-year-old Lilias and his sister-in-law Agnes. It was all that he had hoped and he wrote a book about his findings, *Rural Denmark*, published the following year, composed in a gentler, more reflective style than his readers had come to expect.

The Danes, he discovered, could not only produce all the crops and dairy products and most of the meat they themselves required but maintained a profitable export trade in farm produce. Lessons could be learned from Denmark, he urged, in the management of smallholdings, with freeholders joining cooperatives. Unlike tenant farmers, those with the security of freeholds or long leases would, he believed, show the enterprise to share storage, transport and expensive equipment. While presenting Danish agriculture as an example, he did not expect the British to emulate them.

> We might change [he wrote], if we wished. The will is lacking, not the way. Perhaps, after all, this feudal system of landlords who do not farm their estates but let them out to others is that which suits us best ... Were we to take another course, which would enable British farmers to adopt and grow rich on the Danish methods of ownership and cooperation ... that intelligent, industrious and charming people might lose their best, if not their only market.[5]

Such resigned pessimism was soothed by his own satisfaction in visiting what he believed to have been the original home of the Haggards. Their name had once been Gyldenstjerne, he had been told, but this was inherited only by the eldest son so that when their ancestor had emigrated to England in the fifteenth century to fight for King Henry V in France, he had taken the name of their Danish home, Aagaard. Their castle had been burned in a peasants' revolt and replaced by a manor house.

> It is an ancient place [Haggard wrote], on a wide, windswept plain. In the wood hard by, encircled by the remains of a double moat, lie the ruins of the old castle of the Gyldenstjernes ... The house is a quaint place built on three sides of a square and having long passages and low, old-fashioned rooms adorned with ancient furniture and brass sconces on the walls.[6]

It was for sale and Haggard had a wild impulse to buy it and return to his roots. On reflection he decided instead to write a novel about a Danish adventurer and began to weave the plot of The Wanderer's Necklace. 'I bade farewell,' he recorded sadly, 'to the ancient and historical manor of Aagaard, its tumuli and its battle-haunted plain, as I suppose for ever.'[7]

He sent a copy of Rural Denmark to Theodore Roosevelt, who since he had relinquished the Presidency had more time to read and to write letters.

> I do not wonder that you feel discouraged and blue at times [he wrote in reply]. It seems a hard and thankless task to hammer into your generation what is vital for them to learn. I half smiled when I read what you wrote, because I so often have the same feeling myself. As President, I tried, and I now continue to try, to teach lessons that I feel ought to be learned by my fellow-countrymen and often wonder how much I am accomplishing by it. Life is a campaign and at best we are merely under-officers or subalterns in it ... We must not be too cast down even if things look wrong because melancholy tends to make us less and not more efficient and buoyancy and good humour and the ability to enjoy life all help instead of hindering a reformer.[8]

Now that Roosevelt was no longer enthroned at the White House, Haggard regarded him as a friend with whom he could comfortably correspond. A patriot and imperialist after his own heart, Roosevelt had been determined to keep his country strong and, as he put it, 'to speak softly and carry a big stick'; he supported Britain and emulated her expansionism by acquiring the Panama Canal and the Philippines and had finally extinguished Spanish power in the Americas; he was wary of Germany and Japan and restricted non-European immigration to the

United States; at home he was both a 'trust-buster' and a strike-breaker; he had been likened to Oliver Cromwell and nicknamed 'Theodore Rex'.

When Roosevelt had first stepped down from the Presidency, he had spent several months in Africa where he met the explorer Frederick Selous, who was often said to have inspired the character of Allan Quatermain. He had visited both men in London the following year and told Haggard how much he admired his 'great work'. Reviewing his *Regeneration* in the New York *Outlook*, Roosevelt enlarged on his admiration:

> Rider Haggard is probably most widely known as a novelist but, as a matter of fact, there are few men now writing in English whose books on vital sociological questions are of such value as his and hardly one amongst this small number who has grasped, as he has grasped, the dangers that beset the future of the English-speaking people and the way these dangers can be met.[9]

The two men shared a practical imperialism, the American writing to the Englishman after his African tour:

> Selous was ... struck by exactly the same thing: the average man who goes to Africa, or goes out West here, or talks of 'progress', seems to be absolutely incapable of understanding what is and what is not of fundamental importance.
>
> In Nairobi, I met Government House travellers and London capitalists who spoke of developing the land and in whose eyes developments merely meant mines and railroads and methods of getting returns for capitalists who live in London; and, if they took up residence on the land, merely treated it as a temporary holiday; who were make-believe settlers, just as in the old days in the West, the average young Englishman came to ranch with the idea of having sport for a few years and then returning home with money, was merely a make-believe settler.[10]

The real settlers in Africa were, he thought, the Boers although he suggested that they should be kept out of Kenya, which should be reserved for the British.

Haggard replied with his usual plea for a return to the land and its social values. 'Doubtless the Golden Calf is the most popular of all gods ancient or modern and he does not build his shrines amongst woods and fields,' he wrote, and condemned 'insider dealing' in finance, adding,

Now in the conditions of a simple pastoral life, dishonesty, even if innate, could scarcely bring such rich rewards ... In most people, the love of Nature scarcely exists; it seems to be the privilege of the highly-educated. But ninety-eight out of a hundred love a gas-lamp.

He was deeply pessimistic about the future.

My opinion is that ... it will involve the practical destruction of the white peoples and that within a measurable time, say, two or three centuries ... Look at Australia. If there were no British Fleet, how long would it be before it received a considerable number of immigrants of the Mongol type?

I think to two alternative conclusions. The first alternative is that the Almighty has had enough of the white races and is bringing about their ruin through their own failings as in past days He brought about the ruin of Rome, purposing to fill their places from the East. The second alternative is that He is pointing out to them their only possible rejuvenation, their only salvation lies in the close settlement of the land which they neglect. Denmark has learned something of this lesson ... But the sporting owner and tenant farmers, both of which classes find things very well as they are, do not share my view and say so with vigour. The future will show which of us is right ... At least one has cried aloud in the wilderness.[11]

Roosevelt wrote back with equally enthusiastic pessimism, deploring the state of his own nation.

To me politics and ethics ought to be interchangeable, and my interest in the former chiefly arises from my interest in the latter. If the whole game is merely one of sound and fury, without any sincerity back of it ... then it is all of as little importance as a contest between the Blues and the Greens in the Byzantine circus.

I am, I hope and believe, a practical man and I abhor sentimentality; but I abhor at least as much the so-called practical man who uses the word 'practical' to indicate more materialistic baseness and who fails to see that while we, of course, must have a material and economic foundation for every successful civilisation, yet that fabric cannot be lasting unless a warp of lofty disinterestedness and power of community feeling is not shot through the roof of individualistic materialism ... [12]

His other close friend with whom he could exchange such resonant echoes, was, of course, Rudyard Kipling. He, too, received signed copies of Haggard's latest books and responded with comforting comments. They stayed at each other's houses, happily spending hours in the study, wrapped in the scent of wood smoke and swapping ideas for plots and musing on the meaning of life. They had much in common: both men were highly successful but subject to carping criticism; both were married to agreeable but unimaginative wives and had growing families – Haggard, three daughters; Kipling, a son, John (known as Jack), and a daughter, Elsie – and both had lost a child to illness.

> I asked K. if his work was ever discussed in his own family [Haggard recorded]. He said it was never mentioned, although he talked over things privately with his wife. His boy Jack said to him the other day on his going to school at Wellington: 'Thank heaven, father. I hope that there I shall hear no more of *Recessional*.' I said it was the same in my own circle. He told me that his children showed no signs of imagination and he was thankful for it. I said *ditto* – ditto.

The two men saw themselves sharing the summit of a private Mount Olympus in Norfolk, or Sussex, from which they could survey the lower slopes and distant peaks. Of one visit to Bateman's in September, 1911, Haggard pencilled in his notebook:

> We talked a gt. deal on many subjects, making plots for books, etc. He read me 2 of his plays and we discussed others specially one that wd. deal with the fall of the B. Empire. He remarked to me on what he called my remarkable power of 'sustained imagination', asking if anybody had made a study of it. I sd. to the best of my belief nobody had ever thought it worth while.
>
> Afterwards apropos of some passage I came across in a history of the Eastern Empire he said words to the effect that in decaying civilisation it was always the case that real gifts were ignored. They devoted themselves to the criticism of style and other details. They had no longer the mind to appreciate mind ... [13]

Such were happy, reassuring times but there were others of melancholy, Haggard feeling that he had completed his life's work and was unable to see any way forward, except in the invention of more fanciful novels. Such musings were brought up sharply at this time when the newly-installed telephone at Ditchingham House rang and a London news agency enquired whether it was true that Rider Haggard was dead.

Although still in the prime of life, he was shocked rather than amused by the mistake and made a sudden decision, which he wrote down:

> Like the storm that I hear raving outside the windows as I write, the elemental forces which are about every one of us will sweep me away as they brought me here and my place will know me no more. Before this event happens to me ... before I, too, ... put on the Purple and have my part in the majesty of Death, it had entered into my mind that I desire to set down, while I still have my full faculties, certain of my experiences of life.

He would write his memoirs and, as a start, he wrote the Introduction, but this only depressed him more. It seemed that he had failed to make a significant mark on his time. He felt he might have succeeded as a lawyer if he had not turned to writing fiction and he declared, 'If what I write should prevent even one young barrister, who hopes to make a mark in his profession, from being beguiled into the fatal paths of authorship, I shall not have laboured in vain.' Closer to the core of his own ambition, he mourned,

> I have never been able to gratify a very earnest ambition of my younger years, namely, to enter Parliament and shine as a statesmen ... So that dream had to be abandoned ...
>
> Thus it comes about that on these lines I have failed to make any mark. Fate has shut these doors in my face.

He conceded that he had been a success as a novelist:

> The issue is that though I feel myself more strongly drawn to other pursuits, such as administration, or politics, or even law, I have been called upon to earn the bread of myself and others out of a kind of by-product of my brain which chances to be saleable, namely, the writing of fiction ... Now, although it may seem much to claim, my belief is that some of my tales *will* live.

Even then he had doubts and clutched at a final straw, his writing about agriculture, perhaps unaware that that would soon be out of date. 'I trust, therefore,' he concluded, 'that should my novels be forgotten in the passage of years, *Rural England* and my other books on agriculture may still serve to keep my memory green.'[14]

With that, he set about writing his autobiography, beginning with the Gyldenstjernes of Aagaard and then the Haggards of Hertfordshire, describing his paternal grandmother as 'a Russian lady, the eldest daughter and co-heiress of James Meybohm of St Petersburg',[15] instead of the daughter of a German-Jewish family living in Russia. The narrative reflected his current melancholy and he was unable to summon up the delight and excitement he had often felt, while seeming to relish the description of the day he heard that Jock was dead. Not even religion – or the contemplation of alternative beliefs – could console him for that loss and he wrote despairingly in his pocket-book: 'We wander mid darkness and the shadow of death. Our successors may have light. The prophets and prophetesses of the early Church may once more appear. As at the beginning, man may come into actual communion with God. Why not? Why should revelation be a stationary thing?'[16] But the implication was that the answers he had sought so long were now unlikely to be revealed to him.

Then, just before Christmas, 1911, as he wrote his life story, which increasingly seemed like a narrative of failure, he received a letter from the Prime Minister. To his surprise, this announced that the King wished to confer a knighthood upon him. A few years before, a Cabinet minister had hinted that he might become eligible for a baronetcy, but he had declined on the grounds that 'baronetcies are for rich men, who have male heirs, not for persons like myself.' Now he accepted the honour, he wrote, not only 'on the ground that it is a mistake to refuse anything in this world' but that 'a title is useful in the public service and especially so abroad' as 'recognition ... for who does not appreciate recognition, particularly after long years of, I hope, disinterested toil?'[17] He was therefore gazetted a Knight Bachelor in the New Year's Honours of 1912. Kipling, who had himself twice refused knighthoods, wrote to congratulate him on his: 'You've done such good work for the State for so long that in this case the State truly honours itself in honouring you.'[18] Yet this was only a beginning. A fortnight later, a letter reached him from Lewis Harcourt, the Secretary of State for the Colonies.

> You are probably aware that at the Imperial Conference of last year it was decided to appoint a Royal Commission to visit the various Dominions and report upon them ... The inquiry will probably extend over three years ... Lord Inchcape is to be the Chairman and the Prime Minister and I are very anxious to try to induce you to be one of the British Commissioners.[19]

Again, there would be no remuneration; just the satisfaction of duty done.

The prestige would be considerable. There would be six Commissioners from the United Kingdom and one from each of the five Dominions. They would report on the current economic, political and social condition of Canada, Newfoundland, South Africa, Australia and New Zealand; their three tours of inspection each lasting several months. Sir Rider and Lady Haggard were gratified that his knighthood had been followed so speedily by an appointment which demonstrated that it had not simply been a graceful nod.

> It is rather remarkable for a writer of fiction to have attained a seat on such a Commission (though I says it as shouldn't) and shows that the Country must take me pretty seriously [he wrote to her]. Also it means that, whatever happens, one cannot be said to have quite *failed* in life. I hope you are pleased about it, dear. I am in a way as it is the end of a long struggle for serious recognition in which I was much hampered by this necessary novel-writing.[20]

His publisher, Charles Longman, gracefully congratulated him on both honours: 'I would rather have heard this than that they had given you a peerage. Anyone can be a peer but to be one of the six men chosen to represent the United Kingdom on a great Empire enquiry of this sort is a real honour.'[21]

The task of the Dominions Royal Commission was to report on the health of the British Empire and recommend any measures thought necessary to improve it, almost as though it was preparing itself for some great, unspecified ordeal. It was to concentrate on natural resources and their development, manufacturing and distribution, food production and trade. This would naturally expand into economics and politics, both domestic, imperial and international; the Empire would be looking at its own reflection through the eyes of the Royal Commissioners. These were, with one exception, to be distinguished industrialists, politicians or civil servants, and that exception, who was to catch the public imagination as he so often had before, Sir Rider Haggard, had only come to public affairs late in life. Now the creator of so many lost civilisations of fiction would concentrate on the reality of an empire, which he believed embodied the best in human endeavour but which also might be at the edge of an abyss which had swallowed up so many others.

There were two preliminary meetings in London, arranged by the

Commission's secretary, Edward Harding, a forceful young civil servant who had been seconded from the Colonial Office. The first of these was held in a conference room in Scotland House on the Embankment, where many of the Royal Commissions on Coast Erosion and Afforestation meetings had been held, and, characteristically, Haggard reflected that 'It was like rising from the dead into the midst of a new generation ... as I looked up to find fresh faces in the places of the old familiar ones that now were gone, two of them for ever.'[22]

Harding announced that their first tour, which would be to Australia and New Zealand, would not begin until early in 1913. So, to make the most of the interlude and to shake off his persistent bronchitis, Haggard decided to make another visit to Egypt, again taking his eldest daughter, Angela, with him. So, well-stocked with opium to relieve the bronchitis, oil of rosemary and citronella to ease mosquito bites and the customary letters of introduction, they set out.

Again it was to be a working holiday and, as well as making notes on the state of Egyptian agriculture, he jotted down ideas for stories: 'The priest Seti looks into the reflections in the water and says, "Behold God" ...'[23] In Cairo, he was particularly fascinated to be shown the mummy of the Pharaoh Meneptah, who was believed to have reigned at the time of the Exodus; 'It was a strange thing to look upon the tall form and the withered countenance of ... that majesty before whom, perhaps, Moses stood ... One day I hope to write a romance of the time.'[24] However, he noted that he had clearly not drowned in the Red Sea but had died in old age from hardening of the arteries. This time he decided not to travel up the Nile to Luxor but settled for nearly a month at the Mena House Hotel near the Pyramids at Ghiza from which they could make daily excursions. They saw temples half sunk in sand, where he posed for photographs in his dark suit and sun-hat, explored painted tombs by candlelight and inspected the most recent finds to arrive at the Cairo Museum. He enjoyed the comfort of the modern hotel with its cool, dim, mock-Moorish halls and high-ceilinged rooms. This, he felt, was particularly necessary for Angela, who, like most Europeans, was prone to minor stomach ailments and the heat, particularly after an excursion across the desert to Sakkara, where a British archaeologist lived near the excavations and his wife had made their house 'very pretty and English-looking', and up the Nile to Memphis. 'I was rather afraid that Angie might be overdoing it,' he wrote to his wife, 'and this morning she is somewhat upset in the tummie, which she attributes to something she has eaten.'[25]

In mid-April, they packed the small treasures they had bought from dragomen – including an alabaster fish and a necklace of crystal and green beads for his wife – and set out for home, travelling by sea to Naples and, after a few days there and in Rome, continuing by rail. Italy gave Haggard another opportunity to complain about rapacious foreigners and their lack of hygiene. Their particular misery was, he wrote to his wife, 'diarhea (I can't spell the blessed word) ... My own tummy is quite enough for me to understand and look after but when it comes to Angie's I'm undone!'[26]

It was a relief to return to the cool springtime of Ditchingham and its pleasant routines. First, there were books to be completed, notably two Allan Quatermain novels, *Marie* and *The Holy Flower*, which were, respectively, about the early conflict between Boers and Zulus and the search for an orchid sacred to an African tribe; and, of course, his autobiography. Then, while he was busily dictating these to Miss Hector, he heard that Andrew Lang had died. The shrewd, whimsical Scot had been a constant source of inspiration and amusement, teasing him when he took himself too seriously and once even collaborating with him on a novel, *The World's Desire*, which had been published in 1890. 'Dear, dear Andrew,' he wrote in his diary, 'how I wish you were here, how you would argue about what I have been writing and turn everything topsy turvy after your aggravating way ... But that quiet voice is still and that kind eye shines no more.'[27]

Grieved as he was, he now had an impetus of his own derived from public recognition and he forged ahead. He also drew comfort from his continuing correspondence with Theodore Roosevelt, who wrote soon after his return from Egypt, returning to the subjects of smallholdings and resettlement on the land, in which he was trying to interest the United States Government.

> I do not know when we will be able to succeed in the great movement for social and industrial reform [he wrote], but I do know that the alternative is a general smash-up of our civilisation – and, succeed or fail, I hold it to be the duty of every decent man to fight to avoid such a smash.[28]

Haggard replied with a long and fulsome letter in which he told Roosevelt that, although he was now styled *Sir* Rider Haggard, he hoped that he would henceforth 'call me simply by my surname as is our custom here'. He further sought to strengthen their friendship by writing, 'I take some credit to myself in that, although we have met but a few times in the flesh, I have yet been able to discern what kind of spirit is in you. I suppose the truth is that as deep calls to deep, like not only draws to, but understands, like.'

He, too, feared that the end of civilisation as he knew it was nigh and continued,

> I, too, hold that the civilized world wallows in a slough worse, perhaps, than the primeval mud of the savage; that it is possible (if not probable) that it may be dragged from that slough, cleansed and clothed in white garments: that it is the bounden duty of all high men to do their honest best to bring this about ...

His own conviction, he said, was that which 'comes home to certain of us with an added force when some of the cables that bind us here are slipped and our being begins to thrill beneath the pull of that tide which flows over the edge of the World'. Suggesting that Roosevelt himself might return to high office, he continued,

> You are confronted by a hideous problem. The other day, in a hair-dresser's shop, I took up one of our illustrated papers. In it was a reproduced photograph of a number of your New York women (members of the upper 400, I think they were named) feeding their lap-dogs, adorned with jewelled collars, off plates of gold. Elsewhere I have read and seen pictures of New York poor starving in the snows of winter. Here in brief is your problem and the problem of every civilized country on Earth. The glutted, foul, menacing cities, the gorgeous few, the countless miserables! And beyond, the empty Land, which could feed them all and give them health and happiness ...
>
> The problem then is this – the Poor *in* the Cities, and the answer should be the Poor *on* the Land, where they would cease to be poor. [He condemned the] bitter fruits [of urban living leading to] an ultimate dearth of Life ... A destruction: with a vision (for those who can see) of the East once more flowing in over the West and possessing it and lo! the toil and intellect of Ages gone. Such may be the will – the design of God ... Yet I think it is more probable that it is the cracked coin in which he will repay the wickedness, or the mad folly of Man. Cannot this torrent be stayed or turned? Here I see no hope of it: Yonder you may have a chance. Our existence as a race (I speak of all

white nations) seems to me to depend upon the answer. If this letter were published in the Press today, I am aware it would be mocked at. But if it could be read one short five hundred years hence I wonder if the readers would call me a fool or a prophet?

I hope this Sunday evening screed will not bore you.[29]

In such a doom-laden mood, he completed his memoirs in September, almost as if his life were at an end. 'And now, "I have spoken!" as the Zulus say', he concluded. 'Thus then, poor sinner though I am, trustfully as a wearied child that, at the coming of night, creeps to its mother's knee, do I commit my spirit to the comfort of those Everlasting Arms ... Farewell!'[30]

In a more positive frame of mind he turned his attention to the British Empire and his coming tour of inspection. Emigration from the British Isles had increased since the beginning of the century and was now running at between 200,000 and 300,000 a year. In the final decade of the nineteenth century, less than thirty per cent of emigrants had settled within the Empire, partly because of depressions in Canada and Australia, but now three-quarters were heading for the Dominions. Writing to one of his godsons, who was planning to make a career abroad, he advised, 'Personally, in no case would I go to any country over which the British flag does not fly', and he suggested Rhodesia, 'where farmers with small capital are welcomed and given land on special terms.'[31]

To Haggard, as to other imperialists, the Dominions with their vast, empty territories were distinct from the colonies, which usually offered both raw materials to be developed and indigenous people to be ruled and 'civilised' but were seldom thought suitable for European settlement. Whatever claims the North American Indians, African tribes, Australian aboriginals might have to land, there was space enough for all. So he saw the Dominions as enormous extensions of the British Isles to be populated by the same stock and creating similar institutions. The Royal Commission's eventual reports and recommendations would be an essential preliminary.

The first tour was to be of Australia and New Zealand and Haggard decided to combine the outward journey with a visit to his daughter Dorothy, or Dolly, and her husband Major Reginald Cheyne, who was serving with the Army in India. He would then travel to Ceylon, visiting Salvation Army missions in both countries, before joining the other Commissioners when their ship called at Colombo.

Before leaving, he paid another visit to Kipling at Bateman's, taking with him the proofs of his novel about Zulus, *Child of Storm*, which had taken him several years to write and revise. There by a wood fire in the dim, comfortable study overlooking Sussex fields, he read aloud long, dramatic passages until, as he said, 'my throat had given out'. Kipling was thrilled, telling him, 'I don't think you're wrong when you say it's the best thing you've done . . . It marches straight off from the first and holds like a drug.'[32] Glowing with this tribute – to be followed by the heartfelt farewell from his friend, 'I *am* glad you're seeing India, old man!'[33] – Haggard sailed for India at the end of November.

On the long passage in the liner *Arcadia*, he passed the increasingly warm days assembling his thoughts about religion with a view to writing an epilogue to his autobiography, which, before leaving London, he had deposited in the safe at the publisher Longman's office with instructions that it was not to be published, or even read, until after his death. He first pencilled a series of notes:

> The Beyond – the whole object of Life. The grt. estate awaiting us.
> The Intellect here most unsafe of guides.
> Faith not easy – acquired by effort. In its essence a gift . . .
> Prayer – the pull of the Unseen. Why no spirit – because invisible and indefinable. The *earthly* personality is invisible and indefinable!
> Imagination – what we can imagine must be realizable . . .
> I take a grander view of man than that he is a mere accident. Through all the winds and voices of the world, I hear the roaring of the looms of Fate . . .
> Our Lord Himself had to have faith. *He* perhaps did not *know* . . .
> What the spirit sows, the spirit surely reaps.[34]

These he expanded and polished in a long essay, *A Note on Religion*, which he finally wrote while the liner was lying in the heavy heat of Aden. In this, he rejected Roman Catholicism for 'its notorious intolerance and bigotry'[35] in the past and because some of its doctrines were not to be found in the New Testament. He expressed his admiration for the Salvation Army, while deploring its refusal to administer the Sacraments. He recoiled from Buddhism as 'a religion of Death, holding up cessation of mundane lives and ultimate extinction as the great reward of virtue . . . Christianity is a religion of Life . . . Who then can hesitate between the two? Who wishes to be absorbed into the awful peace of Nothingness?' Yet he hankered after the idea of reincarnation:

Compare the world to a great ball-room wherein a Puck-like Death acts as Master of Ceremonies. Here the highly-born, the gifted and the successful are welcomed with shouts of praise, while the plain, the poorly dressed, the halt, are trodden underfoot; here partners, chosen at hazard, often enough seem to be dancing to a different tune and step, till they are snatched asunder to meet no more; here, one by one, the revellers of all degrees are touched upon the shoulder by Puck-like Death, who calls the tune, and drop down, down into an impenetrable darkness, while others who knew them not are called to take their places. But if we admit that every one of these has lived before and danced in other rooms, and will live again and dance in other rooms, then meaning informs the meaningless. Then those casual meetings and swift farewells, those loves and hatings, are not of chance; then those partners are *not* chosen at hazard after all. Then the dancers, who in turn must swoon away beneath that awful, mocking touch, do not drop into darkness but into some new well of the water of Life.[36]

Such speculation seemed to strain even Haggard's imagination and credulity and he fell back upon the rock of Christianity; or, to be precise, the Church of England, which had shaped his family, his childhood and his subsequent attitudes. He shied away from spiritualism, while maintaining that it could offer some genuine, weird but dangerous, experience. So finally he returned to his mother's creed 'That all Love is immortal ... that Christianity is true, although I do not understand and have no right, as yet, to understand the origin of its mysteries.'[37]

Haggard travelled through India and Ceylon as a tourist. He admired the Taj Mahal more than he had the Alhambra and told a journalist, who interviewed him for *The Statesman* in Calcutta, that the mosques and palaces of Delhi and Agra were 'perfect creations ... the mind of man, as it were, at its highest ... through a perfect simplicity of grace'. Indeed, he declared, their builders 'had a gift, which is denied to us in the West, at any rate today'. In Benares, with a blithe disregard for the sensibilities of the newspaper's Indian readers, he said that he had marvelled at the brightly clothed crowds thronging the temples for benediction from 'a fantastic god, figured like nothing in heaven above, or earth beneath', driven by 'a faith, which we Westerners cannot imagine as anything that appeals either to our reason, or to a sense of helpful religion ... It seems to me sad that this great quality of faith, which is now in many instances fading from the horizon of the West, cannot be directed towards a worthier or a truer object.'[38]

In Ceylon he found himself even more of a celebrity than was usual because an effusive article about him in an English-language magazine had reported that, in London, 'His views on great political questions were eagerly sought by Statesmen and Divines and all those who came in contact with him did not fail to go away impressed by his magnetic personality and his breadth of view.'[39] While there he was painted by an expatriate English artist, seated on the knee of a large stone Buddha, his hat in his hand and his face thoughtful and on the back were written the lines:

> Some sun-smit Eastern stairway I will find
> About whose foot the warm blue water slips
> While a stone-carven god with changeless lips
> Stares unremembered from his ruined fane
> Forgotten now of all the joy and pain
> That once made prayer and proffered costly things.[40]

At Colombo, when the *Medina* – the ship carrying the rest of the Royal Commission to Australia – duly arrived, he began to draw his official allowance but, of course, no pay. Edward Harding, the secretary, was wary of Haggard as someone from a world beyond his own and wrote home after a few days at sea that, while he would suspend full judgement, his immediate impression was that 'he is of the temperament which has very ordinary Imperial ideas and thinks they are extraordinary. Perhaps that is the result of being a novelist with a really keen imagination.'[41]

'Australia is a fearful way off,' Haggard wrote from the ship to his Norfolk friend and neighbour William Carr* of Ditchingham Hall, as they sailed onward.

> You steam day after day over a positively empty sea. It's like travelling to the planet Mars – everything one knows seems to fade away behind – till at last one evening, hid in a red glow, Mars, or, rather, Australia, appears. It is a beautiful, a wonderful land and vast, vast. You could chuck Norfolk down anywhere and never find it again: it would be like a lost sixpence.[42]

The ship arrived at Fremantle on 13 February 1913, the day on which

---

* The rich and cultivated Carr family had moved to Ditchingham Hall from Yorkshire towards the end of the nineteenth century. They had invested wisely in the development of railways and William Carr's wife had inherited a fortune from the import of Marsala wine.

work began there on the Western Australian end of the new Trans-Continental Railway. In Perth there was a formal lunch and speeches before sailing for Adelaide, Tasmania and New Zealand; then returning to the south-eastern cities of Australia and a final spell in Melbourne, then the federal capital.

It was at Adelaide that Haggard quietly presented himself as the natural spokesman of the party. When newspaper reporters swarmed abroad, Harding grudgingly conceded that 'Haggard is used to them and, though he would disclaim it, obviously rather likes them.'[43] They, of course, were more interested in him as a famous novelist than as a Royal Commissioner, but he refused to be drawn and *The Age* of Melbourne was to report, 'The last thing Sir Rider Haggard desires to talk about, apparently, is his own work as a novel writer. Statistics of immigration, the state of the rural population of the United Kingdom, the resources of the Commonwealth, these and similar matters are at the forefront of his horizon.' Another report noted that, 'He does not look like a writer of fascinating romances and does not talk like one . . . '[44] He had, wrote one reporter, 'a pleasant manner and a strong face, mobile and full of expression but on occasion inscrutable, like a sphinx's. He wears his beard trimmed to a point and his sharp features denote an ever-active mind.'[45]

It was he, rather than his less sophisticated and more status-conscious companions, who gave the interviews, made the spontaneous speeches and presented an urbane presence to their hosts. He seemed more at home in concentrated enquiry than the others because this was akin to his research for *Rural England* and *Rural Denmark*. He noted both immediate impressions – for example, at Oodnadatta in South Australia the edge of the tin-roofed settlement was 'a sea of rusty tins and broken beer bottles – great marks of the white man's progress in all lands'[46] – and major statistical trends, such as the farming population of Western Australia having risen by fifty per cent and that of Victoria fallen by twelve and a half per cent since the beginning of the century. He noted that, despite Australia having 'land enough for everyone',[47] the numbers engaged in primary production had been falling throughout the same period. In committee, he proved himself efficient, leading the interviewing of thirteen witnesses over three days in Cairns, for example; filling notebooks with evidence whether at meetings, tramping over farms or through factories. He was continually amazed by the emptiness of the land.

The Northern Territory alone, I believe, is as big as most of Europe and very fertile, though hot [he wrote to William Carr], but there are in it only about 1,000 men and 100 women. The other day at a state luncheon given to us at Melbourne by the Federal Govt. with some of the prominent officials connected with that province I got a great laugh in the speech I made by saying that I had enjoyed the honour of lunching with *most* of the population of the Northern Territory. Of course there was, and meant to be, a sting in the tail of my little joke.[48]

But interviewed by a reporter from the Adelaide *Advertiser*, he was optimistic about the future of Australian agriculture. 'Where irrigation is possible, what cannot you grow with your climate?' he asked, adding that Queensland alone could produce far more than Ceylon. 'If you have enough men working the land, you can grow sufficient produce to supply half the world.' Manpower was the problem, he stressed, warming to his ideas for mass immigration.

My own idea is import families from the towns in England ... Bring them out and place them in settlements under the charge of some charitable institution such as the Salvation Army ... There would be a certain number of failures undoubtedly but you must consider the children that would be coming on. In a few years they would be useful members of the community.

Asked if he would be writing a book about Australia, he replied that as a Royal Commissioner he would write no more than an official Blue Book but that he might consider a novel with an Australian setting. The reporter was delighted, speculating,

Possibly Sir Rider's fertile brain will be able to imagine one of our dusky aborigines as a fearless Umslopogaas, perhaps the mirages of Central Australia will suggest a weird story like Ayesha, who was called She; maybe the snow-capped Kosciusko, where the Murray flows, like 'Sheba's Breasts' points the way to some fabulous hoard as inaccessible as the treasure in *King Solomon's Mines*.[49]

In New Zealand, he was diligent in studying agricultural methods, including the meat-processing plant which produced enough sausage skins each year to stretch twice round the the world. He was always ready with such fanciful but illuminating detail and allowed his own feelings for animals to obtrude into his notes as when, at one slaughterhouse, he wrote of the sheep standing, 'dumb before their murderer'.[50] Also in New Zealand, he found Maori dancing at a *Haka* festival 'novel and exciting' and was moved to lecture on 'The Virtues of Barbarism',[51] yet feared that 'the Maori race is doomed'[52] and would disappear within a century because of mixed marriages, imported diseases and drink.

When the tour of both countries ended late in May, Haggard had formed the opinions he would express in his report and in conversation. Broadly he approved of New Zealand as having a practical agricultural economy, although he worried about the Maoris. Australia, on the other hand, had depressed him and his daughter Lilias was to put his views succinctly:

> Rider was greatly interested in Australia, in this wide, new country with 'land enough for everybody' but without a past, or traditions and, in his opinion, too little imagination as regards its future. He feared for its sparse population because he considered they were improvident, pleasure-loving, undisciplined and blinded to the fact that the very low birth-rate and stringent immigration laws imperilled their existence ... He thought Australia's danger lay in lack of population, her recurring violent labour troubles and the growing tendency of the country families to drift into the cities. He did not think they realised that the whole safety of Australia was bound up with the safety of the Empire.[53]

Throughout the tour, his favourite description of the Empire had been, 'The great house with the empty rooms.'

The journey home was across the Pacific to San Francisco, across the United States by train and the Atlantic in the liner *Mauretania*. While living in luxury on board the great ship, where a single walk round the promenade deck covered a quarter of a mile, Haggard drafted his report and worked on a dramatised version of *Child of Storm*, which the actor Oscar Asche had persuaded him to adapt for the stage. On arrival in London he heard from his agent that the new film industry was showing interest in his books and several companies were anxious to bid for serial rights.

It was a new world that was evolving fast around him. The English Channel had been crossed by aeroplane; submarines were in service with the Fleet; stainless steel had been invented; assembly-line production was being pioneered by Henry Ford in the United States; vitamins and isotopes had been named; even in Norfolk lanes, a motor-car might force

Haggard's bicycle into the hedge. Otherwise, Ditchingham was much as it had always been in June: the orchids needed no furnaces to be stoked in their greenhouses and the grass grew thick and green around Jock's tombstone by the chancel door.

CHAPTER ELEVEN

'A dawn of blood'

THE YEAR 1914 began quietly. There were the customary tensions between the great industrial nations of Europe and unrest in the Balkans but the most violent occurrence in the British Isles was the slashing of the Velazquez painting of Venus in the National Gallery by a suffragette campaigning for women's franchise. At Ditchingham House, the Haggard family were preparing for more travel. The second tour of the Dominions Royal Commission was to be in South Africa and Sir Rider Haggard was looking forward to it keenly. It would be a final look over his shoulder before facing whatever else the year might bring.

The tour was due to begin in Cape Town at the end of February, so he decided to leave early in January with his wife and youngest daughter and spend a fortnight on Madeira, where they could join the liner carrying the other Commissioners. The Haggards tended to suffer from 'weak chests' and winter colds, so loved the soft, oceanic climate of Madeira. Indeed, so beguiled were they by the island that they talked of buying a house there for winter visits, much as the Kiplings had taken to staying at the Cape of Good Hope. So they awaited their ship amongst the camellias, magnolia and tulip trees and were sad when she finally anchored in the bay. Arriving on board, Haggard startled Harding by pointing out a large building on the mountainside, which, he said, had been built a few years before by the Germans, ostensibly as a sanatorium for consumptives but actually for use as barracks after they had invaded Madeira; a plan frustrated 'at the last moment' by the vigilance of the Foreign Office in London.

The Royal Commission's secretary was bewildered by Haggard, who was a constant source of eclectic and recondite scraps of information, or ideas, but who could also match any of the others in the grind of committee work. He was therefore intrigued to meet his wife and daughter and noted in his diary:

175

As to Lady Haggard, she improves greatly on acquaintance. She is stout and placid and what might be called an 'outdoor person', very practical and full of commonsense – just the reverse of Haggard ... Miss Haggard is a curious mixture of her Father and Mother – she has some of the placidity of the one and some of the nervousness of the other: the result is rather nondescript ... Anyhow, she is quite good fun.

However, it was his duty to keep the party happy and cohesive, having realised on the first tour that they were liable to bicker and be resentful of each other's status; particularly that of those the others called the 'belted knights'. So he wrote a jolly rhyme called *The Alphabet of the Dominions Royal Commission*, which included the lines, 'L is for the ladies, all five very taking' but also 'R is for Sir Rider's yarns, queerer and queerer.'

As they arrived off the Cape, Haggard leant on the ship's rail remembering the time nearly forty years past. 'I have passed from youth to age since then,' he wrote in his diary, 'but it was with pleasure mingled with a certain sadness that I saw the cloud-cap hanging like poured water down the kloofs and steep sides of Table Mountain ... Much has changed but the sunshine is still the same.' Ashore he found an almost unrecognisable city of modern, stone-built office-blocks and hotels, built in the British municipal style. The administration was an unaccustomed mixture of British and Boer with Louis Botha, who had led a Boer commando against the British at the turn of the century, now Prime Minister of the Union of South Africa.

The two men talked without rancour about the Anglo-Boer wars. Haggard warmed to Botha, noting, 'There is no "down on the Kaffir" about Botha; in every way he impresses me enormously.' Such was not his view of Sir Abe Bailey of the diamond-mining industry with whom he argued over the outcome of the Jameson Raid, which Bailey said was positive since it led to the Second Boer War and subsequent commercial success. When Haggard pointed out that the war had cost twenty thousand British lives, Bailey remarked, 'What matter? Lives are cheap.' Still angry at this Haggard wrote in his diary that night, 'Well, they have won the game' but, he added, 'Also out of this evil good has come, as there seems to be little doubt that the racial animosities are beginning to die down. So at least Botha and everyone else of weight to whom I have spoken declare with emphasis.'[1]

It was a delight to find his old friend Judge Kotzé alive and thriving at the Cape. 'Ah! Haggard, how young we were, the youngest Judge and the youngest Master of the Court who had ever held office under the Crown,' he said in greeting. 'You used to think that you had travelled a long way along the road – but you were only twenty-one and I just twenty-seven!'

After a fortnight of official entertaining, inspections and interviewing, some of the party travelled north by train, breaking their journey to Port Elizabeth to inspect an ostrich farm. The Haggards surprisingly chose to miss this, and they travelled there and to Durban by sea. On the road to Maritzburg, Haggard took his wife and daughter to Newcastle and to 'the last place on earth I ever expected to see again,' Hilldrop. Lilias watched her father closely and recorded,

> Rider wandered through all the rooms, so little changed that in the sitting-room he turned round to look at the spot where his pipe-rack used to hang upon the wall, almost expecting to see it there still. He glanced into the room where Jock was born more than thirty years ago, then turned quickly away and went out across the *stoep* into the garden, stretching out his hand to pick an orange ... He wandered along the sloping gardens ... to the place where they had made bricks. There lay some of the bricks ... Rider picked them up and turned them over in his hands, filled strangely enough with more emotion than he had felt all that day. 'Well, they are not bad bricks,' he said quietly.

Lilias noted that he had reverted to his pioneering ways, ignoring the bed-bugs which swarmed in the inn at Newcastle, not bothering to change his sweaty flannel shirt, smoking pungent Boer tobacco and riding the small, rough veldt ponies with ease and enjoyment. At Maritzburg, however, he became depressed as the ghosts he remembered as vigorous young men gathered, particularly those who had died on Majuba Hill. But not all were memories, for his old Zulu servant, Mazooku, who had once rescued him when lost in the bush, appeared and greeted him with, 'Chief of old! Father! Here am I returned to serve you.' This he did, remaining with Haggard as his servant for the rest of the tour.

Increasingly, as Haggard said, he felt like Rip Van Winkle, 'for few remember the defeats and tragedies of my generation in Africa'. As they passed the huge hump of Majuba, he mused, 'There poor Colley rests with all the others.' That night they reached the new capital of the Union of South Africa, Pretoria, to find the old town of wide, dusty streets, Dutch barns and ox-teams replaced by a modern city of grand Edwardian buildings of stone with porticoes and French pavilion roofs. They stayed at a new hotel facing the square where he had outspanned – unyoked –

their ox-drawn wagon thirty-six years before. 'The whole aspect of the place has utterly changed,' he remarked wistfully. 'Oh, I hate this grandeur – give me the Pretoria of the 'Seventies – Rip Van Winkle, Rip Van Winkle – alas, as well might I ask for my lost youth!'

He walked beneath tall gum trees, which he and Arthur Cochrane had planted, to 'The Palatial', the house they had shared, which had been given the name 'Jess's Cottage' from his early novel. It was now a boarding-house with a corrugated-iron roof instead of thatch and 'its pretty English furniture and engravings on the walls' all long gone. The garden was an overgrown tangle and there he wandered. 'I felt as one returned from the dead. I seemed to forget all the intervening years and grow young again ... I saw the sapling gums, the new-planted roses and gardenias – I went away with a sad heart – Oh, where are the friends of my youth?' One Boer contemporary he did meet – now a senior administrator – had watched him hoist the Union flag at the ceremonial annexation of the Transvaal, and told him, 'At that moment, I would gladly have shot you!'

While Louie and Lilias went sight-seeing in Zululand, he travelled to Rhodesia, which was said to be so suitable for settlers of modest means, and the recently discovered ruins of Zimbabwe. These were being shown to tourists as the original of Kôr and the abode of She; two hills had been named Sheba's Breasts after the mountains in *King Solomon's Mines* and a road after Allan Quatermain. In vain he protested,

> When I wrote *She*, I had only heard in the vaguest way of the Zimbabwe ruins ... Those early romances were entirely the product of my imagination. As to these ruins, who was this skilled and mighty race who built those huge walls of sloping granite stones, chains of forts and vast stronghold temples? People of Semitic race, possibly of Phoenician blood. Business took them to South Africa, where they were not native, and business kept them there ... They vanished, that is all; probably the subject tribes, having learned their wisdom, rose up and massacred them to the last man ... The place has a very strange atmosphere, almost uncanny indeed.

Haggard paid his respects at the grave of Cecil Rhodes before returning to Durban to see his wife and daughter before they sailed for home. Then he, accompanied by the faithful Mazooku, headed for Zululand. It was thrilling to tread again the grassland trampled by the running legions of the tribe he had called the Romans of Africa. Much had changed here, too. Even the residence built for his friend, Sir Melmoth Osborn, after Haggard's own last visit to the country, now looked old. But he delighted to hear the Zulu language and their speech, which suggested that of the ancient world. He visited the site of Dingaan's kraal where the Boer emissaries had been murdered seventy years before and saw their bones lying scattered among the remains of cairns that once had covered them.

On the battlefield of Isandhlwana he walked beneath the great crag where the British had died, and picked up cartridge cases and a broken cricket stump and ball. He stood by the cairns that covered

all that is left of so many whom I once knew; Durnford and Pulleine and many other officers of the 24th, George Shepstone and the rest ... The swift tropical night was falling, the stark mount had become very black and solemn, a trembling star had vanished and of the falling crescent of the young moon but one horn appeared over the hill. It looked like a plume of faint unearthly fire burning upon Isandhlwana's rocky brow. A quiet place for man's eternal sleep – but the scene that went before that sleep!

Finally, on the battlefield of Ulundi he met an old Zulu who had taken part in the final, forlorn charge of the impis against the British Gatling guns.

Haggard was accompanied by three Englishmen who also admired the Zulus and whose company he found refreshing after that of so many newcomers to South Africa.

To ninety-nine out of a hundred a native is just a native [he wrote in his diary]. A person from whom land may be filched upon one pretext or another, or labour and taxes extracted, and who, if he resists the process, or makes himself a nuisance, must be suppressed. 'Make haste, boy – bring my horse – go hoe my corn – pay your taxes in malt or meal – or, see, here are whips and rifles.' It is the dominant note of that tune to which white men have made them dance. Fortunately not all men think thus.

He was amongst those who thought otherwise and when he finally parted with Mazooku on their return to Maritzburg, the emotion was mutual and Haggard made sure that he had provided his old servant with money and a new home 'away from the white man'.

He had seen a newly leaderless, demoralised, almost detribalised, Zulu nation. Amongst the young he found a desire for education and opportunity but they were mocked by their elders who had fought for Cetewayo, one telling Haggard, 'Our children would be white but white they never will be.' Dismayed, Haggard determined to take action. So on his return to Durban, during a short visit to East Africa and on the voyage back to England, he began writing another report. In addition to the survey of the South African economy, he drafted an impassioned plea for the Zulus, which he delivered to the Colonial Secretary on his arrival in London.

The Zulu peoples are crushed and bewildered [he began]. They were defeated in war and, like a nation of warriors, accepted the issue with resignation, hoping and believing that they would be taken over and nursed by their victor, the Queen and her successors ... Instead of this ... the Boers and others were allowed to rob them of their hereditary lands.

It is, I am sure, a great mistake to suppose that the native does not feel, or forgets harsh treatment. On the contrary, I believe that at the bottom of that secret mind of his, which so few of alien race have the imagination and the sympathy to understand at all, he feels a great deal. Also his memory is very long ... The reign of chiefs is finished, the pageant, the spoils and the pomp of battle have gone with it into the limbo of the past ... The son of him who slew our soldiers by the fatal mound of Isandhlwana, or rushed through a storm of bullets until he fell pierced on Ulundi's plain, often the man himself, walks along the hills and valleys of Zululand with greasy trousers for his kilted uniform, holding a tattered parasol in the hand that once grasped the shield or stabbing spear ...

I think that, even now at the eleventh hour, much might be done to give these people something to replace all that they have lost ... In the case of the Zulus, civilisation has one of its great opportunities, for certainly in them is a spirit which can be led to higher things ... If so, it seems to me, that we shall incur a heavy responsibility towards a bewildered people that we have broken and never tried to mend, and suffer evils to arise of which the effects will not be endured by them alone.[2]

This report, Haggard was gratified to hear, was later printed for circulation in Whitehall.

This time, the interval between the Royal Commission's tours was to be brief, so Haggard had little time to do more than enjoy a short summer holiday at Ditchingham, made more agreeable as the Kiplings, to whom he had lent Kessingland Grange, were only fifteen miles away and he found they shared his delight in its theatrical maritime character, describing their stay as like living on board ship. In London on 1 July, he attended a meeting of the Royal Commission on Imperial Communications, to which he had also been appointed. At this, he asked the manager of the Marconi Company whether they could look forward to a time 'when a subscriber can have a telephone in his house by which he can telephone all over the world?'[3] and the witness replied that he would not like to go as far as that in his claims.

It was a glorious summer but the European tensions, to which all had become accustomed, had suddenly been heightened at the end of June by the assassination of the heir to the throne of the Austro-Hungarian Empire, the Archduke Ferdinand, and his wife in Sarajevo by a Bosnian revolutionary. For the Dominions Royal Commission there were more pressing matters for attention, for it was time to pack for their next tour, which was to be of Newfoundland and Canada. They sailed from Liverpool on 17 July and, after a difficult crossing through fog in which they could feel the chill of invisible icebergs, arrived at St John's, Newfoundland, on the 25th. There they found Government House rife with reports of a crisis in Europe, arising from the assassinations. Haggard wrote in his diary on that day, 'At dinner I sat next to Sir Walter Davidson, the Governor, an able, forceful man. He told me that ... somewhat serious trouble had arisen between Austria and Servia (*sic*), which looked as though it might cause European complications.'[4]

On 28 July, Austria-Hungary declared war on Serbia and the Governor's young aide-de-camp was excited over the possibility of a European war and his own prospects of active service. 'Today we heard that there is a grave peril of a European war, news which racks us all with anxiety,' Haggard noted next day. 'It is strange how suddenly clouds spring up in what seemed to be a spotless international sky. Poor England – without an adequate army! I am *very* anxious and wonder whether Armageddon has come at last.'[5]

The tour began, crossing the desolate landscape of Newfoundland: 'Rocky lands ... whereon grow clovers, scrub and grasses ... not a house nor a soul to be seen ... a barren, unpeopled land ... bordered far away by low mountains. Still it has a beauty of its own ... So is the solitude after its own fashion,' wrote Haggard in his diary. He visited the sawmills which provided the London *Daily Mail* with wood pulp and Lord Northcliffe's 'palatial abode ... full of old English furniture and engravings', which he had only visited once or twice. On 1 August, Germany declared war on Russia and next day Haggard, made restless by prolonged entertaining for which he had no stomach, recorded, 'All day long I have been tormented by the war news, or rather the lack of any accurate news. I find the suspense terrible and most depressing and am in no mood to listen to bands playing on the lake in the wet.'[6] They watched the mining of iron ore in Newfoundland, then crossed to Nova Scotia to see its smelting for steel. Meanwhile, on 3 August, Germany invaded Belgium and declared war on France.

On 4 August they were in the Canadian wilds and tried to enjoy a walk in the woods before taking the night train to Halifax, where, next morning, Haggard wrote,

> We learned that England had declared war against Germany on the ground of the violation of the neutrality of Belgium by that Power. It is terrible and of this business none can foresee the end. For years some of us have known that such a war must come ... but always one hoped vaguely that it would not be in our day ... Now the thing is on us in all its horror and, ready or unready, we must fight – and win, or go under! God save England![7]

Then he added, 'It is very hard to sit here taking evidence on canned lobsters ... when the Judgement Day of nations has dawned upon the world.'[8]

Desperate to take some action he sent a telegram to 'my belongings at home,'[9] telling them to look after themselves, although he did not doubt that they would, and another to the publisher, Longman, suggesting that he be commissioned to write a history of the war. Then, on the 7th, they heard 'apparently on the best authority (an officer from the local War Office tells me that the despatch arrived in the Admiralty cipher and was also wired on by the Governor of Newfoundland) of the utter defeat of the German fleet in the North Sea'. Seventeen enemy ships were said to have been sunk and nineteen captured while the British flagship, the *Iron Duke*, had been lost and Admiral Jellicoe, the Commander-in-Chief, killed. 'Thanks be to God!'[10] declared Haggard, only to hear next day that the report was wholly untrue. But it had stirred his criticism of the lack of any warlike mood in Canada and, in particular, their reluctance to take any practical steps in maritime defence.

At St John in Newfoundland, on the following day, a cable arrived from the Colonial Office in London, ordering the Royal Commission to complete its tour of the maritime provinces and return home; the over-wrought Commissioners immediately disagreed, some demanding to continue across Canada. While there, they were entertained to dinner at the Union Club, where their hosts were clearly offended by their refusal to make speeches. After the formal toasts, muttering began and then, as Haggard noted, 'from all round the room there arose a veritable storm of cries of, "Haggard! Rider Haggard!"' Eventually the chairman motioned to him to rise and then, as he wrote in his diary, he

> spoke for 3 or 4 minutes only 'but with my heart', as the Zulus say, indeed everything that had been simmering in my mind for days seemed to rush to my lips, the difficulty being to know what thoughts to choose and in what words to clothe them. The effect of my utter-ance, totally unprepared and bad enough though it was, can only be described as startling.[11]

A Canadian journalist, who was present, reported, 'Sir Rider Haggard was deadly pale and seemed nervous and highly strung and he spoke with a kind of repressed fervour that made the effect strange in the extreme.'[12] He had said,

> I doubt if those present, indeed if those in this country, realise the state and appreciate the peril in which this Empire stands tonight. I believe that few of them really understand. Do the men and women in your great country of Canada, whom I notice laughing and talking daily in the streets, understand that the Empire is at grips for life and death? I know that Canada is glad to give her aid and I know that England is glad to accept your help, but do you all understand that *you* are England? Do you understand that if we fall, you fall? Do you under-stand that if Germany and her allies become masters of England, they become masters of the world; and that in two or three years time there will be no British Empire? ... The Angel of Death appears in a dawn of blood; the Armageddon, which has so long been foretold, has at length fallen upon us ... [13]

When he stopped speaking, the journalist continued, 'there was a silence in which a pin could be heard dropping,'[14] and, as Haggard himself put it, 'when I sat down it was in the midst of a dead silence, during which men – all leaders of thought in the city – looked at each other.'[15] One listener who was not impressed was Edward Harding, who wrote to his mother, 'Haggard distinguished himself by making a speech which some people think the extreme of pessimism, and others a "trumpet-call" ... I think the speech in the very worst of taste. But Haggard prides himself on his diplomacy!'[16]

He himself declared that it had had 'a great effect throughout Canada and did not a little to arouse its population to a sense of the terrible realities with which they are confronted'. Confident that he had spoken 'at the right moment',[17] Haggard's sense of the dramatic enhanced the news that same night that a nearby grain elevator had caught fire and been destroyed; he noted that it had contained wheat bound for England and that therefore it must have been the work of German agents. Next day, gratifyingly, 'stout ladies rushed at me with autograph books and strangers, appearing from round corners, silently shook my hand – testimony to the effect of last night's speech.'[18]

The curtailed tour ended with a voyage up the St John River to Fredericton, by which all were charmed but where the licensing laws infuriated Haggard, who declared 'total abstinence seems to produce a certain flatness and tameness of mind and to tend to a strange lack of imagination ... For the most part water-drinkers are dull dogs.'[19] From thence they travelled to Prince Edward Island, where they continued taking evidence, now on oysters, lobsters and arable farming. Then it was by ferry and night train to Quebec, where they stayed at the grand new Hotel Chateau Frontenac to await a ship for England. 'So ends our Canadian trip, or as much of it as we can do,' Haggard recorded. 'What with ... dissensions, anxieties and uncertainties, I consider that it has been a failure.'[20]

The Atlantic crossing was to be made in the liner *Virginian*. Haggard noted that to reduce her visibility at sea, brown paper was being pasted over windows and scuttles and the funnel painted black as there was fear of German commerce-raiders, said to be waiting on the shipping routes west of Ireland. They sailed on 21 August and, as they reached the supposed danger-zone, steaming through fog, which was welcomed as a protection from the enemy, Haggard noted, 'It has been a strange voyage, rushing through ice and reek in this dumb and shrouded ship.' The captain, who had been so reassuring about the advantages of fog, now added that

the whole position as regarded German cruisers was quite uncertain. No one seemed to know where they were. Also he remarked that there is such a thing as fog in which they might slip out of the Kiel Canal and work havoc … If met with, there was but one thing to expect, namely to be sent to the bottom.

At night the ship was darkened while 'dodging about on an unusual northern course' and 'black as a tomb and not a sound to be heard … Thank heaven we have met no cruiser; if we had I do not think I should be writing this.'[21]

All was forgotten when the liner steamed up the Mersey and Haggard arrived in London in time to hear of a real naval action off Heligoland, in which a German cruiser had been sunk; then on to Ditchingham where he found a dreamlike unreality with 'all well and the harvest up'.[22] A meeting with the Colonial Secretary recalled him to London immediately and took him to the edge of realities. Harcourt told him that the Dominions Royal Commission must go into 'a state of suspended animation' and that no report need be written until after the war, which he expected to last two or three years. Meanwhile Haggard and his fellow Commissioners could study ways for Britain to usurp German trade. Finally, he denied the persistent rumours of Russian troops passing through England (with snow still on their boots, it was said) en route for France, which he said had been caused by the arrival of Gaelic-speaking Scottish regiments.

Visiting his former publisher Charles Longman in the vain hope of the commission to write a history of the war, a task which had spurred him to keep a fuller and more self-conscious diary, Haggard found him depressed and worried about his son serving in France. Haggard said that he, too, was worried about his nephew Mark – Bazett's son – who was an officer in the Welch Regiment with the British Expeditionary Force. He saw Oscar Asche and tried to persuade him to postpone his production of *Mameena* – the stage version of *Child of Storm* – as inappropriate to the times, but failed and rehearsals began. The newspapers were full of reports of German atrocities in Belgium and Haggard suggested to the Colonial Secretary that another Royal Commission should be convened to enquire into them; Harcourt raised this idea with the Cabinet but it was dismissed as unnecessary.

Back in Norfolk, he found the countryside full of soldiers. The Cheshire Regiment and some gunners had been sent to bivouac at Ditchingham without tents or even blankets and found the misty September nights so cold that they had to walk the lanes to keep warm. He himself was invited to address a recruiting rally at Bungay and did so with thundering rhetoric, later having ten thousand copies of his speech printed and distributed under the title *A Call to Arms*.

Then one Saturday evening he wrote in his diary,

> I have just heard over the telephone from my daughter Angie that her brother-in-law, my nephew Mark Haggard, 'died of wounds' ... All honour to him who has died the best and greatest of deaths ... I write this at the dining table where so often he has sat and almost it seems to me that he answers my toast to him from that Valhalla whither he has passed.[23]

Major Haggard had been fatally wounded leading a patrol which had attacked a German gun position, himself first killing three of the gunners. It was the sort of end that Haggard accorded his Viking or Zulu heroes.

Daily news of the fighting in France – the retreat from Mons, the Battle of the Marne and finally the stabilising of the front in the trench systems – appalled Haggard, who thought the British people were 'too much occupied with party politics, football, cranks and the works of the late Oscar Wilde'[24] to appreciate their danger. In Norfolk, he wrote:

> The bulk of the population do not seem at all to understand the seriousness of the crisis ... Numbers of the elder women, being better off than formerly, are drinking a great deal, while the younger ones rejoice whole-heartedly at the presence of so many soldiers in their midst ... No stranger from another planet would guess that there was a life and death war in progress, though he might suspect autumn manoeuvres. For instance, as I write the guns of the partridge-shooters are popping merrily in the fields.[25]

Despite his oratory at Bungay, recruiting had slackened: 'The keen ones have joined and the others do not wish to join. Also the *women* are the great obstacle. Hundreds of them refuse to allow their sons to go. In that class of life, women as a body seem to lack patriotic spirit, which is a great argument against giving them the vote.'[26] There was no risk of that happening in his own household for he became tireless in repeating the latest rumours, particularly of atrocities, while convinced that the truth about the war was being kept out of the newspapers by censorship.

He was as depressed by the mood in the capital.

> It is a curious place just now [he wrote in his diary]. The light is about as bright only as that which I remember as a boy when the gas lamps were few and burned dully and electric lamps were unknown. This is

to avoid Zeppelins ... Consequently, the town looks melancholy and so are its inhabitants ... There is gloom in the air. Everybody reads more and more papers and yet more papers with the same news dished up again and again and nothing else. Business is shocking ... All of which means that the war is beginning to come home. Well may it do so with searchlights stabbing the skies and a dim something floating aloft, which I took to be a guardian airship (perhaps it was nothing but a cloud with the moon behind it).[27]

Haggard's own depression was partly induced by the sense of futility surrounding the winding up of the Royal Dominions Commission and all that he had hoped it might have achieved in setting the British Empire on the foundations for growth.

We are engaged in holding a quarter of the Earth with a white population considerably less, all told, than that of the German Empire alone, say, 60,000,000 of whom 40,000,000 live in these islands, against, say, 80,000,000 Germans [he wrote]. 'Let us suppose that Germany is beaten and out of action for a generation or so, which is as much as we can hope for. Would not Russia remain and is it conceivable that in time to come we might find ourselves face to face with Russia with her 250,000,000?[28]

He was convinced that in the short term there had to be conscription of all able-bodied men and then, if the Empire survived, the population of its Dominions had to be increased with Anglo-Saxon stock.

Even so there was an income to be earned, which meant fiction to write. His novels were not in such demand as they had been and since he parted from Longman in 1911 his agent sold them where he could, notably to Cassell and Hutchinson but also to lesser publishers. That autumn, he completed *The Ivory Child*, a sequel to *The Holy Flower*, telling the story of Allan Quatermain's rescue of the beautiful Lady Ragnall, who had been abducted by an Egyptian sect because of her likeness to the goddess Isis. He then began planning a sequel, *The Ancient Allan*, in which Quatermain joined the lady in reverse reincarnation with the aid of a hallucinatory drug taken in her private museum, like that at Didlington Hall. In London, he attended the opening of *Mameena* and, although he still felt that it should not have been performed in wartime, enjoyed it and the critics were generous for it was the same escapist entertainment as in his novels. Oscar Asche himself was to write:

London had never before seen what appeared to be real Zulus in all their war rig-out. At the end of the wedding dance, in which over eighty dancers sang and danced till the curtain fell – and then was raised time after time – even the jaded first-nighters got up on their feet and sang the tune and stamped their feet in rhyme.[29]

Then it was out into the darkened streets: 'London grows gloomier and gloomier at night. It is now so black that at times, especially in rain, it is difficult to find one's way about.'[30] Haggard was apprehensive of air attack.

> The 20 miles of Channel is no longer a complete protection to us. Soon there will be guns that can shell across it ... Dreadnought submarines and frightful air vessels which can make a mock of space with many other as yet undreamed of developments of war ... This war lacks the grandeur and picturesqueness of old time.[31]

He hankered after the wars of his imagining:

> There are no great battles, only one large hideous slaughter in the trenches. In the same way, where now is the majesty of Nelson's battles on the sea? In their places we have mines and sneaking submarines ... Yet, as of old, great deeds are being done ... It is only the visual grandeur of the thing that has gone.[32]

On 7 November he attended the final meeting of the Royal Dominions Commission. They signed their report on Newfoundland, then adjourned to the Cheshire Cheese tavern in Fleet Street for lunch of lark pie and toasted cheese. Convinced that he would be called to further duty by the Government, Haggard took a flat in London within walking distance of Whitehall. But the year ended without such a call and his depression increased. After writing to *The Times*, urging the appointment of a Minister for Food, he had hopes of some appointment in that connection and applied to the Minister of Agriculture, who replied, as he recorded, that he found it 'impossible to make use of my services in any capacity'. A plea to his acquaintance Lord Curzon, the former Viceroy of India, brought the reply that 'he will bear me in mind ... "since you are just the man who ought to be employed at such a time".' But, added Haggard, 'I don't suppose he will hear of anything.'[33]

Perhaps his task was to inspire the young men to fight? In his diary, he mused,

> How often have I been violently attacked for writing stories that deal

with fighting rather than with sexual complications ... I am not in the least ashamed for trying to inculcate in the mind of youth the ancient and elementary facts that their hands were given to them to defend their head – also their King and Country.[34]

Again he wrote:

In some ways I think the war is doing good in England. It is bringing the people face to face with elementary facts ... How often have I been vituperated by rose-water critics because I have written of fighting ... 'Coarse! bloody! brutal! uncivilised!' such has been the talk. Well, and today have I done any harm by inoculating a certain number of the thousands who are at the front with these primary facts, even though my work has been held to be so infinitely inferior to that of Oscar Wilde, Bernard Shaw and others?[35]

Much fiction of the time – particularly that for boys – dealt with heroism but little matched Haggard's bloodthirsty descriptions. He himself had never actually had to fight, although he had been on the fringe of the Zulu War and the First Boer War and, like all travellers on the frontiers of the Empire, had been exposed to risk. But the sort of feat with which he credited his fictitious heroes sprang from a hyper-active imagination and, perhaps a twinge of guilt that he had not been with his friends at Isandhlwana, or Majuba.

Now aged fifty-eight, he burned with revenge for real or alleged German atrocities; listening to the latest rumours in a London club until, sated, protesting, 'They are no good sauce for mutton cutlets.'[36] At the beginning of 1915 there was some relief in being invited to become chairman of the Belgian Agricultural Restoration Committee, although this was of little importance and was soon absorbed by another. That did not, of course, assuage his longing for action so he bought a Lee-Metford rifle and joined the Bungay Volunteer Defence Corps with which he occasionally drilled, when he could laugh at himself – 'The spectacle was distinctly funny ... a lot of determined old gents stumping about and doing their best to execute manoeuvres which they did not understand'[37] – but he did become a platoon commander.

This was not, as he recognised, a serious contribution to the war effort and he felt old and unwanted. Even drilling on the village green had to stop when he went down with influenza and, for convalescence, stayed at St Leonard's, a fashionable resort on the Sussex coast. It was mild and soothing but the sight of other elderly gentlemen – such as he classed himself – being pushed along the esplanade in wheeled, wickerwork Bath chairs deepened his depression and he wrote, 'It would appear that men like myself who have lifelong experience and accumulated knowledge are of no value to the country ... Or perhaps it is right and nobody is of value now save those who can shoulder a rifle or wield a hammer. Yet foolishly enough, perhaps, I feel sore.'[38]

Kipling's home at Burwash was within reach for a day's visit and he was of some comfort, although he, too, was aghast at the casualty lists: one of seven hundred and twenty-four officers killed in the fighting at the beginning of 1915 prompting his exclamation, 'Heaven save us from more such victories!' Haggard noted that

> he is greyer than I am now and, he says, his stomach has shrunk, making him seem smaller. I expect that anxiety about the war is responsible. Their boy John, who is not yet 18, is an officer in the Irish Guards and one can see that they are terrified lest he should be sent to the front and killed as has happened to nearly all the young men they knew.[39]

Charles Longman's son had been killed, just as his father has expected; his son-in-law, Reggie Cheyne, had also been wounded. 'Old, gentle-born families like our own bear a large share in the national defence,' he wrote in his diary. 'Would that I were not too old to take my share!'[40]

In contrast, Kipling, worried as he was about the prospects of his only son, was surprisingly optimistic about the war, considering a campaign of attrition by trench warfare against Germany was practical and that the landings at Gallipoli of that April – during which Haggard's nephew Geoffrey, had been taken prisoner when his submarine was sunk – might well succeed. But in East Anglia, to which the Haggards returned in the summer, the war was coming closer: German warships had already bombarded the coast and now Zeppelins were dropping bombs and, in August, an air attack on Lowestoft was so heavy that windows rattled and clocks stopped at Ditchingham. This seemed to strengthen rumour of an impending invasion of East Anglia, beginning with a landing at Harwich. Credence was also given to the stories of German atrocities when a nurse from Norfolk, Edith Cavell, who had been working in Brussels, was executed by the Germans for helping British soldiers to escape.

Then, on 7 October, Haggard entered in his diary:

Poor John Kipling, R.K.'s son, whom I have known from a child, wounded and missing but there is still hope that he may be a prisoner as he was not severely hurt when last seen. Poor Kipling, I know how great have been his anxieties about this boy ever since he entered the Irish Guards about a year ago; now they must be terrible.

Conflicting reports followed and then, shortly before Christmas, he met Kipling in London and recorded, 'He has heard nothing of John and evidently has practically lost hope. He says from all accounts that he can gather that the boy made a good end in his first action, that he liked his men and was liked by them. Poor lad! He added that he was very fond of me ... '[41]. Haggard took it upon himself to make enquiries about the young man's fate and managed to find a Guardsman Bowe, who had been with John Kipling in the battle near Loos and himself wounded, and he asked him to lunch. Bowe, a shy, nervous youth, had, when questioned, first replied, 'As far as I knew he had been blown to pieces. I saw Mr Kipling about 40 yards away from me before we went into the wood. A shell dropped near him and when the smoke cleared away in about half a minute there was no sign of him ... He was leading his platoon when he disappeared.'[42] It was also possible that he had been buried by the shell. Later Bowe remembered that he probably *had* seen Kipling again after all and Haggard wrote in his diary:

> Bowe now says that as they left this wood he saw an officer, who *he could swear* was Mr Kipling, leaving the wood on his way to the rear and trying to fasten a field dressing round his mouth which was badly shattered by a piece of shell. Bowe would have helped him but for the fact that the officer was crying with the pain of the wound and he did not want to humiliate him by offering assistance.
>
> I shall not send this on to R.K.[Haggard added]; it is too painful but, I fear, true. Still it makes J.K.'s disappearance still more of a mystery. A shell must have buried him, I think.[43]

The second account would have been particularly agonising for the Kiplings. They had been told by another, who had been with their son at the time, that when last seen he had been smiling.

John Kipling's body was not found* and eventually his father and his friend could discuss another experience they had in common: the loss of

---

* He was finally identified in 1992 as already lying in a Commonwealth War Graves Commission cemetery under a headstone bearing the epitaph composed by his father for the unidentified dead, Known Unto God', and this was replaced by his name.

an only son. Kipling asked how much older Haggard was than himself and when told ten years, remarked, 'Then you have the less time left in which to suffer.'[44] Later, the latter wrote:

> Poor old boy, John's death has hit him very hard. He said today that I was lucky to have lost my son early, when I still had youth to help me bear up against the shock and time in which to recover from it, at any rate to some extent (which I never have done really). 'If he had lived to see this war,' he added, 'he would now have been dead or mutilated, perhaps leaving a family behind him.' Maybe he is right.[45]

The two men discussed the possibility of life after death and the alternative of extinction. Haggard asked whether Kipling could 'contemplate without dismay separation eternal from all he loved – John, for instance. He replied that he was never happier than when he knew that, as a child, his boy was asleep in the next room.' It was almost the same image that Haggard, when considering such possibilities, had applied to the boy lying outside the chancel door at Ditchingham.[46]

CHAPTER TWELVE

'A job of great and imperial importance'

'THIS IS XMAS EVE,' wrote Haggard in his diary, 'and reflecting on all that has happened since last Xmas, I have come to the conclusion that had I been an agnostic at Xmas, 1914, I would have come to believe in God by Xmas, 1915.' This was not because of surviving in the war itself – despite the disaster of Gallipoli and the bloody stalemate on the Western Front – but because, he explained,

> nothing short of the goodness and protection of God could, in my opinion, have preserved this country during the last 12 months from reaping the fruits of ruin from the seeds that it has been busy sowing for over a generation.
>
> Communal hysteria of the most unimaginative sort, selfishness, lust for money, rejection of the burdens of maternity and of citizenship, such as National Service, low ideals, deafness to all warnings, blindness to all inconvenient truths, veiled corruption, such as is evinced by the notorious sale of Honours ... and Parliamentary self-voted pay, love of comfort and conventions, hatred of honest work, worship of party politicians plotting for their own and not their country, neglect of the land and its population in favour of the vote-giving cities, discouragement of Home-food supplies in favour of sport and pleasure – such are some of the seeds. And the fruits are unreadiness, incompetence, vain-boasting, confusion, dwindling birth-rate of our fit, class-hatred, envy and malice, refusal to face facts, subterfuge, lack of statesmanship and the substitution of cunning for wisdom in Government, lack of skill in the business of war, lack of munitions for its successful prosecution, lack of great men in high places, civil or military ... [1]

Only God, he was sure, could have saved the nation from itself. The war seemed to have brought out the worst and the best in people; and the best was being squandered on the battlefields. At home, those gentlemanly qualities that Haggard so admired appeared to have been lost. This was not just a failure of etiquette on a grand scale but, as he saw it, a portent of doom for the Empire, which he believed to be founded upon those qualities, and that meant the collapse of civilisation.

But it was not Germany and its Austro-Hungarian and Turkish allies that Haggard saw as the main threat to the British Empire. He had been reading news from the Far East and again it was there that he saw the potentially fatal danger. The particular news was of Japanese demands on China for industrial, mining and railway concessions and that no more of the Chinese coast should be leased to other foreign powers. These he saw as early signs of the domination of China by Japan 'with the object of organising her vast resources of men and of developing her incalculable wealth'. The final outcome, he imagined, was that

in a day to come – say 50 years hence – the countless yellow races, armed to the teeth and practically unconquerable, may be in a position to do what Germany has done, but with better success, that is to attempt to obtain the supremacy of the world. If once Japan can make her cause that of China also and enter on the struggle with all China's resources at her back, such an aspiration would certainly pass out of the region of dreams ... I will not pursue the problem, which is probably one which the following generation will be called upon to solve, but should very much like to learn what ideas are working in the brains of the astute and unchanging Japanese statesmen at this moment ... Mine is that Japan is taking the first step on the long road to a national Tipperary of its own.[2]

As the Japanese sent troops into China, Haggard worried that his fellow countrymen were so obsessed with the European war and the current social problem of alcoholism that they were oblivious to long-term danger. 'China and Japan are far away', he continued, 'while Germany is near and the great drink problem nearer still'.[3]

Australia – under-populated and, as he saw it, complacent – would be most at risk, followed by New Zealand. Canada, albeit distant, was equally under-populated and had no concept of self-defence. South Africa might no longer be so fragmented as it had been in his youth but the potential for schism remained and its natural riches made it tempting to any potential aggressor. The answer to all these degrees of risk was population: strong, unified, hard-working populations of English-speaking Anglo-Saxon and Celtic stock. This had been Haggard's theory since he had first ridden across Natal and the Transvaal and it had been strengthened whenever he visited the Dominions.

But now he knew that the exact method he had advocated in the past was flawed. The foundations of the new populations would be small holders but those already fitted for the life were needed in the British Isles. He had – together with General Booth of the Salvation Army, and, since his death in 1912, alone – proposed the settlement of the urban poor on the land after training in independent farming. Yet these were mostly of poor stock, he realised, and while he had maintained that their children would become the men and women that were needed, it was more likely to be their grandchildren and great-grandchildren; and they, in the light of his present scenario, might come too late.

In March, 1915, Haggard had been appointed to a new committee which had taken over the study of such emigration from the Royal Dominions Commission. But the Committee on Land Settlement, under the chairmanship of Earl Grey, who was also chairman of the Royal Commonwealth Society, had not the slightest idea of the complexities involved, he thought. But from this first meeting an idea arose, which to Rider Haggard became his Holy Grail, bringing together his experience, practicality and ideals.

The settlers on the empty lands of the Dominions would not be the narrow-chested consumptive sweepings of the slums but healthy young men of determination who had earned the 'homes fit for heroes' they were already being promised. The settlers would be the surviving soldiers, sailors and airmen, who were now fighting and, for them, the same training and subsidies would be available as for the Salvation Army's derelicts and the same opportunities; but they, at least, would be of the sturdy stock needed to populate what would, in effect, be Great Britain beyond the seas. For the soldier-settlers – hundreds of thousands of them, perhaps – it would be a reward with an historical tradition for it was in this way that veteran Roman legionaries had been given land in England, and Cromwell's in Ireland.

In July, Haggard joined a deputation from the influential but unofficial Royal Colonial Institute to Andrew Bonar Law, the recently appointed Colonial Secretary of the Board of Agriculture, to present the idea for what was wistfully spoken about as 'after the war', unimaginable as such a time might seem. He wrote in his diary, 'Sir John Taverner, the ex-Australian Agent-General, who also spoke, suggested that I should be sent round the Dominions to find out the minds of their governments on this and kindred matters, at which Mr Bonar Law nodded his head'.[4]

Yet, despite the nodded head, the idea aroused little interest in a Government concentrating on the war and the assembly of new armies for a great offensive on the Western Front in the following year. They could not bring themselves to think about the future of those soldiers once they had won the war, nor, indeed, of the Empire itself. So, on 4 August, the first anniversary of the outbreak of war, Haggard wrote in his diary:

> Bonar Law writes ... that he is not prepared 'at present' to recommend that a mission should be sent to enquire into land settlement for soldiers in the Dominions. This means, of course, that enough pressure has not been put on by the Dominions Govts. Indeed it is doubtful whether these really want immigrants, especially in the case of the Australian Labour Govt.[5]

So it would have to be Rider Haggard's own vision of the British Empire, as it might become, against the lack of vision of those in power. Here was a noble cause for a crusade, albeit fought by one crusader – himself.

Yet all was not lost, for the Royal Colonial Institute had shown interest in the possibilities and formed a small committee to consider it further. On 4 September, it called upon Haggard to present his case and described it as 'very interesting'. But, he noted, 'Whether it will encourage them to urge the country to spend a good many millions in a land settlement experiment of great size I do not know. Personally I have grave doubts of the success of the venture, altho' nobody can hope more than I do that it may succeed'.[6] He came to London from Norfolk on 29 October to attend another meeting – his bus from Liverpool Street Station being delayed by vast crowds waiting outside St Paul's Cathedral for the memorial service to Edith Cavell, the nation's martyr – afterwards recording sadly, 'It is obvious that the Govt. will do nothing to help this forward and the question arose as to whether the Royal Colonial Institute should not undertake the work and send me to the various Dominions to interview their Govts.'[7]

Just before Christmas he was again called to London by the council of the Institute, which was now prepared to make him their ambassador on such a mission, beginning with a tour of Australia and New Zealand. Yet lack of government interest was proving more of an obstacle than anticipated.

I am a Royal Commissioner [he wrote in his diary], more or less, I presume, under the control of the Govt., even while the Royal Commission is indefinitely adjourned. Now the Colonial Office is against this mission, fearing, I imagine, with the prescience of officials, that it might result in giving them trouble ... Therefore it is quite possible that Mr Bonar Law will put a spoke into our wheel and stop me from going. Somehow I begin to doubt whether I shall ever get off to Australasia. I think it would be a good bit of Empire work, which I should be very glad to put in as my offering, since I am too old to fight, but if the Govt. chooses to thwart it, as up to the present it has thwarted it in every way ... well, I have nothing to say.[8]

The year ended with mixed expectations. Haggard was depressed by the mood of the nation but more hopeful about the war for there was talk of a great offensive to break the Germans on the Western Front. On 1 January 1916, he wrote in his diary, 'I enter on this year with high hopes, believing, as I do, that it will see the downfall of Germany and the triumph of the Allies'.[9] Next day, as he recorded with delight, 'I received my marching orders from the R. Colonial Institute – S. Africa – Australasia – Canada – a long and arduous business. I can only hope that the Mission will be fortunate and fruitful ... Here is my war offering!'[10]

He would be away working for several months without pay but he was heartened to hear from his literary agent that the film rights for six of his novels had been sold. He had been promised a male secretary to accompany him on the tour but otherwise he would be alone and he was glad. Instead of sharing whatever success was achieved with others – including the politicians, who would have authorised an official tour – all the credit, or all the blame, would be his.

In his diary he resisted any temptation to draw a romantic parallel between himself and a Viking ancestor embarking upon a saga of salvation for his people. He kept his expectations at a low key and even Kipling's response to the news of his mission was a muted postscript to a letter: 'You're in for the deuce and all of a big job'.[11] A farewell luncheon was to be given for him by the Royal Colonial Institute at the Hotel Cecil on 1 February but Kipling was unable to attend, writing rather mysteriously to his friend in January that, 'I have undertaken certain work, which I have to do when I am asked to do it and it so happens that the next call cuts into the beginning of next month'.[12] This work was simply visits to ships of the Royal Navy at sea to write articles and verses to be published as a short book, *Sea Warfare*. The importance of Haggard's work was suitably conveyed by Lord Curzon, whom he sometimes met at the Athenaeum, who wrote to him, 'As usual, you are about to undertake a job of great and imperial importance, patriotically, devotedly, gratuitously', a eulogy Haggard described as 'Curzonic'.[13]

Meanwhile active planning began. Haggard was delighted when Sir Owen Phillips, the chairman of the Union Castle Line, the principal carrier to South Africa, told him that, if the soldier-settler plan was adopted, he would guarantee to ship out 'the wives and families or sweethearts of settlers free for a period of two or three years'.[14] Heartened, Haggard went on to the Royal Dominions Commission to see the chairman, Lord d'Abernon,* and the secretary, Harding, from whom he now felt a pleasing independence, to ask if he could make any enquiries on their behalf during his tour and was gratified when they asked him to do so. Then, with his first achievements in hand, he returned to his new base, the Royal Colonial Institute.

There was the question of a secretary to accompany him round the world. The Institute had suggested Andrew Corbett, a suitable young man with some diplomatic experience, whom Haggard liked, but he was told 'some secret Committee at the Foreign Office'[15] had vetoed the appointment and he had to devote a week to lobbying before the opposition was withdrawn. Then Corbett's first task was to accompany his master on visits to others who might prove helpful, including Canadian shipping and railway companies, all of whom promised help.

The farewell luncheon for two hundred and fifty guests at the Hotel Cecil was a splendid affair, attended by relevant notables, representatives of the Dominions and the press and also by Louie and two of his brothers – the eldest, now Sir William Haggard, the diplomat,† and the youngest, Arthur‡ – and by his daughters. The toast to Haggard was proposed by Lord Curzon, who said that 'with that blend of imagination' – he spoke of 'the astonishing series of works of fiction, showing that our guest possesses a gold-mine of rich and creative fancy' –

and common sense, which is his leading characteristic, he is about to undertake war work which would inure to the benefit of the people of our race for generations to come ... Some say that when the war was over we will slip back into the old groove. There are others, of whom I

---

* Now also Chairman of the Liquor Board, which introduced the licensing laws to restrict drinking.
† Appointed Minister to Venezuela in 1897, Argentina in 1902 and Brazil in 1906.
‡ A former major in the Army, he wrote such novels as *The Kiss of Isis* as 'Arthur Amyand'.

myself am one, who earnestly hope that most things will be entirely different ... A great host of men – possibly from one to two millions – will come back to a country where the labour market will be congested ... We do not want these men to go to America; we want to keep them as British citizens and thus to add to the economic and industrial strength of the Empire.

When the cheers had died away, he quoted the doggerel about the day when

> ... the Rudyards cease from Kipling,
> And the Haggards ride no more.

He was glad, he said, 'that our Rudyard still Kipled to the advantage of the Empire and that our Haggard still rode and that he was about to ride forth on what would in all probability be the most beneficent quest in his long and useful career'.

In reply, Haggard acknowledged that, as a writer of fiction,

It is something, after all, to have amused millions of mankind. Imagination is apt to be decried among the British people, some of whom think that if a man has imagination he can do nothing else. There are many who do not understand that imagination is the soul of things and that without a spice of imagination nothing real is ever done ... [Then, speaking of his quest,] I can imagine that fifty million white people might well find a home in Australia. The world might be filled with Anglo-Saxon people if they would only avail themselves of these stretches of territory. The great need of the Empire today is population ... [16]

His enthusiasm spread as it became clear what particular settlers he imagined setting out for the outback, the prairies and the veldt. Most people in the country were related to, or knew, young men with the armies that had been recruited in the eighteen months since the outbreak of war. Many had been facing an uncertain, insecure future before they had volunteered; some were unemployed, or in poorly paid drudgery, while others had not yet made up their minds what to do with their lives; others had volunteered with friends, forming the 'pals' battalions' of the industrial towns, or public schools battalions, or joined the Artists' Rifles. Such were the young men whom Haggard and his supporters saw as giving new population, vigour and intelligence to the

Dominions, forming a British nation around the world. It was as vibrant an idea as any that Rider Haggard had imagined.

The next few days were spent conferring at the Dominions High Commissions and with Lord Milner, the former British High Commissioner to South Africa – 'an extraordinarily able man who is a *man*',[17] thought Haggard – who promised his support; and he was entertained to a farewell dinner at the Authors' Club, attended by a hundred and fifty, to whom he spoke of his mission. It had aroused much interest in the British and Dominions press but suddenly became controversial following two letters to *The Times*, one declaring that men who had fought for their country were entitled to a home and work and not to exile overseas; the other, that there was plenty of uncultivated land in the British Isles for the settlement of ex-soldiers. In reply, Haggard wrote that many would emigrate in any case, and that in one year after the Boer War a quarter of a million had done so, half of them choosing to go to the United States; this time the Empire should claim its own.

At the same time the Land Settlement Committee set up in the preceding year to study the prospects of resettlement of ex-servicemen on the land in England and Wales published its report. It recommended that the Board of Agriculture should acquire land for agricultural communities, much on the lines recommended by Haggard after his enquiry into the Salvation Army's settlements, but initially involving only five hundred men. The Committee added that they 'cannot look with equanimity on the prospect of losing the flower of our agricultural population, even to the Dominions', insisting that the same opportunities could be offered at home. However, in a leading article, *The Standard* declared that 'a man lost by England to one of the Dominions is a man-and-a-half gained by the Empire', concluding, 'Sir Rider Haggard's mission Overseas to inquire into preparations for the reception of newcomers after the war loses none of its interest or importance by reason of the report on settlement in England and Wales'.[18]

On 9 February, Haggard saw the editor of *The Times* (' ... on my side, or so he said',)[19] and, next day, he and Corbett were accompanied to Paddington station by Louie, Angie and Lilias and an official party, including Lord d'Abernon, where they boarded the train for Plymouth. It proved a tiresome journey since a stranger sat himself in their reserved compartment and tried to alarm them with stories of impending Zeppelin raids on London which would kill fifty to a hundred thousand people in a single night. On arrival, they boarded the *Edinburgh Castle*, bound for

South Africa and before she sailed on the 11th, a sheaf of farewell telegrams arrived on board for Haggard. One was from Earl Grey, the President of the Royal Commonwealth Society, saying that 'intermigration between England and Dominions should now be regarded in same way as migration from one part of England to another ... settlement vacant Dominion lands with Britons will contribute strength and safety to Empire'. The last copy of *The Times* to come on board showed that the editor had kept his word and published a leading article condemning current misrepresentation of Haggard's mission as 'grotesque'.[20] Then the ship steamed past Plymouth Hoe for the open sea and the Empire beyond.

As he felt the rise and fall of the deck, it is possible that Haggard felt an affinity with his fellow Norfolkman, Horatio Nelson, and the letters he had written to Emma Hamilton as he sailed towards Trafalgar, for now he wrote to Louie:

My dearest, dearest Wife, I feel parting from you and the children very much indeed. I am under no delusion as to the risks of this journey, but I felt it my duty to go, hoping and indeed believing that I shall emerge safe out of it at the end ... You know whatever comes I shall always be thinking of you, my dear.[21]

Despite the risk of submarine attack and the consequent darkening of the ship at night, the voyage was peaceful. But, while others were playing deck games between meals or, wrapped in tartan rugs, were sipping *bouillon*, Haggard was in his cabin revising a new Allan Quatermain novel, *The Ancient Allan*. His fellow passengers might have been surprised to know that this tall, brisk Norfolk squire was busily imagining the hero, with whom he identified, and the seductive Lady Ragnall – she dressed in the transparent robe of an Ancient Egyptian priestess – taking drugs in her private museum in order to revisit their earlier, melodramatic lives.

The first sign that the war was now distant came on sighting Madeira lit by the moon and electricity, Haggard noting, 'Its bright lights shining in squares and lines and running high up the encircling mountains. One can judge by their brilliance how necessary darkness is to cities that can be raided by Zeppelins'.[22] As the ship steamed south, news of the war was received by wireless and, he wrote bitterly:

I wonder whether the English politicians, upon whose head this burden rests and whose hands are red with all this blood, ever suffer in their consciences. Not they, I imagine: they are far too tough. Am I justified in writing that these men, Haldane, Lloyd George, Churchill, Asquith,* for instance, to say nothing of the galaxy of minor lights, are responsible? I think I am. They knew what was coming ... And what did they do – they, the Trustees of the Nation? Did they preach a crusade – did they warn our blind and ignorant population? Not they. They, good, practical men, considered all in the light of votes and of their party prospects and cut down the artillery and army, which now at fabulous cost they have been obliged to raise to 4 million men or more ... [23]

These millions were those for whom he saw himself as the ambassador, blazing the trail towards a future which would reward their sacrifice. Arriving at Cape Town on 28 February, he was greeted as such; the last time, he had been one of a number of Royal Commissioners but now the honours were for him alone. Although without government support, he was able to go ashore with a cable that had just reached him from the British South Africa Company promising to give half a million acres of land in Rhodesia to soldier-settlers. This, combined with the earlier offer of free passages from Britain, gave him something tangible to present to his hosts and he noted with satisfaction that this was 'something of a personal triumph for myself'.

Next day he had tea with the Prime Minister, General Botha, whom he had met and liked on his last visit, and now thought to be 'one of the few really big men'. In confidence, Botha told him that he was working 'on Imperial lines' and, although himself a Boer, was 'deeply anxious to get British population into the Union'. He met other politicians and officials: 'I holding forth on all my theories about the land and its bearing on Western Civilisation, etc.'[24] He was delighted at the positive reaction, which included the promise to waive immigration restrictions for ex-servicemen and their families after the war. This was particularly gratifying in view of the inherent racial problems of South Africa; particularly the divisions between the white English- and Afrikaans-speaking populations, although Botha had told him that anti-British feeling amongst the Boers would subside when, and if, the Allies won the war. Yet once he got away from officialdom he discovered that 'the usual African hell's broth

* Haldane had been Secretary of State for War (1905–12) and Lord Chancellor (1912–15); Lloyd George, Chancellor of the Exchequer (1908–15) and Minister of Munitions (1915–16); Churchill, President of the Board of Trade (1908–10), Home Secretary (1910–11) and First Lord of the Admiralty (1911–15); Asquith, Chancellor of the Exchequer (1905–8) and Prime Minister (1908–16).

is on the boil' with racial tensions and that 'Botha is much hated by perhaps a majority of the Boers ... because he is supposed to be too "English"'.[25] Much of the anti-British feeling amongst the Dutch was social, he was told, they objecting to their own people taking up 'polite ways of life, such as playing lawn-tennis and even dressing for dinner with the result that they are no longer hail-fellow-well-met with the roughest most uncouth back-veldt Boer'.[26] Amongst the English-speakers, the solution was to bring out more British settlers and, as the fear of a third Boer War was at the back of their minds, it would be useful if they were ex-soldiers.

But there were optimistic, specific proposals, too, one of them for settlement in the Transvaal, north of Pretoria, where a new dam could irrigate ten thousand acres of barren land, enabling it to support cattle or grow wheat, tobacco or any tropical or sub-tropical fruit. Then the Cape Publicity Association offered to reprint their handbook and send huge quantities to British regiments and, at a later stage, to provide advisers to help the soldiers when they arrived to make their homes at the Cape. It was said that a settler should be able to create a satisfactory life for himself and his family on a smallholding of about seventy acres if he began with capital of £1,000, which would presumably be a government loan, at which Haggard suggested the setting up of smallholders' cooperatives as in Denmark. He examined the scope for settlers in gold and diamond mining and even in ostrich farming but always came back to the ideal of the smallholding he had cherished for so long.

There was another meeting with his old friend Judge Kotzé and he noted that his unmarried daughters were 'curiously early Victorian in appearance'.[27] He sometimes felt Victorian, too, remembering the hopes and optimism of his youth. He was nearing the age of sixty and the judge was six years older and seemed more. Haggard would continue his journey round the world so, unless he was sent back to South Africa to choose land for settlement, as had been suggested, it was unlikely that they would meet again. The sequence that had begun by his accompanying the squire of Heydon to Natal as an unpaid, unspecified attendant was ending with his return, perhaps to take the future of South Africa in his hands.

'I wish however that this opportunity of handling State affairs had come to me earlier in life', he wrote to William Carr. 'Now it is late in the day. Still I hope to put in a stroke or two for the Empire yet, before I am myself knocked out, if God wills it'. He told Carr of the half-million acres he had already been offered and that he had also

> succeeded in getting the Union Immigration Regulations modified so that any white soldier or sailor throughout the Empire, whatever his state of health or pocket, can now enter here unquestioned ... Also I have got *en train* preliminaries for the establishment of an Imperial Route via the Cape to Australasia.[28]

On 13 March, Haggard himself set sail for Australia with a message of congratulations and farewell from the Governor-General of the Union of South Africa, Lord Buxton, to give a fair wind to the next stage of his odyssey. On board ship he lectured to wounded, homeward-bound New Zealand soldiers, whose presence illustrated the motive of his mission. He began work on a book, *The Empire and the Land*, but automatically his imagination began throwing up ideas for novels. 'One watches the albatrosses sail', he mused in his diary, 'sail day and night eternally ...';[29] three days later, he noted, 'I have evolved the plot of a new story called *The Fatal Albatross*, of which the scene would be set in some of the desolate islands we are passing, the Marion group perhaps. Or it might be called *Mary of Marion Island* ...'[30]

An 'apparently endless voyage'[31] ended on 3 April with their arrival at Hobart, the capital of Tasmania, and an immediate welcome at Government House. At once Haggard began giving interviews and making speeches, not only to explain his ideas for settlement, but the reason for their urgency.

> Now, what is our Empire [he asked]? It covers fully one-fourth of the globe and it is held by about 60,000,000 of white people of whom 40,000,000 dwell in the United Kingdom. It is just all that we can do to hold the Empire with the population ... Now is the opportunity for the Empire to try to secure for that land ... the finest settlers in the world – men who have been thoroughly disciplined, who know what stress and danger mean and who know how to face opposition of every kind ... Then there is the debt we owe to our sailors and soldiers, for if it were not for ... their heroism, where would we be today?[32]

He was shown virgin land that would be suitable for settlement and enthusiastically detailed the initial requirements: 'A railway must be made for 14 miles, then the land must be laid out with proper irrigation ditches and houses built, etc.'[33] Elsewhere, he noted, 'It appears to me most of the land will grow perfect apples ... At present, however, population and capital are wanting to clear and cultivate the land'.[34] It was obvious that Haggard's scheme struck the Tasmanians as original and exciting and in a burst of enthusiasm, the Prime Minister promised that Tasmania would give land and organise and finance the settlement of three hundred ex-soldiers and their families; many more, if the British Government would help with subsidies.

The prospects of future trade, Haggard told his hosts, would be enhanced by the four months of the year when their fruit would have no competition from British growers. So the visit ended with another burst of enthusiasm and, on 8 April, he and Corbett took the ferry to the Australian mainland, landing at Melbourne. Again there were interviews, speeches and long reports in the newspapers. But it was his answer to a question about his work as a novelist that led him to describe, in effect, his present mission. 'How do I write my books?' he replied. 'The maker of romance must write straight on, or he loses the thread of his story. Of course, one has to sketch everything out ... but, as the story develops new situations occur'.[35]

The new situation for his mission was the Australian attitude to the motherland. A nation with its ancestry amongst the enterprising but dispossessed; penniless and resentful younger sons; roving fortune-seekers; seafarers and convicts; prospectors and speculators, they did not listen with any reverence to advice from those who had remained, as they imagined, comfortably at home. In particular, the leaders of organised labour were unlikely to welcome imported competition for the work available.

'In Sydney ... they were very hostile', he wrote home. 'The Labour Party and all the six Australian Governments do not favour British immigration – especially the Minister for Lands was dead against me.'[36] Even so, the Australians were fascinated by their visitor and the unexpected reason for his visit. But it was a strain and he confided in his diary:

The burden is hard for one man to carry. Speech-making, diplomacy, interviews, bores, endless arrangements and negotiations fill the day so full, to say nothing of the strain of thought. I hope I shall pull through the job all right but it is very, *very* tough. Especially trying are the continual new names and faces and the difficulty of remembering them all and avoiding mistakes and *faux pas*. Then the speeches! These are a

nightmare but so far I have managed all right. And the cranks! Corbett
had almost to wrestle one lady today who tried to force her way into
my office. She wanted me to write her life...[37]

There were meetings, interviews and speeches after luncheons and
dinners (with *Bombe Colonial* for pudding), he was once introduced as
the author of *Far from the Madding Crowd*, and 'giving back chaff for
chaff' when he 'poured out floods of the best eloquence I could muster in
every direction...I have been shouting all over the place until I am sick of
the sound of my own voice and tired to my bones'.
But it brought results. The newspaper reports were fair and sometimes
enthusiastic.

For some reason or other I am popular in Australia [he wrote home].
They think I am something of an orator, which of course I am not...
They like men who have made a success, even if it is only writing
romances. Also they think me honest ... My appearance in a *private*
capacity has proved no drawback.

It was this that won him sympathetic listeners and then allies. Australians
were delighted to find an English celebrity who did not try to patronise
them, a squire who treated their opinions with respect and talked like the
practical farmer he was. In Sydney, when he addressed the trade unionist
of the Typographical Association and the Bakers' Association, both of
which could have been expected to be hostile, he recorded: 'Never, ever
in Australia, did I have such a reception. I thought the cheering would lift
the roof. They are very good fellows if only you know how to deal with
them'.[38] It was reciprocated.

No man could be more free from even the suggestion of 'frill' ... that
the great novelist [reported a Sydney newspaper columnist]. Rider
Haggard, tall and ascetic-looking, has the breezy manner of a frank
schoolboy. The years sit lightly on his lean and wiry frame and he is
probably almost as tireless physically as he is mentally.[39]

Ministers, too, listened to him, liked him and tried to help him. The
governments of Victoria, New South Wales, South Australia, Western
Australia and Queensland all agreed to offer the same help to British
ex-soldiers as to Australians. New South Wales also promised to enlarge
a projected irrigation scheme to increase the number of settlers on the
land by a thousand, preference to be given to the British. His greatest
triumph was in Queensland, where the Prime Minister offered to provide

a million acres of land suitable for dairy farming, or arable crops, for the exclusive settlement of the British. It was an encouraging start, even if most of the Australian politicians had been reluctant to commit themselves too deeply, and an exhausting six weeks. But, in the light of the initial Australian reaction and what he had been warned to expect, it was something of a triumph because the mass settlement of British ex-servicemen had now been accepted in principle.

Before he left Sydney on 25 May for New Zealand, he heard of the death of his brother Alfred,* whom he described in his diary as 'intrinsically the ablest of us, yet the lack of some qualities and the overplus of others made his abilities of no avail'.[40] There was other bad news from Europe: Ireland was in revolt; the carnage at Verdun continued; and in Mesopotamia, the British garrison of Kut had surrendered. Soon after he arrived at Wellington after a rough passage on 1 June he heard the news that on the preceding day and early that morning a great battle had been fought between the British and German fleets in the North Sea. It had long been expected but, as became increasingly evident, it had not been another Trafalgar for British losses seemed to have been far higher than the German. 'At best it is a sad business and a great blow', noted Haggard. 'A melancholy event to be published to the Empire on the King's birthday ... Wanted, a Nelson!'[41]

Haggard was exhausted by the voyage through one of the most violent storms he had experienced, in which the ship had almost capsized, and was all too aware that in three weeks' time he would be sixty. But again there was a heartening welcome with an invitation from the Governor-General, Lord Liverpool, to stay at Government House. At once he felt it his duty to do what he could to counter the shocking news of what appeared to have been more defeat than victory at sea. At a reception in Wellington, he rose, reported a local newspaper, a 'tense, earnest look in the large-featured bony face, the same suggestion of nervous energy – and reserves of temper ... The audience hung upon his lips and thrilled in sympathetic accord with him'[42] as he declared that he must speak

at a time like this when the whole Empire has been thrilled by the news of a great battle in the North Sea ... It is easy for me to imagine what happened there – the rough misty Northern Sea, the low coastline, then the appearance of English torpedo-boats tempting on the Germans; then the rush of all the great German fleet upon our weaker squadron;

Alfred Haggard had served in the Indian Civil Service.

207

then the hours of desperate fray ... and through the night the sinking ships of both sides, the unequalled valour upon both sides; finally the approach of the great British battle-squadron and the flight of the foe – leaving the sea covered with wreckage and with dead. Sir, the Germans claim a victory. It is a lie![43]

Later news arrived that British losses had indeed been far higher than the German and later still it became clear that while what came to be called the Battle of Jutland had been a tactical victory for the Germans, they would never again present a challenge at sea to the British, who could therefore claim a strategic victory.

Although this had conjured up patriotic excitement, it did not affect the reception of Haggard's proposals. New Zealand was more akin to England than was Australia and the owners of its fertile farmland were as wary of any scheme for smallholdings as had been British landowners, fearful for their large estates. Even before Haggard arrived, a newspaper published a leading article under the headline 'Fight First, Then Exile',[44] protesting against the idea of shipping returned British soldiers away from their motherland, where there was plenty of uncultivated land suitable for their settlement. Again Haggard stressed the abiding threat of Germany – 'Attila again walks the earth ... The German population will be restored in 20 years, with every man imbued with one desire that had cleared their pitch and spoiled their game'.[45] But he did not mention the 'Yellow Peril' any longer, because Japan was now an ally.

More meetings, more touring, more interviews, this time in a temperate, comfortable country of rich lowlands and valleys and magnificent mountains with a placid, self-satisfied population. This time there was no promise of land, nor even an offer of equality of opportunity for British and native ex-servicemen. The Prime Minister, William Massey, wrote to Haggard, supporting his aims but adding, 'unfortunately the good land available is limited in area and the members of the New Zealand Expeditionary Force and its reinforcements have first claim ...' They had to be settled first but 'next to them ... we shall be most happy to give favourable consideration to any soldiers of the British Army who desire to settle in this Dominion'.[46] After a fortnight of handshaking and speechmaking, Haggard and Corbett set sail for Vancouver.

The two-week voyage across the Pacific to Vancouver was regarded as safe because the German commerce-raiders had long since been sunk, or driven away. The ship board routine was as in peacetime complete with concert half-way across with passengers singing *All the Girls are Lovely by the Sea*, *My Beloved Queen* and *Little Grey Home in the West*, reciting *My Mate Bill* and playing *Ragtime Medley* on the piano. This concert was held on 22 June and he wrote in his diary:

> A very lonesome birthday amidst all this crowd of strangers in whom I take no interest and who take no interest in me – except as a penny peep-show, some of them ... Today I have definitely entered upon old age – for at 60 a man is old ... Let me look round ... For me the world is largely peopled with the dead; I walk amongst ghosts ... Well, ere long I must join their company ...

Sunk in gloom he continued,

> The work, for the most part lies behind me, rather poor stuff, too – yet I will say this, I have *worked*. My talent may be of copper not of gold – how can I judge of my own abilities? My opportunities have not been many, and for the most part I have made them for myself; the book-writing, the agricultural research business, the public work, for instance. Of course, I might have done more in the last line by going into Parliament. But this I have really never been able to afford since, except in the case of the Labour Members, it has designedly been made to suit the rich alone. Also it is hardly the place for a self-respecting man ... [47]

His fellow-passengers irritated him, even when sitting alone on deck after dark: 'There was dancing and, after the dancing, just noise that made my head ache. I have rarely heard such female screams, even from a kitchen, or such high-pitched and continuous laughter ... But Heavens! – how common the world has become even in my time'.[48]

On arrival at Victoria on Vancouver Island on 1 July 1916, he was met by his sadly unsuccessful brother Andrew and by the news that his godson Rider Greiffenhagen, the son of his illustrator, had been lost in a submarine. His first meeting ashore was with the manager of the Canadian Pacific Railway, who told him that he had a low opinion of British immigrants and preferred, as Haggard put it, 'those of enemy nationality, viz. Hungarians'.[49] Soon after he was told that the Government of British Columbia had decided on a post-war land-settlement scheme exclusively for British Columbian ex-servicemen. So he immediately called on the Prime Minister and persuaded him to revise the legislation to include the British: 'A great triumph',[50] he concluded.

Other news was crossing the Atlantic. A great British offensive – the long-awaited 'Big Push' – on the Western Front had begun at dawn on 1 July. The new armies of volunteers, who had waited so long, were advancing eastward from their trenches on a wide front to the north of Verdun in the *département* of the Somme. The news seemed to add purpose and immediacy to his mission and he set off across Canada by train. There was more encouragement when, before boarding the train for Edmonton, he was told that the Grand Trunk Pacific Railway Company had proposed to the Geographical Board of Canada that a peak and a glacier in the Rocky Mountains be named after him. 'Here they give my name to a towering Alp', he wrote in his diary. 'In Norfolk they would not bestow it on a pightle.* Truly no man is a prophet in his own country'. He was flattered and delighted by Mount Sir Rider and the Haggard Glacier, joking that the former would make 'the best of tombstones'.[51] He had also heard that the Dominions Royal Commission were to visit Canada, which he thought would be 'foolish and useless' and that because of 'the infinitesimal results of so much ponderous and costly labour'[52] he could achieve more on his own. Indeed, when they did come and were admiring the mountains, Harding was to note ungenerously and inaccurately that when Haggard had been there he 'had induced the railway authorities to give his name to quite an outstanding one'.[53]

In Edmonton, Calgary, Regina, Saskatoon, Winnipeg and Montreal there were more luncheons and speeches, which, he complained, suffered from the iced water which was the obligatory drink with the meals. The last call was at Ottawa, where he was received by the Prime Minister, Sir Robert Borden, who had given him vague but non-committal assurances of a favourable Canadian attitude to the settlement plans, which Haggard realised was the most he could expect. Yet again his persistence bore fruit and more positive letters began to follow him from the state capitals he had visited. One of the first was from the Prime Minister of Ontario, telling him that all British ex-servicemen suitable as farm settlers would be given the same help as returning Canadians.

Most heartening to Haggard personally was a telegram from Theodore Roosevelt inviting him to Oyster Bay near New York, where he was living. In high anticipation he travelled by steam-heated train through the sweltering American summer to meet his old friend, who was awaiting him on the front steps of his house, Sagamore Hill. 'He has grown older

* A small field.

and stouter', Haggard noted, 'and at times his burning manner of speech is nervous in its intensity'. Then began what he described as 'a solid three hours of the most delightful intercourse I have perhaps ever enjoyed with any man'. They discussed politics – American and international – and the war, and Roosevelt said that he wished he had stood again for the Presidency. They talked about Haggard's books and Roosevelt inscribed and gave him a photograph of himself taking a jump on his favourite horse. They discussed old age and agreed that, ideally, they would both choose to end their days in Africa. When Haggard had to leave and had boarded the train for New York, he mused, 'I wonder if we shall ever meet again. No, I do not wonder for I am sure we shall meet *somewhere*. We have too much in common not to do so, though it may perhaps be in a state unknown'.[54]

Next day, 22 July 1916, Haggard and Corbett boarded the liner *St Louis* at New York and sailed for Liverpool, their mission ended. On the seventh and last night of the crossing, as they steamed through the darkness north of Ireland, where German submarines were most active, Haggard was kept awake as 'passengers, mostly Americans, who antici-pated torpedoes, sat up all night by the boats and kept their spirits high by talking and singing at the tops of their voices'.[55] Next morning they docked and Haggard reached London by train late that night and was met by Louie and Angie at Euston. Next day, he was warmly welcomed at the Royal Colonial Institute and, later, at the House of Commons, where he gave an initial report of the results of his mission. He looked worn yet commanding; less like the Viking adventurer, who had set out, and more like a returning crusader, who had seen Jerusalem.

Yet, as he talked of his mission to men of affairs, politicians and journalists, the realisation grew that the scenario that had inspired it might no longer be as it had been at the beginning of the year. The great offensive in France was still grinding slowly forward, as the buffeting of ear-drums in south-eastern England by distant gunfire and the optimistic daily communiqués bore witness. Heavy casualties in any 'big push' were to be expected but, this time, they were more than heavy. On that first day, it was being said, twenty thousand British soldiers had been killed and thereafter the dead had been counted in many more thousands. They were young men, for whom he had been seeking future homes and land in the Dominions, and now they had settled for ever on the chalk downs of the Somme.

CHAPTER THIRTEEN

'An excellent scribe in very truth'

RIDER HAGGARD WAS too tense to sleep on his first night in London, or on the second night, which was spent at home in Ditchingham. On the next night, the Zeppelins kept him awake. He blamed the raid on his neighbour William Carr's chauffeur, who had been told by the police to switch on his headlights while bringing Carr's daughter and Lilias Haggard home from a dance at Bungay and believed this was mistaken by the airships' crews for a spy's signals indicating targets.

After the explosion of the first bomb, recalled Haggard,

> confusion and scurryings ensued in the house till at length we all found ourselves in the cellar, clothed in precious little. Well, there we stopped till nearly three in the morning, servants and all, while the Zepps, of which an officer tells me he saw three over the Common, disported themselves around. We must have heard over 50 bombs ... The nearest fell about 100 yards from the house, smashing trees and windows and making a large hole.[1]

Next day they found the bomb-craters in his fields: 'They are terrific, but only killed a rabbit and stunned a gold-crested wren.'[2]

A month later there was another raid and bombs burst all around Ditchingham House. 'It was hellish,' he wrote in his diary, 'the whirr of the machine above, the fearful boom of the bombs and the crashing of glass in the greenhouses...'[3] They, of course, were now empty of orchids, which had been replaced by tomatoes, and their fate had been the beginning of the end of Haggard the farmer. His farms were no longer economic and now a land agent advised him to sell and he reluctantly accepted the advice, although he postponed a final decision for another year. 'I have done my best,' he declared, 'but the adventure is scarcely possible for a gentleman in East Anglia.'[4]

His mission now was the preparation of such a life on the land for the survivors of the battles of France and Flanders. He returned to London to urge action by the Government and when he told Bonar Law of his fear that, after the war, the United States would lure away the best of returning British servicemen, he was relieved to be told that passport regulations might be changed to prevent them from settling outside the Empire. Then the Colonial Secretary changed the subject to the immediate threat to shipping and the nation's food supply by German submarines. It was clear that all minds in Westminster and Whitehall were upon the war and not upon what might happen when, and if, it was won. With that – and a handsome letter of congratulations from the Duke of Connaught, the Governor-General of Canada, whom he had not been able to meet on his tour – Haggard's work for the Royal Colonial Institute ended. There was talk of 'an Imperial Board'[5] being convened to study post-war soldier-settlers further but also a feeling that the idea was simply being filed for possible future reference.

Action was now the responsibility of others. In November, Haggard happened to meet Lord Curzon at Waterloo Station and asked if he knew whether his recommendations were being acted upon. He replied that he, too, had asked Bonar Law, who had said that he did indeed plan to appoint a board to consider matters further. Haggard remarked sadly that nothing seemed to be happening and, he noted later, Curzon 'replied with sarcasm, "Nothing ever does happen!" He promised to stir Bonar Law up again.'[6] In the event, he was stirred by other events: in December, the Asquith administration fell and Law was invited to form a Government. He failed but Lloyd George succeeded. 'I have often in bygone days criticised Mr Lloyd George,' Haggard reflected, but now regarded him as 'a great man, one of the very few among our millions who can not only understand a situation but face and deal with it.'[7] He had taken charge only just in time, for, a few days before, Haggard had written in his diary, 'Never did things look blacker for England and the Empire.'[8] The great offensive on the Somme stalled in rain and mud – with a quarter of a million British dead and missing – and the U-boat blockade threatened to strangle the British Isles, so seeming to vindicate Haggard's campaign for the increase in smallholdings to enable the country to feed itself.

The year ended with dank cold and fog and Haggard took his immediate family – Louie, Angie, Dolly and Lilias – to stay in a rented house at Budleigh Salterton in Devon, where it would be milder. Christmas was a sad time and he had not the heart to propose the customary toasts. When dinner was over and the others had gone to bed, the doorbell rang and there on the doorstep stood Dolly's husband, Reggie Cheyne, on unexpected leave from France, where he had been commanding an infantry battalion, and Haggard was to remember:

> That impressive, and war-worn figure, laden with heavy equipment, his uniform covered with trench mud, haggard, exhausted, almost speechless with laryngitis, coming suddenly in out of the winter night and standing in the warm, firelit room, asking for his wife.

Cheyne did not seem just a son-in-law but a representative of hundreds of thousands. 'So might the ghosts of thousands of his generation come in from the shadows and with outstretched hands demand of us the things that for our sakes they had surrendered... '⁹ Looking with awe and pity at the gaunt figure at his fireside, Haggard could at least feel that he himself had kept faith with those who would survive.

Despite his preoccupation, Haggard continued writing fiction. He had completed *Love Eternal*, which drew on his early experiences with spiritualism, and begun *When the World Shook*, based on an idea of Kipling's about a gigantic natural gyroscope that controls the rotation of the planet. Its originator was thrilled with what his friend had done with his suggestion ('On it came, dancing, swaying and spinning at a rate inconceivable, so that it looked like a gigantic wheel of fire...')¹⁰ and wrote to him that 'It held me like a drug. That's your d—d gift!'¹¹ He was also working on another historical novel, *Moon of Israel*, about the Israelites in Egypt at the time of the Exodus and, although he did not identify with Jewish ancestors as enthusiastically as with the Viking, guarded sympathy for them was apparent. Again Kipling was to be flattering: 'What is your secret, Old Man? It goes and it grips and it moves with all the freshness of youth ... Also you have developed what Scripture made plain, but which no one else dwells on – the essential turbulence and unaccommodativeness of the Israelites in captivity.'¹²

For Haggard, this creativity was still a mixture of necessary money-making and relaxing pastime and no more. He saw his life's work as that of an agricultural, social and imperial reformer and, most immediately, architect of a post-war British Empire repopulated by its returned soldiers and sailors. So it was particularly gratifying when in March, 1917, he was elected Vice-President of the Royal Colonial Institute and, a month later, the Government announced that, at his instigation, it was to establish an Empire Settlement Committee with himself as one of its members.

The dominating issue at the beginning of 1917 was whether the United

States would at last enter the war on the side of the Allies. 'If America really comes in *con amore*, it will make a great difference ... I believe that the sovereignty of the world must ultimately pass to America,'[13] he wrote in his diary. Had Theodore Roosevelt still been President there seemed little doubt that war would already have been declared. Haggard had been delighted to hear that Roosevelt had enjoyed his visit to Oyster Bay as much as himself, having written, 'I shall not forget your visit here. It was one of the most enjoyable afternoons I have spent with any friend.'[14] Roosevelt was furious at President Wilson's* apparent reluctance to commit his country to war, writing to Haggard in March:

I am sick at heart and burnt up with fiery indignation at Wilson's timid shuffling and hesitancy. He is as baneful to this country as an overdose of morphine to an invalid. We should have been in the war six weeks ago. He has not even been preparing. He seems impervious to every consideration of national honour and right; and he has behind him the solid alliance of the utterly base materialists, the utterly silly sentimentalists and all that portion of the population which is at heart traitorous.[15]

The position is intolerable for America [Haggard agreed]. It comes to this: that the German blockade is effective against her, inasmuch as her ships cannot sail ... This cannot endure. Either Germany must give way, or the States must accept the position and, in fact, become her vassal. Or – America must fight.[16]

But they were not to be frustrated much longer. On 2 April, the President called a special session of Congress and, two days later, declared war on Germany. Haggard wrote in his diary, 'The event is of stupendous importance in the history of the world and to what it can lead none can say, possibly to an alliance between the English-speaking peoples and a league to enforce peace on the world.'[17] He wrote a reply to Roosevelt:

Your letter astonishes me, in that on March 14 you – even *you* – did not know what the President was going to do. Either the secret must have been very well kept indeed, or there must have been a very sudden change of attitude ... Everyone rejoices at this new development for which I, for one, had ceased to hope.

He marvelled at the transformation of the outlook since they had last met: 'Ah then, my friend, how little we knew what lay hid in the womb of

* Woodrow Wilson had succeeded William H. Taft as President in 1912.

Fate', and he reminded Roosevelt how his own forecasts were being proved right, particularly over blockade by submarine. Reminding him that he had forecast this in *Rural England*, he continued,

> In 1901, we did not reckon much of submarines ... Generally ... all I wrote has proved itself to be true, although the miserable party politicians mocked me at the time. One of them, I remember, wrote to me that he 'suspected quackery'. Now a very different tune arises from that full-throated choir![18]

But Roosevelt still felt frustrated because, at the age of fifty-seven, he wanted to fight and had presented to President Wilson a plan for him to recruit and lead volunteers himself ... He wrote to Haggard:

> The President, in the smallest spirit of party and personal politics, has refused to allow me to raise and take abroad the divisions. However, I did force him into sending some troops abroad. He represents a common type in the politics of democracies, the purely selfish rhetorician, who has no thought except for his own advancement, who has no sensitiveness about either his own, or the country's honour, and who has been trained in the dreadful school that treats words as substitutes for deeds. However, I am enormously grateful we have gone to war. Under him, we shall not accomplish one-tenth of what we would accomplish if there were a genuine man in the White House...[19]

Instead Roosevelt fought the war vicariously, three of his sons serving in France and a fourth alongside the British in Mesopotamia.

Haggard's intimacy with the former President had become known at the War Office and, after this exchange, he was approached by General Maurice, the Director of Military Operations, and asked if he would write to his friend putting discreet questions on his behalf. The letter would be sent secretly via the diplomatic bag to the British Embassy in Washington and thence by messenger to Oyster Bay. So he wrote at length, explaining that he was acting for 'an eminent friend on the General Staff of our War Office' and would be grateful for his opinions on 'points, which are ... somewhat vital to the interest of both our countries'. Would it be possible for the United States to send troops to Europe soon, even if they had to be armed and equipped by the British? Could large numbers of military aircraft be sent over by the following April, even if they had to be incorporated in British squadrons? Could Russia be reinforced by sending troops from San Francisco to Vladivostok, if necessary taking over and managing the Russian railway system, and then setting up American military bases in Moscow and elsewhere in western Russia? Could the Americans help in organising Armenians against the Turks? Might financial aid be possible for Greece? These questions, he concluded, 'I do not lay before you merely to satisfy idle curiosity.'[20]

General Maurice asked him to make changes before it was shown to the Foreign Office, which then feared that President Wilson would be offended if he discovered that the British had gone behind his back, using a popular novelist as intermediary; so it was never sent. The experience reinforced Haggard's view that most enterprises that the Government undertook – were likely to flounder in indecision and inaction and that he was far more effective as the lone warrior, driven by his own conviction and initiative.

He was even apprehensive for the future of the new Empire Settlement Committee, which seemed to have become the reincarnation of the defunct Royal Dominions Commission, even sitting in the same committee room. This was particularly galling since it had just been announced that Lord d'Abernon and Edward Harding were both to be decorated for their work with the Commission, although the five years' work of the Commissioners themselves were not to be recognised. Indeed Harding had been appointed secretary and there were thirty-five members, the whole becoming so unwieldy that sub-committees had had to be formed, he himself serving on those concerned with 'general purposes', agriculture and industry. Yet there were some grounds for optimism because Lloyd George, the vigorous Prime Minister, had publicly stressed 'the great importance of what I may call the preparation for peace. That will involve ... such after-the-war questions as the migration of our own people to other parts of the Empire, the settlement of soldiers on the land ... ' Also the War Cabinet had been renamed the *Imperial* War Cabinet; a sign that the Empire intended 'to run its affairs jointly',[21] he believed.

The war was showing no signs of reaching a climax. As the slaughter on the Western Front continued, Haggard worried about the lack of imagination shown by the Allied leadership. 'The only way to win this war,' he mused, 'is by a much more extensive use of aircraft, which cannot be held up by trenches ... We could destroy Krupp's and every arms manufacturer and chemical works in Germany and thus make the continuance of war impossible. Of course, if tens of thousands (or even ten thousand) of machines were used there would be many losses, but, after all, these must be as nothing compared to the numbers sacrificed in land warfare ... The idea is too novel to be adopted.'[22] Similarly, at sea, he believed. 'The day of the big battleship has gone by,'[23] and that 'the Germans are now said to be building U-boats with a displacement of 6,000 tons ... What is to happen to the world when the sea is full of such monsters and the air of swift machines flying at such a height as to be invisible?'[24]

While his imagination speculated on future technology, his friend Kipling's eye was upon the present, writing about the grey silhouettes of British warships slipping through the North Sea fog, protecting the motherland from invasion. The two friends began to see more of each other in 1917 because the Haggards had taken a flat in London – 26 Ashley Gardens – and in the autumn moved to another at St Leonard's on the Sussex coast – 28 Grand Parade – to avoid the East Anglian winter and this was within easy reach of the Kiplings at Burwash. They discussed the war and, as usual, Kipling, recognising his friend's current lack of self-confidence, flattered his writing. Haggard responded with the compliment that 'There are two men left living in the world with whom I am in supreme sympathy, Theodore Roosevelt and Rudyard Kipling.' Both shared his views about the lead that the English-speaking nations should give in human evolution. If this should lead to the rule by those higher up the evolutionary ladder of those lower down, then that was part of the process. All agreed that the highest practical ideal was that of honour, of gentlemanliness. All strove to understand the purpose of human life, or, at least, to take an intellectual stance from which it could be discussed without bewilderment.

At Bateman's, Haggard and Kipling talked about religion, the former writing of the latter in his diary, 'He is no unbeliever, only, like the rest of us, one who knows nothing and therefore cannot understand.'[25] They considered the concepts of God and the Devil and of free will, agreeing that

the enormous power of the Roman Catholic religion lies in its support of the individual – whereby his spiritual cares are lifted from his shoulders. He 'touches the button', his church does 'the rest', where the English Church for the most part does nothing, but tells him to worry through with his doubts and sins and troubles as best he can.

They agreed that 'every year which passes draws back a curtain, as it were, and shows us to ourselves in yet completer nakedness.' A humble mind was essential and Haggard thought that 'the small man is the vain man ... Thus, of all the men I know, I think that Roosevelt and Kipling are the humblest.' As for himself, he thought that 'now in my age I feel – well, I cannot express how *stripped* I feel of all merit and value. Perhaps it is well to be thus and then we may be clothed in other garments which *we* did not weave.'[26]

Despite the comfort he took from philosophical conversations with Kipling, he longed for certainties. Wary of spiritualism since his early dabblings, he was fascinated and repelled by the theories of his two acquaintances, Sir Oliver Lodge and Sir Arthur Conan Doyle, and the upsurge in interest brought about by the loss of life in the war. The latter had been lecturing on the subject and

> giving details of our life-after-death, which, he says, is so happy that no one wishes to return therefrom. If only he would prove it! We hear these things again and again but when it comes to the proofs – what are they? Things so trivial that no reasonable person can accept them, sometimes things vulgar and even revolting – the 'cake-walk', synthetic whiskies and sodas and comic songs ... for instance. It seems cruel to play with the aspirations of humanity in this fashion and to give them such soap bubbles in place of the bread they crave. All my life I have been trying to find out the truth of this great matter but, whenever I approach it, it melts away into trivia and vague generalities.[27]

His thoughts strayed to earlier religions when his eye was caught by two Ancient Egyptian statuettes on his desk, one of a priest named Roy, 'like me, "an excellent scribe in very truth", who died between three and four thousand years ago. There he sits staring with calm eyes and fixed, sweet countenance at the centuries as they flow past him. One can almost envy Roy in his repose'; the other of the god Osiris, 'who died that men might live, like another Saviour, whom in those days men did not know'.[28]

Yet he did not give up and wrote to another acquaintance, Dean Inge of St Paul's Cathedral, whose pragmatic pronouncements on spiritual and current affairs had won him the nickname 'The Gloomy Dean'. In a summing-up of his own attitudes, rather than beliefs, Haggard wrote:

> It seems to me that Christianity is Occultism in a sense – perhaps Spiritualism would be a better term – for instance, the Materializations

on the Mount. To put it widely: does not Christianity cover Spiritualism at its best? (What, for instance, is meant by 'The Communion of
Saints'?) But undoubtedly there is a worst as well as a best. When I was
a young fellow, I saw a good deal of the Spiritualism of the day and
certainly it was not elevating. What it is now I do not know for certain,
as I have never been to a séance for over 40 years. But even then I
witnessed things I could not explain.

He cited Conan Doyle's views, adding, 'I think it would be a good thing
... if our Church would seriously investigate all this business – thrash it
out without fear, prejudices or favour, as a Royal Commission thrashes
out a matter and report thereon.'[29] A year later, Dean Inge was to address
the Church Congress on spiritualism and immortality and speak of the
view of the dead that 'they had not lost them because love was stronger
than death.' Haggard, recording this in his diary, added, 'There is our
only hope, that love is stronger than death and that God is love.' He toyed
with the idea of reincarnation as 'a more reasonable explanation of the
many mysteries by which we are surrounded', but expressed doubts and
concluded, 'God is Love and God is also Wisdom and in the hands of the
Infinite Love and Wisdom we must be content to rest – and wait.'[30]

All such comfort was to be needed. At the end of July, the British
armies began a massive new offensive at Ypres, which became bogged by
rain and mud from the smashed irrigation system and developed into a
new slaughter on the gentle slopes of Passchendaele. Amongst the tens of
thousands of those killed was Haggard's nephew Lance, Arthur's son;
and amongst the dead in East Africa was Frederick Selous, so often
likened to Allan Quatermain. German submarines tightened their blockade of the British Isles; Russia was engulfed in revolution; Italy had been
defeated in battle by the Austrians.

Haggard himself faced a hard decision: his farming had never been
profitable and he finally decided to give up; in September, 1917, the stock
was sold and the land let. At the same time he presented the bound
manuscripts of his novels, together with some of the more important
letters he had received, to the Castle Museum at Norwich as if he were
putting his affairs in order at the end of his life. He did not linger and
returned to St Leonard's, where, at the end of the year, he bought North
Lodge, a small house adjoining the gatehouse that spanned the road
leading down to the sea through the wooded valley where Decimus
Burton had built an estate of villas. He took the room over the archway as

his study so that he could look south through the mullioned windows, over the tree-tops to the English Channel and the horizon.

The year ended full of sorrows. In April, 1918, his eldest brother William decided, on his retirement, that he could no longer maintain the family seat at Bradenham and that it would have to be sold. When Rider had last visited the house, two years before, he had written in his diary,

> Every bit of furniture, every picture on the walls, every stone and tree brings forgotten scenes before the eye, or finds tongues and talks. Scenes in which dead actors played, voices that can stir the air no more. Where are they all, oh where do they hide from the searchlight of our love?[31]

Now it was all going to go and, as he now wrote, 'doubtless soon the axe will bring down all its familiar woods and even the great copper beech on which every one of us cut his name ...'[32] He was right: the estate was sold to a timber merchant and all the great trees around the house and in the Long Plantation and the Great Wood were felled. At the auction of contents he had left bids but many of the pieces he wanted went for higher prices and he was left with only a few mementoes, among them the bed he had slept in as a boy and the remains of his mother's blue Copeland breakfast service. 'I find it hard to forgive my brother for having ordered the sale of these relics,'[33] he confided in his diary.*

In March, 1918, the Germans launched a tremendous counter-offensive on the Western Front and for a time it seemed that they would break the Allied defences, flood through and win the war. But, despite fearful losses, the armies of the British and French empires held and then began to push the exhausted Germans back. If they could maintain this momentum there seemed a chance that they might continue to the Rhine and achieve final victory. Even so, Haggard was full of foreboding:

> Unless vision fails me ... Germany will shut down the war as soon as she can for about a generation ... She will employ this period in exploiting the vast annexed territory filled with her slaves and extract-ing therefrom enormous wealth as well she knows how to do ... She will recruit its countless manpower into her armies, which will be thereby almost doubled; also that during that time she will breed up her own on stud-farm principles, choosing the finest fighting stock for

---

* During the Haggard family's final years at Bradenham – perhaps when it was let – the house was said to have been the setting of the love affair which inspired the novel *The Go-Between* by L. P. Hartley.

sires. That then, at the end of the thirty years from the conclusion of the forthcoming peace, she will attack and lay all Europe beneath her feet ... Britain will go with the rest ... there will be but one hope for her inhabitants, to flee to America.[34]

Such pessimism could find an echo in Kipling, who had been ill and been aged by the loss of his son. But Theodore Roosevelt was usually a source of vigorous optimism. However, early in the year, it was announced that he was seriously ill with abscesses in both ears; and, a few weeks later, he wrote to Haggard saying that he was better but his capacity for work reduced. One of his sons had been badly wounded in France but he was glad his country was at war, although regretting it had not been declared two years earlier. Haggard replied that, 'The prolonged strain of this hideous war is not conducive to health', adding that they had both 'foreseen the day when Britain and America would stand side by side with their backs against the Gate of Destiny, fighting for the Freedom of the World.'[35] Then, during the summer, Roosevelt's youngest son Quentin was killed in air combat over France. The bonds between Haggard, Kipling and Roosevelt were strengthened by his loss.

Haggard's pessimism took a curious turn when Japan, an ally since 1914, moved troops into Siberia to counter the Bolshevik revolution. His own fear of Orientals seemed to have abated, or changed:

In all of European blood there lurks a secret fear of the East and a doubt of its ultimate aims [he wrote in his diary]. It is not one that I share myself for two reasons. The first is that I think there is much good in the East and perhaps more true civilisation, although of a different sort. The East has a greater grip on essential things. For instance, her peoples are lovers and cultivators of the land; also they believe that it is the duty of every race to increase and multiply ... They, or the best of them, are thinkers and philosophers though they may have reached conclusions that vary from our own and they are not vulgar until they have been leavened by the West ... I consider the Easterners are almost our equals, or, if they have not attained to our highest levels, they have shown that they possess the capacity to do so. Now for my second reason. I look upon their advance into and possible penetration of much of the West as inevitable – a decree of Fate. Our civilisations have in them the seeds of death ... Rome fell before the hordes sent out by the fringe of the East and it may well be that other modern civilisations will partake of her fate . . . though in a different and perhaps more powerful fashion.[36]

Peace was still only a hope at the back of all minds in the summer of 1918. In July, the Bolsheviks murdered the Tsar of Russia and his family, the Allies began another (they hoped, final) offensive on the Western Front and, in September, the Americans launched theirs. In that month and October, the Ottoman Empire collapsed and Turkey was defeated and the Allies marched into Constantinople on 1 November. Then it was Germany's turn: mutiny in the High Seas Fleet, a revolution in Berlin, the Kaiser abdicating and, on 11 November, an armistice between Germany and the Allies silenced the guns.

That night in St Leonard's, Rider Haggard wrote in his diary, 'There is Peace . . . Flags hanging flaccid in the November damps, a few bells rung out of time (for lack of ringers), some cheering from recruits of the Essex, Norfolk and Suffolk regiments, who now will never be called upon to feel a wound or crawl down a ditch of Flanders mud . . . '[37] Amidst the gloom that had settled upon him over the past four years, he allowed a spark of hope:

So it comes about that our nation emerges from the struggle more potent, more splendid than ever she has shone before, laughing at all disloyalties, with mighty opportunities open to the grasp. How she will use them in the years to come, I shall never see. The Germans will neither forgive nor forget; neither money nor comfort will tell with them henceforth. They have been beaten by England and they will live and die to smash England – she will never have a more deadly enemy than the new Germany. My dread is that in future years the easy-going, self-centred English will forget that just across the sea there is a mighty, cold-hearted and remorseless people waiting to strike her through the heart. For strike they will one day . . . [38]

Haggard himself now looked as old as he felt: lean, lined, grey-haired, his face sad but noble. It was not just the war and the news of so many deaths that had aged him. His chronic bronchial trouble had led to emphysema and, early that year, he had had to abandon a new appointment as an inspector for the Agricultural Wages Board in the West Country, in which he was again to have had Arthur Cochrane as his assistant. His novels were no longer selling as they once had, nor were they automatically reviewed in all the newspapers. 'Oh, I grow weary of storytelling,' he complained, describing himself as 'the deadest of dead letters'.[39]

Above all, his great wartime crusade for 'homes fit for heroes' in the Dominions seemed to have failed. The Empire Settlement Committee, of which he was a member, had recommended the setting up of an Emigration Authority to control the post-war settlement of ex-servicemen in the Dominions but, in June that year, the Government's endorsement of this was defeated in the House of Commons by one vote. Whatever was to be done – and Haggard feared that it would be little – would remain in the provinces of relevant departments of the Civil Service instead of a new and independent authority. The Emigration Bill, which included traces of his own proposals, again came up before a Grand Committee of the House of Commons but could not be discussed because a quorum was not present. Protests from the Dominions seemed to have no effect and Haggard maintained, 'if it gets the chance, the Government will drop it altogether.'[40] He even urged that the Royal Colonial Institute send him, despite his poor health, on another tour of the Empire to drum up support for action. Within a year of the war ending, he noted, there were four hundred thousand demobilised soldiers out of work and the Government was said to be paying at the rate of £200,000,000 a year in unemployment benefit.

But, at the very time when action should be taken, the politicians seemed to have lost interest and their former enthusiasm began to look like a cynical diversion to distract attention from the war. For Haggard himself there was to be a sop and in the New Year's Honours he was appointed a Knight of the British Empire – particularly for his services on the Royal Dominions Commission – which would not involve a new title since he was already Sir Rider, leaving him pleased but disappointed that he was now unlikely to be accorded the recognition he wanted most as a Privy Councillor. Yet official indifference had not quite killed his idea, for a month later the newly appointed Under-Secretary for the Colonies Colonel Leo Amery, invited him to discuss emigration. 'They want to make use of me in some capacity in connection therewith,' he noted 'Probably it will boil down to a seat on the advisory council – or to nothing at all.'[41] Within a year, The Times correspondent in Australia reported that there was little emigration from the British Isles, 'although there is ample land and opportunities are plentiful'. Three years had passed since Haggard had been given promises of land, or of help, but, he noted, 'these promises are lapsing, or have lapsed. It is heart-breaking!'

At the end of December, 1918, Haggard received another letter from Roosevelt, saying that, 'Like you, I am not at all sure about the future.'

Ten days later, in the first week of the first post-war year, he died suddenly of 'a clot of blood upon the lungs' and Haggard mourned for his friend 'for the world's sake', musing, 'A great man indeed.'[44] Now there was only Kipling to whom he could open his heart and mind.

With his compulsion to work, Haggard remained busy. Although he had refused an approach to stand again for the East Norfolk constituency as a Conservative, since not only did he detest political parties but his own politics were an idiosyncratic mixture of Conservative, Socialist and Imperialist, he did allow himself to be recruited, together with Kipling, into a new anti-Bolshevik movement called the Liberty League, backed by the newspaper magnate Lord Northcliffe. This was ill-conceived and finally disintegrated in a scandal involving the embezzlement of its funds, but not before it had been lampooned by the press, particularly with a rhyme running,

'Every Bolsh is a blackguard,'
Said Kipling to Haggard.
'And given to tippling,'
Said Haggard to Kipling ...
'That's just what I say,'
Said the author of *They*.
'I agree; I agree,'
Said the author of *She*.[45]

He kept writing novels so that his publisher always had a stockpile, some of them completed several years before publication date; indeed, a dozen of his books were published after the end of the Great War.* They were not as popular as they once had been and his agent had difficulty in selling the serial rights but the booming international film industry found his stories ideal for the new medium and profitable contracts were signed for the filming of seven novels. He wrote articles for newspapers and magazines on subjects ranging from the Boy Scout movement to Egyptian archaeology and the racial mixture of the British Empire to 'My Favourite Holiday'. There were no fees for letters to newspapers, nor for speeches, but he wrote or delivered both on the future of the Kaiser, the vulgarity of film publicity, the current novel, taxation of land, the Castle Museum at Norwich, art, the birth rate, Danish agricultural policy, the

When the World Shook, The Ancient Allan, Smith and the Pharaohs, She and Allan, The Virgin of the Sun, Wisdom's Daughter, Heu-Heu, Queen of the Dawn, The Treasure of the Lake, Allan and the Ice Gods, Mary of Marion Isle and *Belshazzar*.

importance of humility, the real Umslopogaas, the need for electric power in rural England 'so that it can be used for all household purposes,'[46] and the future of the British Empire.

'In a way,' wrote Haggard in his diary towards the end of 1919, 'the British Empire is at the apex of its glory and, if only it can recover itself at home, its future is splendid and assured.'[47] But, within a month, he was adding, 'Never has the general and social outlook been darker than at present. Everyone is excited, everyone is dissatisfied; abroad there are endless troubles and at home prices go up and up; the Government blunders about like a bull in a china shop and the crockery crashes.'[48] Instead of the war, he worried about industrial unrest, political agitators and strikers. Looking about for scapegoats he became infected by the currently virulent anti-Semitism, which had been growing since the mass immigration of the late nineteenth century.

Haggard was, of course, part-Jewish himself – although he still preferred to romanticise his 'wild Russian blood' – and he admired the historical Israelites as idealistic and determined. In the view of the English upper-middle class, it was not quite proper to be 'linked with trade,' as were so many Jews, except at a distance, and he had also noted the number of Jewish intellectuals in the socialist movement and among the Bolsheviks in Russia. So he was prone to anti-Semitic outbursts, writing early in 1919, 'In Poland, the Jews are being persecuted, in England they are persecuting us. Jews seem to be at the bottom of much of this Bolshevism and labour trouble. Why cannot we clear these undesirable aliens out of our country?'[49]

Kipling was more prone to such prejudice and, at the end of the year, Haggard wrote:

Kipling, who had been lunching here today, is of the opinion that we owe all our Russian troubles, and many others, to the machinations of the Jews. I do not know, I am sure, but personally I am inclined to believe that there are Jews and Jews. If, however, they are as evil as he believes, the evil that they do is likely to recoil on their own heads since in extremity, the world has a rough way of dealing with Jews.[50]

Always receptive to the dramatic rumour, whether it was of heroism or atrocity, Haggard had a tendency to repeat even the most grotesque stories about 'The Jewish Peril', which seemed more immediate than 'The Yellow Peril'. Indeed, he was unable to accept even the most distinguished Jews as equals, remarking, with unconscious irony, after hearing a speech by the Marquess of Reading,* 'It was rather absurd to listen to this member of an ancient Semitic race, declaiming with a somewhat forced enthusiasm about the glories of being an Englishman.'[51]

When the mandate of Palestine became a British responsibility in 1920, Haggard noted that it was to become the Jewish national home, a prospect he had strongly supported eight years before. 'It is a far cry to the days of Titus and strange it seems that Palestine should once more return to the Jew, this time under the Protectorate of Britain in place of that of Rome. But will the Jews make it their home? Not in great numbers, I think, for in Jerusalem there is little money to be made.'[52] Having once endorsed the Zionist cause, Haggard now began to disparage it, particularly when he was comparing the British and Roman empires; later remarking that 'most Englishmen are in a very similar mood to that of the Romans under the Emperors of the Fall' and would not be eager to defend 'the Jewish state that, for some reason, which has never been adequately explained, we have set up in Palestine'.[53]

Partly, perhaps, such attitudes were induced by his feelings of failure. It was probably this, too, that prompted him to accept invitations to sit on unpaid and time-consuming government committees – those concerned with the national birth rate and the relief of allies amongst them – but, in that year, the Haggard family sold their London flat. He now had a routine of spending the summer at Ditchingham and the winter at St Leonard's and would stay at a hotel when in London for a garden party at Buckingham Palace, or for a dinner at which he would be the guest and speaker. He was always ready with trenchant opinions, warning of the renaissance of Germany, or of Jewish manipulation, or of Irish savagery in 'The Troubles', which produced the atrocities the Germans had once provided.

Now that the war was over, there was no need for tact towards the Japanese ally and Haggard again raised fears about the dynamic Orientals moving into the empty Dominions.

It is my belief [he declared] that within a short time, say two hundred, or three hundred years, the East will make war upon the West and conquer it, or at least permeate it, so that our existing civilisations become absorbed. Such are my conclusions and, perhaps to a less degree ... were those of my late friend Roosevelt.[54]

Appointed Viceroy of India in 1921.

He quoted 'rather an excited article about Australia' in *The Times* by Keith Murdoch* supporting the 'white Australia' policy, asking, 'Will Britain ... if needs be fight for a white Australia?' To this Haggard replied, 'Britain probably would fight to prevent Australia being invaded and captured by the yellow races to whom her empty lands are a great temptation. But, to prevent immigrants of that blood from landing on her shores – well, I am not sure.'[55] That possibility could have been made less likely by his settlement scheme of 1916, which he considered a tragically wasted opportunity. The question that should be answered, he maintained, was not 'Are we willing to fight for a white Australia?' but 'Are we willing to fight for an empty Australia?' He quoted an estimate that the Northern Territory, which had a population of one or two thousand, could support thirty million and also the view that this was 'a far more dangerous powder magazine than Germany ever was to Europe'.[56]

His constant repetition of his vision of the Dominions populated by the British was, however, a factor in persuading the Government to take some action and, at the end of 1921, the Empire Settlement Bill was laid before the House of Commons. This would allow the Government to subsidise public or private settlement schemes in the Empire with grants to meet half their cost to a maximum total of £3,000,000 a year for the next fifteen years. It would not promote emigration on anything like the scale Haggard had envisaged but it was at least a start and he felt satisfaction that it would for the first time put it on 'a sound, continuous basis'. When the Bill was given its second reading in the Commons in April, 1922, he added,

> Although my share in the business is now forgotten, I look upon this advance with some pride since surely I have had some part in bringing it about. The real forward movement towards the State recognition and support of emigration dates from my mission round the world in 1916 that brought about the appointment of the Empire Migration Committee,† on which I served, and whose recommendations in the main are now being acted upon. Still nothing would have happened had it not been for the dreadful unemployment of the present time ...[57]

It was something, but it would not, he knew, be what he had imagined and it would not be enough.

* The future Sir Keith Murdoch, the newspaper magnate, and father of Mr Rupert Murdoch, present owner of *The Times*.
† Otherwise the Empire Settlement Committee.

CHAPTER FOURTEEN

'Imagination ... a terrible steed to ride'

AT THE BEGINNING of 1921, Maurice Greiffenhagen, who had illustrated many of Haggard's novels, completed a portrait of him and it was exhibited at the Royal Academy.* It showed him seated in a chair; a gaunt, handsome figure wearing what one of his sisters-in-law described as 'your The-end-of-all-things-is-at-hand-and-on-the-whole-it-is-better-so expression'; Haggard himself gave it the title 'Wrinkles'.[1] It did show him as an Old Testament prophet in modern dress, wary but wise and with a tranquillity that his daughter Lilias was to notice. 'Strangely enough these years were full of happiness,' she wrote of the post-war period. 'As if the river of his life had passed the deep pools and troubled shallows of its earlier course and had spread out into quiet, sunlit waters, lipped on the horizon by the sea.'[2]

There was plenty to worry about if he so wished. In January, 1922, Haggard and Kipling exchanged visits in Sussex and, as was their custom, talked about a wide range of subjects and, as always, the British Empire. The latter's fear was of another Indian Mutiny and he had heard that already 'no white ladies and children are ever left alone, especially at outlying stations.' The future of the British presence in Egypt was in question and Ireland was a recurrent nightmare of violence. Indeed, after their final conversation at Bateman's, Haggard reported that Kipling 'even went so far as to say that it looks as though the Empire were going to fall to pieces. The only hope he could see was in young men, who may arise, but when I asked him where these young men were, he replied he did not know.'[3] Many were, of course, in the military cemeteries of

---

* Sir Rider Haggard wrote in a note on the back of the painting, which is now in the possession of the Cheyne family, that some 'Royal Academicians ... declared to me that it was one of the very finest portraits that had ever crossed their doors and an "immortal work" ... and would have been bought by the Trustees of the Chantrey Bequest for the Nation had not it been for the fact that Greiffenhagen was a member of the selecting committee ... Whether it does or does not make me too sad, old and marred, it is a brilliant piece of artistry and colouration.'

France and Flanders and Haggard might have added that others should by now have been new settlers giving muscle and drive to the Dominions.

Writing to his Norfolk neighbour William Carr about county affairs at this time, he recounted a debate about the origin of a marble bust he had bought in a Norwich antique shop and believed to be Greek. One authoritative friend had said that it must be Roman because the treatment of the hair was too free and had been carved two centuries after Christ, while another insisted that it was Greek after all. 'Such things now interest me more than anything else,' he explained, 'except observing world events.'[4] Feeling an old man at the age of sixty-five, he saw himself as the prophet-like figure of Greiffenhagen's portrait, almost an Egyptian seer, or Greek oracle, unable to direct but able to warn.

Towards the end of the year, news reached London that galvanised him and he entered into his diary on 30 November:

> Mr Howard Carter, whom I know and who, I believe, now works on behalf of Lord Carnarvon, has made a marvellous discovery in the Valley of the Kings at Thebes. There, below the tomb of Rameses VI, he has found a sealed cache of several chambers full of all the funerary furniture, also the chariots and throne of Pharaoh Tutankhamun, who was one of the shadowy successors to Akhenaten, the heretic Pharaoh. Whether his body is in one of the chambers that remains unopened is not yet known.[5]

At once he was being asked for his reaction by newspapers and the *New York World* sent him a reply-paid cable asking his view on 'the efficacy of magical curses against despoilers, placed around ancient mummies'. In the same entry in his diary, he noted that Kipling was aware of the cloud of mock-mysticism the discovery had aroused: 'Rudyard asked me on Tuesday if I had noticed how every sort of superstition was becoming rampant in this country, which ... always presaged the downfall of great civilisations.'[6] Certainly he himself drew comfort from such contemplation of ancient beliefs.

As further news of discoveries in the tomb of Tutankhamun were reported, Haggard became a champion for the respect due to the pharaoh, although 'he had avowed a faith different from our own'. In a letter to *The Times*, he warned that when his mummy was removed from its gold sarcophagus he

> may be stripped and, like the great Rameses and many another monarch mighty in his day, laid half-naked to rot in a glass case of the

museum at Cairo ... to be made the butt of merry jests by tourists, as I have heard with my own ears. Is this decent? Is it doing as we would be done by? ... Now that they are so helpless, from the dust they pray us to protect them.

His solution was simple but dramatic. Tutankhamun and the other exhumed pharaohs should be 'examined, photographed and modelled in wax ... laid in one of the chambers of the Great Pyramid and sealed there with concrete in such a fashion that only the destruction of the entire block of acres of stone could again reveal them to the eyes of man.'[7]

Curiously, the Egyptian king and the Norfolk squire had something specific in common. There was one particular place where they were at home. For Haggard, it was not Ditchingham, where there were constant reminders of his failed farming; nor Bradenham, where there were too many desecrated memories; nor London, which he loathed; nor St Leonard's, which was simply a comfortable retreat. He had long felt most content in the Pharaohs' capital, now the riverside town of Luxor, and there he was determined to go for a final visit.

His principal companion was to be Lilias but a nephew, a niece and several friends were coming, too, and, after another stormy passage, they reached Port Said on 23 January 1924. As they arrived, the ship's wireless officer reported that, in London, the Conservative Government had fallen and been replaced by the Socialists under Ramsay MacDonald. Here indeed was a subject to inspire Haggard's pontification but, after a night in Cairo, when they boarded a steamer on the Nile, the twentieth century faded. They stopped at Memphis and Sakkara and at once there were reminders of the callous behaviour against which Haggard had protested in his letter to *The Times*; after visiting one ancient site, he complained in his diary, 'They are still pulling out the poor corpses by dozens so that the whole necropolis is littered with fragments of humanity.'[8]

Arriving at Luxor, an Egyptian fortune-teller came on board, squatted, smoothed a pile of sand upon the deck and began tracing lines in it with a finger. As the passengers gathered round, Haggard advised his nephew against asking questions as he might be told something unpleasant. Hearing the tone of his voice, the Egyptian looked up and said, 'You call me a common cheat – is it not so? Then what of the son of whom you always think?'[9] Only Haggard and Lilias heard this and she recorded that her father made no reply, but walked across to the rail and stood looking silently over the Nile to the long range of the Theban Hills that hide the Valley of the Kings.

> We have had tumultuous days at Luxor visiting the temples, the tombs, the Colossi, etc [wrote Haggard in his diary]. Lilias and I were honoured with an invitation from Howard Carter to inspect the tomb of Tutankhamun ... It is small and, for a Pharaoh, rather a mean tomb ... The gilt shrines however – what we could see of them – are wonderful and the gold on them glitters as if it were laid on yesterday ... Howard Carter looked very worn and tired[10]

by the constant stream of visitors, squabbles concerning the newspaper coverage and trouble over the concession from the Egyptian Government.

Haggard found peace and satisfaction in the temples on the Nile at Abydos and Denderah, and was photographed in the Hall of Osiris at the former, which had always been known for its extraordinary air of sanctity.*

> Sometimes it is possible to separate oneself from the many companions of the tourist season in Egypt [he recorded], and sit alone in some hall of one of the great temples, as I did today in that of Abydos, perhaps the divinest among them. I looked about me in the silence that was broken only by the hum of bees and the twitter of the building birds. Everywhere soared great columns ... everywhere rose the sculptured walls where kings made offerings to painted gods, or goddesses led them by the hand into some holy presence. Here was the place where, for tens of centuries, priests marched from Sanctuary to Sanctuary, following the order of their ritual: where proud Pharaoh – himself a god – bent the knee before other gods, whose company he soon must join ...
>
> Surely such a spot should be holy ... What does it all mean? It means that this, and many other sanctuaries, expressed the faith and spiritual aspirations of dim forgotten millions. They believed that here dwelt God ... It is terrific to think that all these hordes were deluded by a faith which we know to be false ... as nine out of ten clergymen would demonstrate. The glorious temples were in vain, the gifts to the gods were meaningless offerings, benefiting none but the priests who re-

---

* Visiting Abydos in 1992 in company with an Egyptologist, Dr Rosalie Davies, who had worked there for many months, the author asked whether she had experienced this and was told 'Every time I entered the temple, there was a feeling of comfort, like swimming into a warm patch in the sea.'

ceived them; the worshippers pursued an empty lie ... If this inference were true, their lot was terrible indeed. But I, for one, do not believe it to be true. I look upon religion from that of the lowest savage up to that of the most advanced Christian, as a ladder stretching from Earth to Heaven – a Jacob's ladder, if you will, whereby, painfully with many slips and backward fallings, Mankind climbs towards the skies. In that ladder, the faith of the old Egyptians was a single rung ...

Once he had left the pillared halls, he was back in the tumult of the tourists' Egypt; its herds of visitors and packs of beggars. Yet he could escape, even on the terrace of his hotel, where, he wrote:

I watched the infant crescent moon, bearing the disc of the old moon, and, not far above her, Venus blazing like a silver point, and in the background the Valley of the Dead Kings austere and solemn in the rosy glow of sunset and, at my feet, the broad Nile, on which sailed a single white-winged boat. Looking at these, vulgarity was forgotten ... Man cannot touch them and, when he has ceased to be, still the crescent moon will ride and the star will shine and the broad Nile flow and the rugged hills look solemn in the sunset.[11]

On their return to Cairo, he wrote 'news from home dribbles through to us':[12] strikes continued, Stanley Baldwin had been re-elected leader of the Conservative Party and President Wilson had died. They had planned to visit Palestine but the lure of Luxor was too strong and, when the other members of the party had left for England, Haggard and Lilias returned there. They visited the temple at Karnak by moonlight and found peace there, too: 'As Lilias says, there is about these ruins no atmosphere of wrath and terror, but rather one of gentle and kindly compassion. They are not a place where one would fear to pass the night alone.'[13] Then even Luxor was overwhelmed by contemporary life: 'floods of Americans touring in ship-loads invade the hotels and make them dreadful, so that one must fly to one's bedroom. The costumes they wear are often strange and, indeed, in the case of stout elderly women, sometimes, to my old-fashioned tastes, positively indecent.'[14]

They returned to Cairo, choosing to avoid the city and stay at the Mena House Hotel near the Pyramids of Ghiza, although 'a stream of motors screeches past bearing American, or German tourists intent on "doing" the Pyramids in half an hour!' His greatest pleasure was, he wrote,

to sit in my room at the top of the house and, as I am doing at the moment, watch the mighty mass of the Great Pyramid gradually devoured of the night. It grows dim, its sharp outlines become blurred; it disappears by degrees till it becomes but a blacker blot upon the blackness. Then it is gone, yet being gone, its presence still is *felt*, something palpable though lost to the eye.[15]

This was his final memory of Egypt for, as he sailed from Port Said, he wrote:

> So, at the dawn, we bade farewell to Egypt. I never expect to look on it again and, indeed, do not wish to do so ... If the old Pharaohs ... could behold it now in all its hateful and brazen vulgarity, I think they would go mad! The ancient land ... is degraded with tourists, harlots and brass bands.[16]

They arrived at Tilbury on 30 March and travelled to London, where his first act was to call on Lord Curzon and give him a pharaoh's signet ring. After visiting the British Empire Exhibition at Wembley soon after it was opened by King George V, he returned to Ditchingham and found spring still awaited. It was a relief to be home for he no longer enjoyed travel as he once had, although his imagination roamed as widely as ever. Now he could worry about labour unrest, continuing troubles in Ireland and the news that the Labour Government refused to strengthen the defences of Singapore, to the dismay of the Australians. Japan would be encouraged, he feared, and 'one day ... when it is ready, it will awake and that awakening will be terrible for America grown soft in luxury and windy with self-pride. Japan and its allies may be beaten in the end but the victory will cost the conquerors dear.' Haggard insisted that what he saw as the 'hatred' of the East by the West was not racial but 'has its root in trade and labour jealousy. The Easterner works harder and more cheaply – that is all.'[17]   With his low opinion of British politicians and his disillusionment over the performance of the newly established League of Nations, he looked with wary but not unfriendly curiosity at the new breed of European dictator, notably Benito Mussolini, who had made himself *Il Duce* in 1922 and was now 'trying to run Italy as a Roman Emperor might have done'.[18] He noted in his diary:

> Indeed dictators are *à la mode* today and it is amusing to watch the attitude of Labour in face of this fact. Obviously it would not mind its own dictator but ... an uneasy suspicion haunts the mind of our

agitators lest one day someone of the sort should arise in Britain and sweep away the privileges of Trade Unions and make people do an honest day's work in return for their pay ... Personally I cannot say that I like dictators. At first, they have all the virtues of the new broom, but when the twigs grow worn either they don't sweep at all, or they sweep too hard and scratch the floor.[19]

In other ways Haggard kept up with new ideas and one of them was aviation. He had already warned of the future threat of aerial bombardment and the development of the aircraft carrier by navies ('Perhaps before another war comes ... vessels of war will be chiefly used for the transport of air machines to the localities whence they can operate')[20] and now he considered travel by air. In 1922, he had seen a seaplane crash off Hastings and commented, 'Nothing will make me believe that these air craft are desirable vehicles of locomotion,'[21] and, as for airships, another accident prompted him to declare that 'any who wish to escape the risk of a horrible death will, I think, be wise to avoid using them just to save a little time.'[22] When an Imperial Airways flight to Paris ended in another disaster, he commented, 'Several of the papers take the opportunity to show how safe and delightful is travelling by air!'[23]

On his forty-third wedding anniversary in 1924 he mused on the changes he had seen at Ditchingham:

We drove away from the wedding at this house in a chaise and four with postilions in the old post-boy dress, a sight which would astonish Ditchingham in this year of grace when even the milk churns go to the station by motor and every child rides a bicycle ... What would those of 43 years ago have said to five-shilling Income Taxes, Super-Taxes, Woman's vote, Doles, perpetual strikes and Communistic Sunday schools? I wonder what this England of ours will be like when another 43 years have gone by?* Well, we shall not be here to see.[24]

His greatest fear for the future was a racial world war and this was aroused by the French policy of granting full citizenship in its colonies. 'Is it not dangerous to train the swarthy nations in the use of arms that may in the end be used indiscriminately against the white communities of the world?' he asked. 'The great ultimate war, as I have always held, will be that between the white and the coloured races.'[25]

For the British, Haggard saw that the most promising leader on the political horizon was Winston Churchill, whom he had met when a boy

* That is, the year 1967.

but whose policies and style he had frequently criticised. On 6 October 1924, he wrote to him, saying that if the Labour Government should fall 'there is no one ... who could form a new Government in the existing House. But I ... think that you might do so. You are of no party but just an anti-Socialist ... Why not put yourself forward?'[26]

A few days afterwards he met a friend and an acquaintance who symbolised, respectively, all that he admired and feared. Lunching with Kipling in London, he recorded:

> In his amusing and allusive fashion he pointed out to me that in the Book of Revelations it is prophesied that the Beast will only be allowed to dominate a third of the Earth and that Bolshevist Russia already occupied a fifth of the third, so that there would not be very much more to go mad and bad, begging me to consult the Bible, on which he was so good as to believe me an authority! I propose to do so tonight.

Afterwards, he continued,

> On the steps of the Duke of York's column, I met H. G. Wells ... and asked him if he were pursuing his blessed Communism ... He replied no, that he was tired of it and of everything and was going abroad to be quiet and 'find his soul'; adding, 'Have you found your soul?' I replied that I hoped so.[27]

This had, indeed, been Haggard's preoccupation for many years and now seemed more urgent for he was taken ill at a climactic moment. On 5 November 1924, he had been chosen as the principal speaker at a dinner in the Stationers' Hall to celebrate the bicentenary of his publisher, Longman. He spoke with wit and grace to a distinguished gathering that included his old friends Sir Edmund Gosse and Sir Arthur Conan Doyle but afterwards suffered 'a most fearful attack of indigestion'[28] and was clearly ill on his return to St Leonard's. However, three weeks later, he felt able to deliver a speech in London on 'The Good and Bad of Imagination'.

> Imagination is power which comes from we know not where [he began]. Imagination is a great gift, but a terrible steed to ride. Those that dwell under the shadow of its wings eat the fruit of both good and evil, for if genius and inspiration is theirs, so also is madness and misery undreamed of by those of more phlegmatic mind.

As he grew old, he said, it seemed to him that

the spirit of man is like those great icebergs which float in Arctic seas –
towering masses of glittering blue-green ice, which yet hide four-fifths
of their bulk beneath the water. It is the hidden power of the spirit
which connects the visible and the invisible; which hears the still small
voice calling from the infinite.[29]

After this speech, too, he was taken ill and his doctor diagnosed a bladder
infection. On his return to Ditchingham, Lilias was shocked by his
appearance: 'He had changed ... in some intangible fashion ... His face
had settled into the brooding sadness so noticeable in the portrait painted
by Maurice Greiffenhagen ... His hands, had grown oddly thin, so thin
that the heavy Egyptian rings which he wore, almost slipped off them.'[30]
It was a mild and sunny Christmas, but he complained in his diary that he
had to

sit through an Xmas Day dinner at which my grandsons, as children do
on these occasions, did justice to their creature cravings and I shall not
forget the experience.* Well, we must suffer what it pleases God to
send us with such patience as we may but I begin to think that my active
career is at an end and that I must resign from all public work.[31]

Just before Christmas, his hopes for the campaigns he had started took a
blow when another campaign was launched by the Minister of Immigration in Ottawa, which seemed to lower a final curtain on his dreams of
a British nation from the Atlantic to the Pacific. This campaign was also
to attract settlers but, declared the Minister,

I expect to secure farmer settlers from Hungary and Hungarian
nationals in Rumania. I can look forward to a large immigration of the
best agricultural type of Yugoslavia ... Increased immigration is
expected from the Scandinavian countries and Switzerland. Arrangements made with the Irish Free State permit of large emigration to
Canada.

But by now Haggard himself was disillusioned and added, 'It is sad to
read this and reflect that there are millions of people who ought to be
moved from this country. The truth is, however, that they do not wish to
go and, if they did, they would not make good migrants.'[32]

Three more blows followed within a month. First, Arthur Cochrane,

* His grandson, Commander Mark Cheyne, remembers Sir Rider telling him at table 'not to eat like a
pig'.

his friend and partner in ostrich farming, died; then his brother, Andrew; finally his Norfolk neighbour William Carr, who had become a regular correspondent. Soon after, Lord Curzon, his grandest friend, also died and Haggard concluded that his career 'magnificent as it was ... was still a failure ... He could never catch the ear of the crowd ... he had not the art of popularity. Possessing everything else, he still lacked this.' This could never have been said of himself for he had caught and held the eyes and ears of the world but, while his public had read his stories with enthralment, they did not seem to have listened to his guidance, nor acted upon it.

Meanwhile his own illness, which he described as 'a horrible disease of the bladder'[33] kept him lying in bed, depressed at the thought that his only close friend still living was Rudyard Kipling. It was now he who came to the rescue, writing on 15 February 1925, 'Dear old man, I heard a day or two ago that you are under the weather at Ditchingham ... In a hell-broth of a winter like this, bed's the best and soundest place there is.'[34] Here began a succession of long, chatty, cheering letters, giving family news, commenting upon international affairs and flattering his sick friend with the occasional hearty metaphysical sally: 'I was overcome by the ancient marvel ... that a man's carcass should be such a disgusting, ill-perfumed, vilely packed bag of tricks while his soul, at the same moment, or almost, should sit cheerily trumpeting above it all!'[35]

Haggard responded by sending Kipling a heavy Egyptian signet ring bearing the seal of the monotheist Pharaoh Akhenaten, explaining, 'my rings fall off my hands and there was a deuce of a hunt for one of them the other night – finally retrieved from the seat of my pyjamas.' At the same time he dictated a long letter to Miss Hector, giving his friend an assessment of his own life's work: his fiction was not mentioned and he concentrated on 'some fifteen years solid ... as one of the great unpaid'. He regarded his work for the Royal Dominions Commission as 'utterly wasted' but maintained that 'the only things that appear to have succeeded at all are what I have done off my own bat.' One of these was the *Rural England* survey and his campaign for smallholdings. The other, his world tour for the Royal Colonial Institute, which he believed, with uncharacteristic optimism, had eventually given rise to the Empire Settlement Act,

which is imperfect and insufficient enough, but still a beginning – an egg out of which great things will, I hope, grow in time – and, honestly,

238

I believe I had something to do with that egg. [He concluded] I am glad to say I am somewhat better. I got up yesterday and sat in the old study … for a little while, but of course my limbs are like sticks … you would laugh to see me being fed with milk puddings from a spoon just like a baby.[36]

Kipling kept up the comforting flow of letters, which continued when he went on holiday in France with long, comic accounts of his travels. He described Lourdes 'getting ready for summer when the miracles begin and the special trains will pour in' and Pau, where the English visitors were 'elderly birds with doubtful lungs in plus-fours'.[37] He gently teased his wife for being '"pityingly sorry" for the male who doesn't understand the joy and solace of shopping' while elaborating his own despair at being unable to buy 'any decent brand of pipe tobacco'[38] and his experiments with a meerschaum pipe being 'like a liaison with a lime-kiln'.[39] He responded to news of Haggard's health, welcoming 'the good news that you've been trekking about in a Bath chair. Hurroo! It isn't quite the same as a Boer pony, or even an ox-wagon; but 'twill serve for a start; and you've got the spring winds in your rear (on reflection, this isn't a happy simile; but I'll let it stand).'[40] Finally, when he heard that his friend was to go to London for further examination and possibly an exploratory operation, he wrote comfortingly,

There is this – and just this to be said – when the big Machine of Fate is felt and realised to have us in its hold, one gets a blessed incuriousness and content on the matter – on all matters; and the odd feeling that somewhere at sometime the self-same thing has happened before and that, try as one may, one can't put a foot wrong. I *know* that that will come over you as you go up to the table – if you've got to – and it beats any known anaesthetic.[41]

Soon afterwards he wrote to Miss Hector, asking her to telegraph any news of Haggard to him in Brussels.

Despite Louie's care at Ditchingham, Haggard deteriorated. In April, the move to a London nursing-home* had been arranged and, as Lilias wrote:

It is obvious that Rider knew the end had come. So in her heart did Louie. On the grey spring morning that the ambulance was coming to fetch him, she was in his room helping with the last-minute prep-

* At 3 Devonshire Terrace, Bayswater.

arations. The nurse had dressed him and left him in a chair, but he looked down at his overcoat as if something was missing, then got up, walked to the table, where there was a bowl of daffodils, and, taking one, pulled it through his buttonhole – then turned with rather a sad little smile to his wife. How many times had she seen him do that. The last little action of the morning ritual in his dressing-room; for every day the gardener brought in a buttonhole, a rose or carnation in summer, an orchid in winter. Rider was never without a flower. The little incident broke her control – 'Rider' she said, 'do you really want to go, dear? You have only to say if you don't and we'll send the ambulance back – are you quite, quite sure?'[42]

He was.

The exploratory operation was apparently a success and, as he re-covered, Louie and her daughters sat with him as he drifted in and out of consciousness. Late one evening, Major Reggie Cheyne – the son-in-law who had strode in out of the night, stained with the mud of the trenches, that wartime Christmas – sat with him. He thought Haggard was asleep when lights and shadows like flames began to play on the wall behind the bed. Cheyne looked from the window, high above the rooftops, and saw that a tall building was on fire. As he turned, he saw Haggard sitting upright in bed, an arm outstretched towards the distant fire, his dull eyes alive with its reflection. 'My God!' thought Cheyne, 'an old pharaoh!'[43] Next morning, 14 May 1925, Rider Haggard died. An intestinal leakage and exhaustion had killed him;* at sixty-eight, he was worn out.

Soon afterwards Lilias went up to his room at the nursing-home, alone and apprehensive. Outside was spring sunshine, blossoming laburnum and may. In her father's room she found that

the blind was drawn and a dim, honey-coloured light flooded the mean tastelessness of the small room; the shabby furniture, all the litter of his personal possessions on the dressing-table – the bed and what lay upon it. The tumbled clothes had been hastily straightened, the unlovely paraphernalia of sickness barely thrust to one side. No flowers, no beauty, no dignity or reverence had served that death-bed – there was only a sheeted figure looking strangely small.

Then, Lilias continued as if describing somebody else:

Death was no stranger to her, but she stood for a moment, filled with

---

* The death certificate gave the cause as, '1. Recto-Vesical fistula; 2. Exhaustion following prolonged suppuration syncope.'

an unutterable dread. For the first time in her life, if she called there would be no answer; if she spoke, no reply. She put out her hand and pulled down the sheet.

Something lay there, wrapped in a dignity and peace which defeated the careless arrangement of the slack hands and crumpled clothes – but, in a moment, the terror of absolute loss, the desolation of everlasting separation fell away. What she had thought so beloved was no more than a cloak dropped from his shoulders, a garment still carrying the impress of his form ... The complete and triumphant conviction born in that dim, mean room, that the body was indeed only a garment; that the spirit, casting off the trammels and humiliations of the flesh, and finished with the winds and weeping of this rough world, had gone on its way rejoicing.[44]

At his own wish, Haggard's body was cremated – possibly to avoid an imagined fate like that of the dead pharaohs – and his ashes were laid in the vault beneath a black marble slab in the chancel of St Mary's church at Ditchingham. The inscription described him as 'Knight of the British Empire, who with a humble heart strove to serve his country'. Another inscription nearby told that his ashes lay close to his son, 'who sleeps without'.

Soon after the death of Sir Rider Haggard, Norfolk squire, imperialist, agricultural and social reformer and novelist, his friend Charles Longman, the publisher, took from his safe the sealed parcel left with him thirteen years earlier, containing the manuscript of his autobiography, *The Days of My Life*. When Haggard had completed it, he had written at midnight on the Whit Sunday of 1912, a note of his final intention, knowing that this would not be read until after his death. 'I dedicate this record of my days to my dear Wife,' he wrote, 'and to the memory of our son, whom now I seek.'

Epilogue

THE BRITISH EMPIRE survived Rider Haggard by a quarter of a century. Most of the colonies and protectorates were granted independence after the Second World War, which he had forecast, and in many cases the veneer of British democratic institutions, which had been imposed, flaked away. His idea of populating the Dominions with Anglo-Saxons – particularly men who had fought in the First World War and their families – did bear some fruit. Although his dream of a global British nation never took wing once his own drive ceased, the Empire Settlement Act of 1922 and subsequent emigration schemes had some success, but they disintegrated after the Second World War with the evolution of 'multi-cultural' societies.

The population of Australia, which had survived the onslaught of the 'Yellow Peril' that he had forecast, stood at seven million at the end of the Second World War and ninety-eight per cent were of Anglo-Saxon or Celtic stock. That population doubled in thirty years and seemed likely to triple by the end of the century. However, by the 1990s, only twenty-six per cent of immigrants originated from Europe, including the British Isles and Russia, while more than half were Asian.

Canada, which Haggard had not seen as so vulnerable as Australia, also changed its policies. Immigration from Britain, which had been well over half the total at the end of the nineteenth century, dropped to well below that by the middle of the twentieth, British immigrants being replaced by those from Italy, Yugoslavia, Hungary and the Netherlands, and their total was further eroded by a high proportion emigrating again to the United States. Particularly after the Immigration Act of 1963, which abolished the quota system, the proportion of Anglo-Saxon and Celtic migrants steadily fell and by 1990 was equalled by that from India, exceeded by that from Poland and was about a third of that from Hong Kong.

The Empire was replaced by the Commonwealth, a loose association of the former rulers and the ruled, and that showed an increasing tendency to shake itself free from even those links. Towards the end of the century a multi-cultural Australia was moving towards independence from even nominal loyalty to the Crown, while Canada seemed ready to split into French- and English-speaking components, the rump of the latter seeming vulnerable to absorption by the United States.

In Britain, the wide horizons which once lay open to the young through the choice of professions or occupations in most parts of the world via an interview in London were shrunk. Only at Ditchingham would Haggard now recognise his world. His daughters have all died – Dolly in 1946; Lilias, herself a notable writer on country life and her father's biographer, in 1968; Angie in 1973 – but his family survive on his land.* It is farmed by his grandson, Dolly's son, Mark Cheyne, who remembers his grandfather, and Haggard would surely be proud of the dynasty he perpetuated through his daughters. Mark Cheyne became a naval officer and won the Distinguished Service Cross in 1943 for gallantry in a destroyer action in the Mediterranean. Four years later, he married Nada Haggard, the adopted daughter of his aunt Angela, who had married her first cousin, Bazett's son, Tom. They have two sons and two daughters; one son now living in Canada, the other three children and their families on the Ditchingham estate. Commander and Mrs Cheyne live in Ditchingham Lodge, while the larger Ditchingham House – 'Mustard Pot Hall' – where Haggard himself lived, has been carefully converted into flats, while preserving some of the character he created there.

As a farmer and agricultural reformer, Haggard would be delighted by the relative prosperity he would see in Norfolk but doubtless appalled by the 'set-aside' scheme for supposedly surplus land in the 1990s. Many of the reforms he advocated were eventually put into practice. Six years after his death, the Government introduced direct financial aid to farmers, including subsidies, quotas and tariffs, and after the Second World War, passed the Agricultural Act of 1947 to lay the foundation of 'a stable and efficient agricultural industry capable of producing such part of the nation's food as is in the national interest'.[1]

What that national interest had become would be no surprise to Haggard for many of his prophecies had been fulfilled. As he had forecast, Germany rose again and a renewed war with Britain came only

His estate was, with all his assets, valued in his will at £61,725, which would have been worth more than £1,600,000 by the 1990s. The total would have been higher had he not been so generous to his relations over the years and had he invested more wisely.

a decade earlier than he had predicted because of Hitler's miscalculation of British reaction to his aggression in Europe. In the Far East, the 'Yellow Peril' materialised in the form of Japanese aggression and its 'Greater East Asia Co-Prosperity Sphere,' threatening Australia with invasion, which was, as he had expected, averted by an American rather than a British fleet; but then he had forecast the dominance of the United States in the West.

The demise of the British Empire would have come as no surprise but would have saddened him. It would be dangerous to guess at his reaction to mass immigration from the former Empire into the British Isles for his views were often unpredictable. Certainly he would have been surprised to know that, by 1993, one in twenty of the British population would be of Asian or African origin; one in five of their number being under sixteen, compared with one in three of the indigenous population. One could imagine him equally enthusiastic over Clement Attlee's Labour Government of 1945 and Margaret Thatcher's of 1979, or, at least, aspects of both. But it requires no effort to imagine his opinions of the resumption of atrocities committed by Irish terrorists.

That there had been no great developments in religious ideas would not have surprised him. But he would be pleased that his recommendation to Dean Inge that the misty area between science, the paranormal and religious belief should be studied by something akin to a Royal Commission has been undertaken in recent years by the Alister Hardy Research Centre in Oxford.

His own works live on. Of course, most of his fifty-eight novels and seven books about social, agricultural and economic reform have faded from public consciousness, although, at the time of writing, four are still in print. However, three of the novels – King Solomon's Mines, She and Allan Quatermain – remained staple reading for the young, although latterly being progressively replaced as entertainment by the attraction of television and video. Yet they survive in dramatised form, for twenty-eight films were made of his stories and some are regularly shown on television, inspiring a genre of imaginative adventure films, such as the 'Indiana Jones' series. Haggard's stories could also be seen as the inspiration for 'The Lost City' pleasure resort, opened in the wilds of the South African state of Bophuthatswana in 1992.

Lilias Rider Haggard's perceptive and affectionate memoir of her father, published in 1951, began a reassessment of him as a writer and as a man. Reviewing it, Graham Greene, the most celebrated novelist of his own day, wrote that Haggard had not only given him a sense of history but had been 'the greatest of all who enchanted us when we were young'. He saw beyond the thrilling yarns to the haunted, questing author:

We did not notice the melancholy end of every adventure, or know that the battle scenes took their tension from the fear of death ... Haggard's own melancholy end, departing from the doomed house with a flower in his buttonhole to the operation he guessed would be final, comes closer to adult literature perhaps than any of his books.[2]

A decade later, Lilias herself said in a radio talk:

Like many Victorians, my father took himself much too seriously and saw everything a bit larger than life. In his loves and loyalties, his triumphs and personal failures, his sorrows and personal short-comings, he scaled precarious heights and plumbed depths which are spared to ordinary humdrum mortals ... He had also a penetrating and sometimes devastating intuition about men and matters which as-sorted ill with his (in some ways) child-like nature. In his psychological make-up there were things which many people do not even guess at: the old, savage, primitive urges of nature worship, the fear of some demoniacal force whose power and depth might easily become beyond human resistance; his belief that all life was indestructible and that a love beyond our comprehension would ultimately solve all problems, if only it was held fast.[3]

When Dr Morton Cohen's clear-sighted biography of Haggard was published in 1960, C. S. Lewis, who went in search of the same Holy Grail, wrote, 'Haggard's best work will survive because it is based on an appeal well above high-water mark. The fullest tide of fashion cannot demolish it. A great myth is relevant as long as the predicament of humanity lasts.'[4] Reviewing the same book, V. S. (later Sir Victor) Pritchett wrote, 'Mr E. M. Forster once spoke of the novelist sending down a bucket into the unconscious; the author of *She* installed a suction pump. He drained the whole reservoir of the public's secret desires.'[5]

Academic assessments of his work was divided. Dr Alan Sandison of Exeter University was sympathetic, believing that it was his 'awareness of flux and change which gave Haggard his humanity and humility', which, 'enabled him to escape the vice of racial prejudice to which so many of his contemporaries succumbed'.[6] But Dr Wendy R. Katz, of St Mary's University, Halifax, Nova Scotia, saw him differently in her *Rider*

Haggard and the Fiction of Empire. Choosing her own quotations from Haggard's multiplicity of opinions, she concluded that he was paternalistic, racist and 'an imperial propagandist', and he can seem so when viewed from the late twentieth century. Yet his volatile writings can lead to many and sometimes contradictory conclusions. For example, Dr Katz, quoting what certainly read as anti-Semitic comments about 'Jewish profiteers'[7] after the First World War, writes that 'Haggard's anti-Semitism prevented him from seeing the possibility of a Jewish political state,'[8] she presumably being unaware of his telegram to the Young Zionists supporting their hopes of final resettlement in Palestine.

In her eyes, and in many others, Haggard's opinions were certainly not 'politically correct'. But he was a man of his time and his opinions were shaped by his own experience. He looked at the advance of late-nineteenth- and early-twentieth-century Britain and then at the societies of Africa and Asia, concluding not only that the former were currently more advanced than the latter but that they might not always be so and thus were not inherently superior. His apparent anti-Semitism is less easy to understand, given the high standards set by Jewish ideas and achievement in his day and his own Jewish blood. But he lived at a time when anti-Semitism was rife in all European countries; born of the fear of clever strangers and rivals and the British resentment of those who made a living by manipulating money rather than exchanging it for produce in the traditional ways, being forgetful of the landless state of the wandering Jews; their fears were sharpened by the part played by Jewish intellectuals in revolutionary movements and by the mass immigration of Jews from Russia and continental Europe. Amongst British writers, anti-Semitism crossed political divisions from the imperialist Rudyard Kipling to the radical H. G. Wells. Yet it is easy to imagine that, had Haggard been born half a century later he would have been an admirer, and probably a friend, of the soldier-archaeologist Moshe Dayan, amongst the many Jews who would have been seen to meet his own standards as gentlemen of ideas and action.

Haggard's ideals were invested in the British Empire and his energy directed towards fashioning it accordingly. He was not optimistic. 'Civilisation is only savagery silver gilt,' he wrote. 'Out of the soil of barbarism it has grown like a tree ... and into the soil like a tree it will once more, sooner or later, fall again, as the Egyptian civilisation fell, as the Hellenic civilisation fell and as the Roman civilisation fell.'[9] For eternal verities it was necessary to stare into the darkness and his eyes strained to do so. Would a man ever see them? 'Stare and study as he will,' concluded Haggard, 'at best ... he sees as in a glass darkly.'[10]

On reflection, his greatest achievement was not as a prophet, a reformer or, indeed, as a novelist. It is pointless to speculate on what he might have become had his father given him the educational advantages enjoyed by his brothers; had he been allowed to marry the girl of his choice; and had his son and heir survived to perpetuate his name; none of that occurred. Rider Haggard became the spur to imagination which would produce achievements both within and beyond the boundaries of his own conceptions. In agricultural and social reforms, his mark is upon those of his successors. The British Empire is gone, as have all the others, and most will accept the inevitable, while some will applaud and some will describe it as a lost civilisation. Rider Haggard saw it as the most beneficent form of social, political and economic order within the bounds of his own experience and imagination; a pattern which should be followed by whichever nation or race stood highest on the ladder of evolution. His ideal, as he saw it in his time, was not unworthy. His aspiration can be seen as the high-water mark of the British Empire; the moment when the last breaker of the tide sweeps up the beach and sinks into the sand.

Sources and Bibliography

The bulk of Sir Rider Haggard's papers are in the Norfolk Record Office, Norwich, to which he presented them. Many other family papers including transcripts of his diaries for the years 1914–25, which he dictated to Ida Hector with a view to publication, and his wife's diary in South Africa, are in the care of Commander Mark Cheyne, his grandson. Other papers are in the United States: in the archives of the Henry E. Huntington Library, San Marino, California, and the Manuscript Library of Columbia University. The Theodore Roosevelt correspondence is in the Library of Congress, Washington, D.C., and there are microfilm copies in the British Library, London. Smaller collections belong to Dr Morton Cohen, Mr Chris Coquet and the author.

Cohen, Morton. *Rider Haggard: His Life and Works*, London, 1960.
— *Rudyard Kipling to Rider Haggard: The Record of a Friendship*, London, 1965.
Constantine, Stephen. *Dominions Diary: The Letters of E. J. Harding, 1913–16, (Lancaster)*, 1992.
Ellis, Peter Beresford. *H. Rider Haggard: A Voice from the Infinite*, London, 1978.
Etherington, Norman. *Rider Haggard*, Boston, 1984.
Haggard, Ella. *Life and Its Author*, London, 1890.
— *Myra, or the Rose of the East*, Norwich, 1857.
Haggard, H. Rider. *Cetewayo and His White Neighbours*, London, 1882.
— *A Farmer's Year*, London, 1899.
— *A Winter Pilgrimage*, London, 1901.
— *Rural England*, London, 1902.
— *A Gardener's Year*, London, 1905.

— *Report on the Salvation Army Colonies*, London, 1905.
— *The Poor and the Land*, London, 1905.
— *Regeneration*, London, 1910.
— *Rural Denmark*, London, 1911.
— *The After-War Settlement and the Employment of Ex-Servicemen*, London, 1916.
— *The Days of My Life*, London, 1926.
— *My Fellow Labourer* and *The Wreck of the* Copeland, Cheltenham, 1992.
Haggard, Lilias Rider. *The Cloak That I Left*, London, 1951.
Higgins, D. S. *Rider Haggard: The Great Storyteller*, London, 1981.
— *The Private Diaries of Sir Henry Rider Haggard*, London, 1980.
Katz, Wendy, R. *Rider Haggard and the Fiction of Empire*, Cambridge, 1987.
Kipling, Rudyard. *Something of Myself*, London, 1937.
Martineau, John. The Life and Correspondence of Sir Bartle Frere, 2 vols, London, 1895.
Sandison, Alan. *The Wheel of Empire*, London, 1967.
Scott, J. E. *A Bibliography of the Works of Sir H. Rider Haggard*, London, 1947.
Thwaite, Ann. *Edmund Gosse*, London, 1984.
Whatmore, Denys. *H. Rider Haggard: A Bibliography*, London, 1987.
Winstone, H. V. F. *Howard Carter*, London, 1991.

The Fiction of Sir Rider Haggard

1884	Dawn		——	Benita
1885	The Witch's Head		1907	Fair Margaret
——	King Solomon's Mines		1908	The Ghost Kings
1887	She		1909	The Yellow God
——	Jess		——	The Lady of Blossholme
——	Allan Quatermain		1910	Morning Star
1888	Maiwa's Revenge		——	Queen Sheba's Ring
——	Mr Meeson's Will		1911	Red Eve
1889	Colonel Quaritch, VC		——	The Mahatma and the Hare
——	Cleopatra		1912	Marie
——	Allan's Wife		1913	Child of Storm
1890	Beatrice		1914	The Wanderer's Necklace
——	The World's Desire		1915	The Holy Flower
1891	Eric Brighteyes		1916	The Ivory Child
1892	Nada the Lily		1917	Finished
1893	Montezuma's Daughter		1918	Love Eternal
1894	The People of the Mist		——	Moon of Israel
1895	Joan Haste		1919	When the World Shook
1896	Heart of the World		1920	The Ancient Allan
——	The Wizard		——	Smith and the Pharaohs
1898	Dr Therne		1921	She and Allan
1899	Swallow		1922	The Virgin of the Sun
1900	Black Heart and White Heart		1923	Wisdom's Daughter
1901	Lysbeth		1924	Heu-Heu
1903	Pearl Maiden		1925	Queen of the Dawn
1904	Stella Fregelius		1926	The Treasure of the Lake
——	The Brethren		1927	Allan and the Ice Gods
1905	Ayesha		1929	Mary of Marion Isle
1906	The Way of the Spirit		1930	Belshazzar

Notes

CHAPTER ONE

1. Ella Haggard, *Myra, or the Rose of the East*, p. 115.
2. Ella Haggard, *Life and its Author*, Intro.
3. Ella Haggard, *Myra*, p. 42.
4. Ibid., Intro.
5. *The Days of My Life*, Vol. 1, p. 24.
6. Ella Haggard, *Myra*, p. 56, fn.
7. Letter from Ella Haggard to Ella Green, 31.8.17 (Cheyne Collection).
8. Ella Haggard, *Myra*, p. 80.
9. Lilias Rider Haggard, *The Cloak That I Left*, p. 29.
10. *Norfolk Life*, p. 33.
11. *Days*, p. Vol. 1, p. 24.
12. *The Brethren*, Intro.
13. *Days*, Vol. 1, p. 29.
14. *Longman's Magazine*, Nov., 1887.
15. *Days*, Vol. 1, p. 11.
16. Ibid., pp. 5–6.
17. Ibid., p. 20.
18. Ibid., p. 35.
19. Ibid., p. 43.
20. *The World*, 29.6.87.
21. *Days*, Vol. 1, p. 36.
22. Ibid., pp. 39–41.
23. Ibid., p. 42.
24. Ibid., p. 45.
25. *Cloak*, p. 32.
26. *Days*, Vol. 1, p. 46.

CHAPTER TWO

1. *Days*, Vol. 1, p. 49.
2. James Morris, *Heaven's Command*, p. 427.
3. *Days*, Vol. 1, p. 48.
4. Ibid., pp. 52–3.
5. Ibid., p. 56.
6. *Gentleman's Magazine*, July, 1877.
7. *Days*, Vol. 1, p. 58–60.
8. *Gentleman's Magazine*, July, 1877.
9. *Cloak*, p. 40.
10. Ibid., p. 43.
11. *Cetewayo and his White Neighbours*, p. 2.
12. *Days*, Vol. 1, pp. 76–8.
13. Ibid., p. 86.
14. Ibid., p. 90.
15. Ibid., p. 104.
16. *Days*, Vol. 1, p. 6.
17. Ibid., p. 107.
18. Ibid., p. 18.
19. *Gentleman's Magazine*, Sept. 1877.
20. *Days*, Vol. 1, p. 112.
21. Ibid., pp. 111–12.
22. Ibid., p. 116.
23. Ibid., p. 117.
24. Ibid., p. 119.

25. Andrew Lang, ed., *The Blue Story Book*, p. 141.

26. *Cloak*, p. 79.
27. *Days*, Vol. 1, p. 134.

CHAPTER THREE

1. *Cloak*, pp. 89–90.
2. *Days*, Vol. 1, p. 162.
3. D. S. Higgins, *Rider Haggard: The Great Storyteller*, p. 41.
4. *Days*, Vol. 1, p. 166.
5. *Cloak*, p. 93.
6. Ibid., p. 96.
7. Ibid., p. 99.
8. Higgins, *Great Storyteller*, p. 43.
9. Louisa Haggard's diary (Cheyne Collection).
10. Ibid. p. 94.
11. *Days*, Vol. 1, p. 173.
12. *Days*, Vol. 1, p. 179.
13. Louisa Haggard's diary.
14. *Days*, Vol. 1, p. 181.
15. Ibid.
16. *The Times*, 28.1.81.
17. *Days*, Vol. 1, p. 182.
18. *Cloak*, p. 105.
19. *Days*, Vol. 1, p. 183.
20. Ibid., p. 184.

21. Louisa Haggard's diary.
22. *Cetewayo*, p. 239.
23. *Days*, Vol. 1, pp. 187–8.
24. Ibid.
25. Louisa Haggard's diary.
26. *Days*, Vol. 1, p. 188.
27. Ibid., p. 190.
28. Louisa Haggard's diary.
29. *Cloak*, p. 108.
30. Louisa Haggard's diary.
31. Morton Cohen, *Rider Haggard: His Life and Works*, p. 262.
32. *Child of Storm*.
33. *Cetewayo*, pp. 96–8.
34. *Colonel Quaritch, VC*
35. John Martineau, *The Life and Correspondence of Sir Bartle Frere*, Vol. 11, p. 415.
36. Louisa Haggard's diary.
37. *Days*, Vol. 1, p. 201.
38. Louisa Haggard's diary.

CHAPTER FOUR

1. *Days*, Vol. 1, p. 221.
2. *Daily News*, 23.8.82.
3. *Days*, Vol. 1, p. 206.
4. Ibid., p. 209.
5. Ibid., p. 212.
6. *Cloak*, p. 119.
7. *Days*, Vol. 1, p. 214.
8. Ibid., p. 218.
9. Cohen, *Life*, p. 83.
10. *Days*, Vol. 1, p. 219.
11. Ibid., pp. 229–31.
12. Ibid., p. 227.
13. Ibid., p. 235–7.

14. Norman Etherington, *Rider Haggard*, p. 44.
15. *Allan Quatermain*.
16. *Jess*.
17. *Days*, Vol. 1, pp. 245–6.
18. *She*.
19. *Cloak*, p. 129.
20. *Days*, Vol. 1, p. 246.
21. Ibid., p. 247.
22. Ibid., p. 249.
23. *The Bookman*, New York, Nov., 1895.
24. *Days*, Vol. 1, p. 250.

Notes

CHAPTER FIVE

1. *Days*, Vol. 1, pp. 256–7.
2. *Cloak*, p. 131.
3. *Days*, Vol. 1, pp. 257–8.
4. Ibid., p. 261.
5. *Cloak*, pp. 132–3.
6. *Contemporary Review*, Feb., 1887.
7. Higgins, *Great Storyteller*, p. 105.
8. Ibid., p. 121.
9. Cohen, *Life*, p. 125.
10. Ibid., p. 128.
11. *Days*, Vol. 1, p. 273.
12. *The Critic*, 15.12.1888.
13. *Cleopatra*.
14. *Longman's Magazine*, Nov., 1887.
15. *Cloak*, pp. 141–5.
16. *Days*, Vol. 1, pp. 289–94.
17. Higgins, *Great Storyteller*, p. 127.
18. Morton Cohen, *Rudyard Kipling to Rider Haggard*, pp. 17–18.
19. Rudyard Kipling, *Something of Myself*, p. 51.
20. Cohen, *Kipling to Haggard*, pp. 28–9.
21. *Cleopatra*.
22. *Days*, Vol. 1, p. 272.
23. *Cloak*, p. 148.
24. *Days*, Vol. 1, p. 24.
25. Ella Haggard, *Life and Its Author*, 1890.
26. *Days*, Vol. 1, p. 25.
27. Ibid., Vol. 1, p. 25.
28. Higgins, *Great Storyteller*, p. 142.
29. *Days*, Vol. 2, pp. 41–2.
30. *New York Times*, 11.1.1891.
31. *Cloak*, p. 154.
32. *Days*, Vol. 2, pp. 42–4.
33. *Montezuma's Daughter*.

CHAPTER SIX

1. *Cloak*, p. 16.
2. *Montezuma's Daughter*.
3. *The Strand Magazine*, Jan., 1892.
4. *A Farmer's Year*.
5. Cohen, *Life*, pp. 147–8.
6. *Days*, Vol. 1, p. 255.
7. *Cloak*, p. 161.
8. *The People of the Mist*.
9. *Cloak*, p. 158.
10. Higgins, *Great Storyteller*, p. 152.
11. *Days*, Vol. 2, pp. 120–21.
12. *Child of Storm*.
13. *Cetewayo*.
14. *Days*, Vol. 2, p. 112.
15. Ibid., p. 111.
16. *Cloak*, p. 167.
17. Haggard to Julia Haggard, 23.3.95 (Cheyne Collection).
18. *The Cable*, 11.5.95.
19. *Norfolk Chronicle*, 20.7.95.
20. *Days*, Vol. 2, p. 114.
21. *The Cable*, 11.5.95.
22. *Saturday Review*, 23.3.95.
23. *The Times*, 20.7.95.
24. Ibid., 23.7.95.
25. *Pall Mall Gazette*, 25.7.95.
26. *The Times*, 29.7.95.
27. *New York Times*, 28.7.95.
28. *The Times*, 29.7.95.
29. Huntington Collection (HM 43406).
30. *Days*, Vol. 2, p. 106.
31. *Cloak*, p. 168.
32. *Days*, Vol. 2, p. 110.
33. Ibid.
34. *The Times*, 13.1.96.
35. Ann Thwaite, *Edmund Gosse*, p. 337.

CHAPTER SEVEN

1. Cohen, *Life*, p. 165.
2. *Punch*, 15.11.99.
3. *A Farmer's Year*, Intro.
4. *Days*, Vol. 2, p. 133.

5. *A Farmer's Year*, 1.1.98.
6. Ibid., 10.1.98.
7. Ibid., 14.1.98.
8. Ibid., 22.6.98.
9. Ibid., 3.9.98.
10. Ibid., 14.9.98.
11. Ibid., 4.5.98.
12. *Cloak*, p. 191.
13. Cohen, *Life*, p. 211, fn.
14. *Days*, Vol. 2, p. 140.
15. Cohen, *Life*, p. 207.
16. Ibid.
17. Cohen, *Kipling to Haggard*, p. 35.
18. *Days*, Vol. 2, p. 131.
19. Ibid., p. 108.
20. *Cloak*, p. 193.
21. Cohen, *Life*, p. 167.
22. *Winter Pilgrimage*, p. 6.
23. Ibid., p. 14.
24. Ibid., pp. 28–9.

25. Ibid., p. 26.
26. Ibid., pp. 38–48.
27. *Days*, Vol. 2, p. 138.
28. *Winter Pilgrimage*, pp. 53–5.
29. Ibid., p. 3.
30. Notebook, Feb., 1901. Norfolk Record Office, MS 4694/2/8–14.
31. *Winter Pilgrimage*, p. 158.
32. *Days*, Vol. 2, p. 138.
33. Notebook, March, 1901. NRO, MS 4694/2/9.
34. *Winter Pilgrimage*, p. 344.
35. Ibid., p. 354.
36. *Rural England*, Vol. 1, p. 3.
37. Ibid., p. 6.
38. Ibid., Vol. 2, p. 321.
39. Ibid., p. 575.
40. Cohen, *Life*, p. 174.
41. Cohen, *Kipling to Haggard*, p. 49.
42. *Days*, Vol. 2, p. 148.

CHAPTER EIGHT

1. Notebook, NRO, MS 4694/2/12.
2. *Days*, Vol. 2, p. 157.
3. Notebook 19.3.04. NRO, MS 4694/2/12.
4. Ibid., 28.2.04.
5. *Days*, Vol. 2, p. 157.
6. H. V. F. Winstone, *Howard Carter*, p. 85.
7. Notebook, 2.3.04. NRO, MS 4694/2/12.
8. Ibid., 14.3.04
9. Ibid., 2.3.04.
10. *Days*, Vol. 2., p. 158.
11. Notebook, 1.3.04. NRO, MS 4694/2/12.
12. *Days*, Vol. 2, p. 158.
13. *Cloak*, p. 196.
14. Ibid., p. 17.
15. *Christian Commonwealth*, p. 75.
16. *Days*, Vol. 2, pp. 160–65.

17. Lodge to Haggard, 26.2.04. NRO, MC 32/5.
18. *Days*, Vol. 2, p. 172.
19. Haggard to William Carr, 23.11.04. NRO, MC 166/89/5.
20. Cohen, *Kipling to Haggard*, p. 53.
21. Ibid., p. 59.
22. Thomas Adams, *Garden City and Agriculture*.
23. *Ayesha*.
24. *Days*, Vol. 2, pp. 173–5.
25. Cohen, *Kipling to Haggard*, p. 59.
26. *Regeneration*, p. 7.
27. *Days*, Vol. 2, p. 217, fn.
28. *Rural England*, Vol. 1, pp. 494–504.
29. *The Poor and the Land*, p. 126.
30. Ibid., pp. 130–33.

CHAPTER NINE

1. *New York Herald*, 19.3.05.
2. *Days*, Vol. 2, p. 176.
3. Roosevelt to W. H. Taft, 4.9.06.

4. *New York Herald*, 19.3.05.
5. *Days*, Vol. 2, pp. 178–9.

6. Roosevelt Papers, TR to RH, 11.3.05. British Library, Reel 337.
7. *Review of Reviews*, July, 1905.
8. Notebook, NRO, MS 4694/2/14.
9. *Days*, Vol. 2, pp. 261–72.
10. *Cloak*, pp. 188–9.
11. *Days*, Vol. 2, pp. 190–91.
12. Ibid., p. 199.
13. Higgins, p. 192.
14. *Days*, Vol. 2, pp. 191–2.
15. Roosevelt Papers, RH to TR, 13.6.05. BL, Reel 55.
16. Ibid., TR to RH, 24.6.05. BL, Reel 338.
17. *The Poor and the Land*, pp. 145–57.
18. RH to Carr, 29.6.05. Author's collection.
19. *Days*, Vol. 2, pp. 195–213.
20. *Cloak*, p. 19.
21. RH to Carr, 29.6.05. Author's collection.
22. *Days*, Vol. 2, p. 206.
23. Cohen, *Kipling to Haggard*, p. 63.
24. Cohen, *Life*, pp. 197–8.
25. *Days*, Vol. 2, p. 208.
26. Cohen, *Life*, pp. 201–2.
27. Cohen, *Kipling to Haggard*, p. 63.
28. *Regeneration*, p. 171.
29. Ibid., pp. 149–50.
30. Higgins, *Great Storyteller*, p. 201.
31. Cheyne Collection.
32. RH to Carr, 4.12.06. Author's collection.
33. Roosevelt Papers, RH to TR, 22.1.09. BL, Reel 87.
34. Ibid., TR to RH, 11.2.09.
35. *The Times*, 27.11.09.
36. Webb to RH, 12.10.06. Coquet Collection.
37. Notebook, 31.5.10. NRO, MS 4694/2/17.
38. Cohen to RH, 9.4.08. Coquet Collection.
39. RH to Cohen. Coquet Collection.
40. *Eastern Daily Press*, 18.2.10.

CHAPTER TEN

1. Notebook, 22.6.11. NRO, MS 4694/2/17.
2. *The Mahatma and the Hare*, p. 163.
3. *Days*, Vol. 2, pp. 166–7.
4. *Cloak*, p. 19.
5. *Rural Denmark*, pp. 274–6.
6. Ibid., pp. 36–7.
7. Ibid., p. 41.
8. Roosevelt Papers, TR to RH, 22.8.11. BL, Reel 368.
9. *The Outlook*, 1.7.11.
10. Roosevelt Papers, TR to RH, 22.8.11. BL, Reel 368.
11. Ibid., RH to TR, 5.9.11. BL, Reel 112.
12. Ibid., TR to RH, 28.6.12. BL Reel 378.
13. Notebook, 30.9.11. NRO, MS 4694/2/17.
14. *Days*, Intro.
15. Ibid., p. 3.
16. Notebook, NRO, MS 4694/2/17.
17. *Days*, Vol. 2, p. 226.
18. Cohen, *Kipling to Haggard*, p. 74.
19. *Days*, Vol. 2, p. 227.
20. RH to LH, 12.4.12. Cheyne Collection.
21. *Days*, Vol. 2, pp. 227–8.
22. Ibid., p. 230.
23. Notebook, NRO, MS 4694/2/17.
24. *Days*, Vol. 2, pp. 230–1.
25. RH to LH, 29.3.12. Cheyne Collection.
26. Ibid., 15.4.12.
27. *Cloak*, pp. 251–2.
28. Roosevelt Papers, TR to RH, 28.6.12. BL, Reel 378.
29. RH to TR, 14.7.12. NRO, MC 32/45/478x7.
30. *Days*, Vol. 2, pp. 232–3.
31. Morton Cohen Collection.
32. Higgins, *Great Storyteller*, p. 213.
33. Cohen, *Kipling to Haggard*, p. 79.
34. Notebook, NRO, MS 4694/2/17.
35. *Days*, Vol. 2, p. 235.
36. Ibid., pp. 242–3.
37. Ibid., p. 259.
38. *The Statesman*, Calcutta, 18.1.13.
39. *Amicus*, Colombo, 6.12.12.
40. Cheyne Collection.
41. E. J. Harding, *Dominions Diary*, p. 65.
42. RH to Carr, Feb., 1913. Author's collection.
43. Harding, p. 72.

44. *The Age*, Melbourne, 18.2.13.
45. *Lyttelton Times*, 1.3.13.
46. Harding, p. 155, fn.
47. Notebook, NRO, MS 4694/2/18.
48. RH to Carr, March, 1913. Author's collection.

49. *The Advertiser*, Adelaide, 12.5.13.
50. Harding, p. 91, fn.
51. Ibid., p. 108, fn.
52. Ibid., p. 107, fn.
53. *Cloak*, p. 216.

CHAPTER ELEVEN

1. Harding, p. 182.
2. *Cloak*, pp. 219–42.
3. *New York Times*, 2.7.14.
4. Haggard's diary, 25.7.14.
5. Ibid., 28.7.14.
6. Ibid., 2.8.14.
7. Ibid., 5.8.14.
8. Ibid., 6.8.14.
9. Ibid., 5.8.14.
10. Ibid., 7.8.14.
11. Ibid., 12.8.14.
12. Higgins, *Great Storyteller*, p. 219.
13. *Cloak*, pp. 245–6.
14. Higgins, *Great Storyteller*, p. 219.
15. Diary, p. 12/8/14.
16. Harding, p. 256.
17. Diary, 12.8.14.
18. Ibid., 13.8.14.
19. Ibid., 15.8.14.
20. Ibid., 21.8.14.
21. Ibid., 28.8.14.
22. Ibid., 1.9.14.
23. Ibid., 18.9.14.

24. Ibid., 23.9.14.
25. Ibid., 14.10.14.
26. Ibid., 25.9.14.
27. Ibid., 4.10.14.
28. Ibid., 12.10.14.
29. Higgins, *Great Storyteller*, p. 220.
30. Diary, 6.11.14.
31. Ibid., 9.11.14.
32. Ibid., 11.11.14.
33. Higgins, *Great Storyteller*, pp. 222–3.
34. Diary, 23.10.14.
35. Ibid., 16.1.15.
36. Ibid., 6.11.14.
37. Higgins, *Great Storyteller*, p. 223.
38. *Cloak*, p. 247.
39. Diary, 23.3.15.
40. Ibid., 17.10.15.
41. Ibid., 7.10.15.
42. Cohen, *Kipling to Haggard*, p. 86, fn.
43. Diary, 28.12.15.
44. Ibid., 22.5.18.
45. Ibid., 15.11.18.
46. Ibid., 22.5.18.

CHAPTER TWELVE

1. Diary, 2.12.15.
2. Ibid., 12.2.15.
3. Ibid., 4.5.15.
4. Ibid., 23.7.15.
5. Ibid., 4.8.15.
6. Ibid., 4.9.15.
7. Ibid., 29.10.15.
8. Ibid., 22.12.15.
9. Ibid., 1.1.16.
10. Ibid., 3.1.16.

11. Cohen, *Kipling to Haggard*, p. 92.
12. Ibid., p. 92.
13. Diary, 5.1.16.
14. Ibid., 10.1.16.
15. Ibid., 15.1.16.
16. Corbett's journal. Author's collection.
17. Diary, p. 8.2.16.
18. Corbett. Author's collection.
19. Diary, p. 9.2.16.
20. Ibid., p. 11.2.16.

21. *Cloak*, p. 248.
22. Diary, 16.2.16.
23. Ibid., 22.2.16.
24. Ibid., 28–29.2.16.
25. Ibid., 4.3.16.
26. Ibid., 11.3.16.
27. Ibid., 4.3.16.
28. RH to Carr, 12.3.16. Author's collection.
29. Diary, 16.3.16.
30. Ibid., 19.3.16.
31. Ibid., 3.4.16.
32. *The Mercury*, Hobart, 7.4.16.
33. Diary, 4.4.16.
34. Ibid., 5.4.16.
35. *The Argus*, Melbourne, 10.4.16.
36. *Cloak*, p. 250.
37. Diary, 22.4.16.
38. *Cloak*, p. 250.
39. Corbett. Author's collection.
40. Diary, 26.4.16.
41. Ibid., 3.6.16.
42. *New Zealand Freelance*, 9.6.16.
43. *Evening Post*, Wellington, 5.6.16.
44. *New Zealand Times*, 30.6.16.
45. *New Zealand Herald*, 10.6.16.
46. Massey to RH, 8.6.16.
47. Diary, 22.6.16.
48. Ibid., 24.6.16.
49. Ibid., 1.7.16.
50. Ibid., 3.7.16.
51. Ibid., 12.7.16.
52. Ibid., 7.7.16.
53. Harding, p. 285.
54. Diary, 22.7.16.
55. Ibid., 1.8.16.

CHAPTER THIRTEEN

1. Diary, 3.8.16.
2. Ibid., 5.8.16.
3. Ibid., 3.9.16.
4. Ibid., 18.8.16.
5. Ibid., 24.8.16.
6. Ibid., 13.11.16.
7. Ibid., 20.12.16.
8. Ibid., 7.12.16.
9. *Cloak*, p. 254.
10. *When the World Shook*.
11. Cohen, *Kipling to Haggard*, p. 95.
12. Ibid., 6.11.18.
13. Diary, 27.3.17.
14. TR to RH, 4.10.17. NRO, MS 21598/20.
15. TR to RH, 14.3.17. NRO, MC 32/12.
16. Diary, 13.2.17.
17. Diary, 7.4.17.
18. Roosevelt Papers, RH to TR, 28.4.17. BL, Reel 230.
19. TR to RH, 1.6.17. NRO, MC 32/12.
20. RH to TR, 19.11.17. Diary, 20.11.17.
21. Diary, 26.1.17.
22. Ibid., 11.6.17.
23. Ibid., 27.4.17.
24. Ibid., 13.7.17.
25. Ibid., 22.5.18.
26. Ibid., 23.5.18.
27. Ibid., 26.10.17.
28. *Cloak*, p. 254.
29. RH to Dean Inge, 30.6.18. Author's collection.
30. Diary, 16.10.19.
31. Ibid., 10.9.16.
32. Ibid., 17.4.18.
33. Ibid., 29.8.18.
34. Ibid., 25.2.18.
35. Roosevelt Papers, RH to TR, 19.2.18. BL, Reel 265.
36. Diary, 7.3.18.
37. Ibid., 11.11.18.
38. *Cloak*, p. 264.
39. Cohen, *Life*, p. 269.
40. Diary, 17.7.18.
41. Ibid., 5.2.19.
42. Ibid., 9.9.19.
43. Roosevelt Papers, TR to RH, 6.12.18. BL, Reel 411.
44. Diary 7–8.1.19.
45. *Daily Herald*, 4.3.20.
46. *The Times*, 25.4.19.
47. Diary, 1.11.19.
48. Ibid., 24.11.19.
49. Ibid., 8.2.19.

50. Ibid., 4.12.19.
51. Ibid., 22.1.20.
52. Ibid., 26.4.20.
53. Ibid., 19.9.22.
54. Ibid., 15.1.21.

55. Ibid., 26.1.21.
56. Ibid., 28.1.21.
57. Ibid., 27.4.22.

CHAPTER FOURTEEN

1. *Cloak*, p. 211.
2. Ibid., p. 267.
3. Diary, 30.1.22.
4. RH to Carr, 14.3.22. Author's collection.
5. Diary, 30.11.22.
6. Ibid., 22.3.23.
7. *The Times*, 13.2.23.
8. Diary, 29.1.24.
9. *Cloak*, p. 275.
10. Diary, 22.2.24.
11. Ibid., 9.2.24.
12. Ibid., 14.2.24.
13. Ibid., 20.2.24.
14. Ibid., 27.2.24.
15. Ibid., 5.3.24.
16. Ibid., 23.3.24.
17. Ibid., 21.3.24.
18. Ibid., 23.12.24.
19. Ibid., 29.9.24.
20. Ibid., 20.7.24.
21. Ibid., 15.3.24.
22. Ibid., 31.12.24.

23. Ibid., 27.12.24.
24. Ibid., 11.8.24.
25. Ibid., 9.8.24.
26. Ibid., 7.10.34. RH to WSC, 6.10.24.
27. Ibid., 14.10.24.
28. Higgins, *Great Storyteller*, p. 240.
29. *The Times*, 26.11.24.
30. *Cloak*, p. 278.
31. Diary, 27.12.24.
32. Ibid., 23.12.24.
33. Ibid., 26.3.25.
34. Cohen, *Kipling to Haggard*, pp. 129–30.
35. Ibid., p. 177.
36. Ibid., pp. 141–6.
37. Ibid., p. 159.
38. Ibid., p. 165.
39. Ibid., p. 163.
40. Ibid., p. 171.
41. Ibid., p. 177.
42. *Cloak*, pp. 278–9.
43. Ibid., p. 21.
44. Ibid., pp. 279–80.

EPILOGUE

1. *Agriculture in Britain* Central Office of Information, London (1955), p. 8.
2. *New Statesman*, 14.7.51.
3. *The Listener*, 22.6.61.
4. *Time and Tide*, 3.9.60.
5. *New Statesman*, 27.8.60.
6. *The Wheel of Empire*, Alan Sandison, pp. 30–31.
7. Wendy R. Katz, *Rider Haggard and the Fiction of Empire*, p. 153.
8. Ibid., p. 151.
9. *Allan Quatermain*, Intro.
10. *Winter Pilgrimage*, p. 344.

Index